ating read: once you start, you won't want to put it down.
iant at painting a colorful picture of the legendary explorer
hey know but don't—a man who draws on the toughness he
ld laborer during the Industrial Age to help rid the tribes of
f slavery, advance the science of his day, and above all serve the
om he loved more than anything and anyone."

—MICHAEL GUILLEN, PhD, FORMER *ABC NEWS* SCIENCE
EDITOR, BEST-SELLING AUTHOR, AND MOVIE PRODUCER

commitment to the abolition of slavery changed the course of
gh his life, we learn much about ourselves and God."

—AMBASSADOR TONY P. HALL, EXECUTIVE DIRECTOR OF
ALLIANCE TO END HUNGER, FORMER CONGRESSMAN

l, this smart, thorough, engaging odyssey reveals the mission-
behind Livingstone's quest to end the African slave trade. Jay
xpertly navigates both the exhilarating and the tragic aspects of
able story. His book makes an important contribution to abolition

—JUDGE KENNETH W. STARR, PRESIDENT, BAYLOR UNIVERSITY

e when missionaries past and present are too often caricatured and
d, it is refreshing to read this gripping study of David Livingstone.
om his official mission work, he was explorer, scientist, anthropologist,
t, and above all, a driving force in ending the East African slave trade.
y invaluable but enthralling."

—PAUL MARSHALL, SENIOR FELLOW AT HUDSON INSTITUTE'S
CENTER FOR RELIGIOUS FREEDOM, AUTHOR OF *PERSECUTED*

and perseverance do overcome evil in our world. Jay Milbrandt's telling
ingstone's trying journey reminds us of God's goodness and grace."

—IMMACULÉE ILIBAGIZA, RWANDAN GENOCIDE SURVIVOR AND
AUTHOR OF THE *NEW YORK TIMES* BESTSELLER *LEFT TO TELL*

ose of us who have dedicated our own lives to the pursuit of global justice
d on the shoulders of giants such as Livingstone, who 'never stopped until
had come to the end and achieved his purpose.' This incredible book will
onate and inspire activists, abolitionists, and explorers for years to come."

—JASON RUSSELL, COFOUNDER, INVISIBLE CHILDREN

PRAISE FOR *THE DA[RK...]*

"A spectacular, ground-breaki[ng]
oughly gripping story. It was
adventurous life of this courage[ous]
Milbrandt also proclaims Living[stone]
quishing the horrors of the global [...]
—ERIC METAXAS,
BONHOEFFER: PASTOR, MARTYR,
ARE, WHY THEY HAPPE[N...]

"Passionate, headstrong, and obsessive[,]
Livingstone strides out of these pages like
interior. Milbrandt's portrait is like an o[...]
grime—a robust challenge to our soft gene[...]
who know the link between the gospel, mi[...]
—O[...]

"Livingstone's life reminds us how God can u[se]
the extraordinary. Milbrandt illuminates Livi[...]
great energy and clarity."
—RICH STEARNS, PRESIDE[NT]
AUTHOR OF *THE HOLE IN [...]*

"Reads like a thriller . . . enables the reader to s[hare]
the passion, the hopes and the hardships of David [...]
travels—and to obtain a glimpse into the faith whi[ch]
and thereby to make a unique contribution to the abo[...]
East Africa."
—THE BARONESS COX, HOU[SE...]
HUMANITARI[AN...]

"A powerful view into the brutality of Africa's slave h[istory]
troubled explorer who exposed its tragedies to the world. [...]
and drive make his story a moving read and cautionary t[ale...]
cares about today's fight to end slavery."
—GARY A. HAUGEN, PRES[IDENT]
INTERNATIONAL [...]

"A fast and fascin[ating...]
Milbrandt is brill[iant...]
everyone thinks t[...]
acquired as a chi[ld...]
Eastern Africa o[...]
biblical God wh[...]

"Livingstone's [...]
Africa. Throu[gh...]

"Full of sou[...]
ary purpose[...]
Milbrandt [...]
this remar[kable...]
history."

"At a tim[e...]
disdaine[d...]
Apart fr[om...]
diploma[...]
Not on[ly...]

"Fait[h...]
of Li[...]

"Th[...]
sta[...]
he[...]
re[...]

"It's a rare moment when an author can tell an old story in way so new that you've forgotten you've ever heard it before. Jay has done just that. He's a maestro."

—JOHNNIE MOORE, SENIOR VICE PRESIDENT, LIBERTY UNIVERSITY, AUTHOR OF *WHAT AM I SUPPOSED TO DO WITH MY LIFE?*

"David Livingstone was a great man, a great explorer, a great freedom fighter, and a spiritual man. Livingstone remains an example of exceptional courage and leadership for the modern world."

—AZARIAS RUBERWA, FORMER VICE-PRESIDENT OF DR CONGO AND BOARD MEMBER, MERCY SHIPS

"The story of David Livingstone needed to be told, and Jay does not disappoint. He is bold and brilliant."

—SUZAN JOHNSON COOK, 3RD US AMBASSADOR AT LARGE FOR INTERNATIONAL RELIGIOUS FREEDOM

"An adventure-packed biography of one man's courage and persistence that finally broke the back of the slave trade and brought the influence of Christianity to the African continent. It's an inspirational read that will encourage Christians as they advance the gospel and the Christian worldview even in these challenging times."

—ALAN TERWILLEGER, PRESIDENT OF THE CHUCK COLSON CENTER FOR CHRISTIAN WORLDVIEW

"Livingstone's story is powerful—a triumph of humanity, faith, and dignity. This is a must-read for anyone with African interests. Government employees, NGO participants, long- or short-term volunteers such as Peace Corps Volunteers or faith-based participants or those who have traveled or are planning on traveling to this amazing continent will all find Milbrandt's insights into Africa, through David Livingstone's eyes and heart, enlightening and inspiring."

—RON TSCHETTER, FORMER DIRECTOR, U.S. PEACE CORPS

"The sympathetic handling of this period stood out, exploring how a man who despised the slave trade so deeply could still end up traveling with, and sometimes admitting to liking, the traders he met. . . . an excellent job of explaining the importance of Livingstone's work to the eventual ending of the slave trade."

—ALISON RITCHIE, PROPERTY MANAGER, DAVID LIVINGSTONE CENTRE IN SCOTLAND

"Fascinating and very well written . . . the story of a determined and tenacious human being with frailties common to us all. I am most grateful for [Livingstone's] relentless efforts and contributions towards the elimination of slavery . . . an inspiration for us to selflessly invest into the lives of our fellow beings!"

—KADITA "A.T." TSHIBAKA, BOARD MEMBER AND FORMER
PRESIDENT AND CEO, OPPORTUNITY INTERNATIONAL

"Impressively researched and compellingly written, Jay Milbrandt's excellent biography of the legendary explorer David Livingstone is a book for everyone. Whether you enjoy adventure or history, or are seeking spiritual inspiration as well as insights into the epic struggle to end the slave trade, this is a must-read."

—BENEDICT ROGERS, HUMAN RIGHTS ADVOCATE AND JOURNALIST,
CHRISTIAN SOLIDARITY WORLDWIDE, AUTHOR OF *ON THE SIDE OF ANGELS*

"It is hard not to compare David Livingstone with another Victorian-era opponent of slavery, William Wilberforce. I suspect each would be surprised to know that there are more slaves today in the world than when they lived. Hopefully, this book will inspire modern-day Wilberforces and Livingstones to take up the cause. But this is also a cautionary tale for those who want to change the world. Livingstone's work often came at the expense of his family and those closest to him."

—ROBERT F. COCHRAN, JR., LOUIS D. BRANDEIS PROFESSOR OF LAW
AND DIRECTOR, HERBERT AND ELINOR NOOTBAAR INSTITUTE ON LAW,
RELIGION, AND ETHICS AT PEPPERDINE UNIVERSITY SCHOOL OF LAW

"Combines the adventure of Sir Ernest Shackleton with the passionate opposition to the slave trade of William Wilberforce. Jay Milbrandt's telling of Livingstone's story is compelling and challenging. The man behind Henry Stanley's famous question is a hero for the ages and a life to be celebrated."

—JAY BARNES, PRESIDENT, BETHEL UNIVERSITY

THE DARING HEART OF
DAVID LIVINGSTONE

EXILE, AFRICAN SLAVERY, AND THE PUBLICITY
STUNT THAT SAVED MILLIONS

BY JAY MILBRANDT

NELSON
BOOKS
An Imprint of Thomas Nelson

Published in Nashville, Tennessee, by Nelson Books, an imprint of Thomas Nelson. Nelson Books and Thomas Nelson are registered trademarks of HarperCollins Christian Publishing, Inc.

Published in association with Yates & Yates, www.yates2.com.

Thomas Nelson titles may be purchased in bulk for educational, business, fund-raising, or sales promotional use. For information, please e-mail SpecialMarkets@ ThomasNelson.com.

**Library of Congress Cataloging-in-Publication Data
is on file with the Library of Congress**

ISBN 9781595555922

Printed in the United States of America

14 15 16 17 18 RRD 6 5 4 3 2 1

For Lisa

No one can estimate the amount of God-pleasing good that will be done, if by Divine favour this awful slave-trade, into the midst of which I have come, be abolished. This will be something to have lived for.

—DAVID LIVINGSTONE, AUGUST 15, 1872

He shall not see the rivers, the floods, the
brooks of honey and butter.

—JOB 20:17

CONTENTS

CONTENTS

AUTHOR'S NOTE

This book is David Livingstone's untold story. In the century since his death, many biographers have recounted and retold Livingstone's life, focusing on his adventures and explorations, highlighting his exploits in scientific discovery. Meanwhile, these traditional biographers have largely overlooked his advocacy for abolishing slavery. In so doing, they have missed the real story—in my opinion the most important story—and, ultimately, the purpose of Livingstone's life.

If David Livingstone pursued one purpose, it was freedom from the African slave trade. This vile desecration bled Africa—"the open sore of the world"—and Africa's wounds ran deep into Livingstone's soul. His search for the mighty Nile River merely powered Livingstone's wheel of abolition.

Livingstone would never know the success of his grand publicity stunt. He would never witness a healing sore. He would never see his legacy. A mere thirty-six days after passing away deep in the heart of Africa, legislation in Zanzibar would make slavery illegal in East Africa. The bleeding would stop. And, to Livingstone, credit was due.

He passed away believing he failed in almost everything in life. For abolition, he sacrificed his career, his reputation, his fortune, his wife, his children, and, eventually, his own life. In perhaps the greatest publicity stunt the world had ever known, he went to his death for a cause in which he faithfully believed.

Livingstone's story is one of failure and falling from grace. But, it is also a story of relentless commitment that brings redemption we may never know, and a story greater than we could ever imagine. This is David Livingstone's legacy.

I hope you will join me in my respect for a great explorer but also discover new admiration for a man who gave his life to heal the wounds of humanity's great atrocities—for a land and people not of his own, no less. May we count David Livingstone among our heroes of faith and abolition.

PART ONE

RISE

1 * HERO

It is something to be a follower, however feeble,
in the wake of the great Teacher and only model
missionary that ever appeared among men.

—David Livingstone

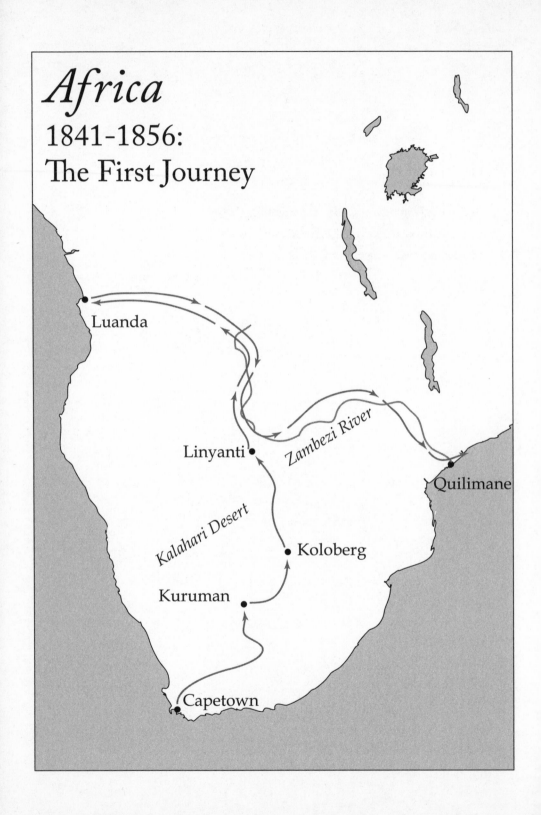

Africa
1841–1856:
The First Journey

Luanda

Linyanti

Zambezi River

Kalahari Desert

Koloberg

Kuruman

Capetown

Quilimane

In the dead cold of an English winter, enthusiastic energy electrified Cambridge University. David Livingstone, Britain's heroic African explorer, had promised to deliver a two-day keynote speech to one of the world's great institutions. Livingstone would headline the university's showcase lecture of 1857—it would be the benchmark event of the decade.

Dignitaries, faculty, and students crowded the Senate House on the wintery Cambridge evening, awaiting stories of African adventure, danger, and unseen wonders. The dark Norwegian oak walls of the auditorium pulsed with palpable energy. The white, ornately designed ceilings resounded the roar of the crowd onto the exquisite black-and-white checkered marble floor.

The man was a celebrity. Returning to England by boat less than one year earlier, Livingstone had stepped onto the British shore and into Victorian-era stardom. In the years leading up to his return, Livingstone's African adventures consumed news headlines and dinner conversations. The Royal Geographical Society hailed his work as "the greatest triumph in geographical research which has been effected in our times."[2] On the streets, crowds mobbed him. In churches, the services turned to chaos as people clamored over pews simply to shake his hand. England adored its iconic explorer.

Livingstone had captured public imagination, immortalizing him. Adoring fans reveled in the gossip of his adventures. Rumors of his audacious exploits swirled through England's tea parlors. Had this man truly survived the jaws of a lion? Had he really walked away with his life from the hands of savage tribes? Had he actually survived unspeakable diseases not once, but *dozens* of times?

Tonight, they would hear the truth from the man.

Cambridge punctuated Livingstone's high-profile lecture tour across England and Scotland—a fitting grand finale. He had spoken at colleges and addressed cities. The Royal Geographical Society installed him as a fellow. The universities of Glasgow and Oxford conferred honorary doctorates upon him. Even Queen Victoria received him privately. Yet no event had matched the enthusiastic audience he found at Cambridge. His triumphant homecoming was a thundering crescendo.

Livingstone took the podium; myth became flesh. His short stature looked two feet taller as he stood before the crowd. He appeared confident, yet noticeably awkward on account of his crooked left arm. His thin, narrow face exhibited the weathering of many days in the blazing African sun. Though only forty-five, he might have passed for much younger. He gazed upon his audience with keen, piercing eyes sandwiched between his sweeping brown locks and bushy mustache.

He spoke slowly, unassisted by notes. An African inflection precipitated his stutter-prone Scottish accent.

"When I went to Africa seventeen years ago, I resolved to acquire an accurate knowledge of the native tongues . . . and speak generally in African languages. The result is that I am now not very fluent in my own . . ."

Laughter erupted from the audience.

"If you will excuse my imperfections," he continued, his lips cautiously forming long-neglected words, "I will endeavor to give you as clear an idea of Africa as I can."

Livingstone's Africa gripped the audience with awe and novelty.

He painted the picture of an Africa that England had never known, an Africa dramatically different from his predecessors' explorations in its dry, empty, resource-scarce northern deserts. Livingstone's Africa was lush, water-filled, teeming with wildlife and fascinating people. Livingstone's Africa had intrigue and mystery.

"I went into that country for the purpose of teaching the doctrines of our holy religion," Livingstone told his audience, "and settled with the tribes on the border of the Kalahari desert."

Upon his first public religious service with these tribes, a chief had inquired about Christianity and the nature of God. Livingstone described to him a vision of heaven: the Lord sitting on a great white throne from whose face the heavens shall flee. The image startled the chief.

"How is it that your forefathers, knowing all these things, did not send word to my forefathers sooner?" the chief asked.

Livingstone explained the geographical challenges between Britain and Africa.

"Will you ever get beyond that with your Gospel?" the chief pointed out to the Kalahari Desert. "We, who are more accustomed to thirst than you are, cannot cross that desert; how can you?"

Later that year, Livingstone stepped out into the Kalahari, leading a team across it. Then he went farther, traversing Africa on foot—Atlantic coast to Indian Ocean—a feat never before accomplished. En route, he became the first person to reach Lake Ngami and majestic Victoria Falls—"scenes so lovely must have been gazed upon by angels in their flight," he said.

Livingstone's rousing tales of adventure and discovery captured the hearts of dispirited Brits at a time when they needed an encouraging distraction. His return to England came on the heels of the bloody Crimean War, while unrest in British India raised the question of whether England had lost her grip on the global empire. The problem of urban poverty engrossed English cities; social tension, unemployment, and child labor ran rampant. Livingstone represented hope and unity.

Success had made Livingstone an icon of the working class. He was one of them. Pulling himself up from poverty and child labor by his own bootstraps, he worked and studied his way to university. He proved success lived in anyone willing to push through fear and suffering. The child had suffered long fourteen-hour days as a "piecer," tying together tiny bits of string at the cotton mill in Blantyre, Scotland. With practically no childhood, Livingstone had early adopted an unwavering endurance for hardship, along with an egalitarian love for the poor and underprivileged. Education offered a means of rising out of poverty. With his family's encouragement, he studied at night, learning Latin and securing a seat in college and eventually missionary medical school.

Livingstone's expeditions had set no speed records. His tortuous trek across Africa, often meandering at the behest of native guides, took three years. The delay served his reputation well—the longer his absence, the more fascinating and extraordinary his persona became. Livingstone's astonishing adventures even bolstered an image of immortality, surviving more than thirty bouts of fever as well as worms and countless undiagnosed conditions. To his riveted audiences, he could as easily have returned from the moon.

Perhaps Cambridge was a curious host. Critics might have shrugged Livingstone off as a reckless daredevil cashing in on short-lived stardom—the luck of a winning hand in a lethal survival lottery. But underneath his brazen adventures, Livingstone possessed a résumé befitting a Cambridge lecturer. In addition to geographic discoveries, he had influenced science and medicine, documenting insects, weather patterns, and geological formations. Among his scientific firsts, he had recorded and described the deadly effects of the tsetse fly. In medicine, the reality of near-constant malaria forced him to experiment with cures, becoming one of the first to institute an effective prophylactic and therapeutic treatment for malaria: a daily dose of quinine.

As he spoke in the Senate House, all present could clearly see this man had sacrificed greatly. He had spent many years away from his family and the comforts of home; he had endured great hardships; and, at the hand of sickness, man, and beast, he had repeatedly stared death in the face.

"People talk of the sacrifice I have made in spending so much of my life in Africa," Livingstone stated.

The crowd quieted for Livingstone's moment of self-reflection.

"Can that be called a sacrifice which is simply paid back as a small part of a great debt owing to our God, which we can never repay? Is that a sacrifice which brings its own blest reward in healthful activity, the consciousness of doing good, peace of mind, and a bright hope of a glorious destiny hereafter? Away with the word in such a view and with such a thought!" he bellowed.

"It is emphatically no sacrifice. Say rather it is a privilege. Anxiety, sickness, suffering, or danger now and then with a foregoing of the common conveniences and charities of this life, may make us pause and cause the spirit to waver and the soul to sink; but let this only be for a moment. All these are nothing when compared with the glory which shall be revealed in and for us. I never made a sacrifice."

Sacrifice—needless, bloody sacrifice—he had witnessed, but not his own. Livingstone steered his podium from science to the matter tearing at his heart. Cambridge, with its regal stature and lofty culture, soon found itself confronted with an unanticipated reality of the African condition: the endurance of the slave trade.

All commerce in Central Africa, Livingstone told them, "is at present only in slaves, of which the poorer people have an unmitigated horror."

He knew, more than anyone in the room—perhaps more than any European in the world—the fear, destruction, and bloodshed of slavery. With the celebrated end of the transatlantic slave trade thirty years earlier, the eyes of the world had turned their attention away from Africa. Few Europeans had witnessed slavery there. Livingstone was one—maybe the only one.

Despite its dreadfulness, Livingstone approached slavery optimistically. The vibrant era of British abolition had run its course through his youth and colored his worldview. Led by parliamentarian William Wilberforce, along with Prime Minister William Pitt, and later parliamentarian Charles James Fox, the men had campaigned persistently against slavery for decades. Their tireless work had ended the trade throughout the British Empire in 1807 and abolished slavery in 1833. Livingstone had British abolition burning inside him.

"I am old enough to remember the dreary time when the brave indignant oratory of Fox, the majestic eloquence of Pitt, and the silver voice of Wilberforce, were heard in vain in St. Stephen's Chapel. When, year after year, the representatives of free England sanctioned and commended a vile unchristian trade in the flesh and blood of the men of Africa."[3]

In South Africa, Livingstone had encountered the twilight of the West African transatlantic slave trade. He had watched as the west coast trade dwindled, largely on account of heavy British naval patrols. He felt confident abolition would win throughout Africa, but Britain had to join the fight.

Livingstone, however, was no Fox, Pitt, or Wilberforce. Politics did not interest him, and he did not possess a platform upon which to legislate. Livingstone was a mere layman—but a layman with a growing voice and reputation.

Compared to his predecessors, Livingstone's still-modest abolition efforts reflected a man forming his convictions. Prior to his years in South Africa, he had attended a public meeting of the Society for the Extinction of the Slave Trade and for the Civilization of Africa. At the meeting, parliamentarian Thomas Fowell Buxton, Wilberforce's successor in the abolition movement, proclaimed Christianity alone would not end slavery—Christianity needed commerce. Africans must trade their own goods, he argued, otherwise chiefs would continue to sell their people to pay for the European goods they coveted.

As a young, wide-eyed missionary stepping onto South African shores, Livingstone had adopted the Buxton philosophy: Christianity and commerce for civilization. Idealistically, he took his theory of engaging Africa to sell something—other than people—to the Makololo Kingdom, where he planned to set up a mission outpost.

He discovered, to his horror, a kingdom under siege. The slave trade had found the Makololo before he did. From the west, the Portuguese had arrived to facilitate slavery; from the east, slave traders from Zanzibar.

The slave trade suddenly became personal and urgent. Convicted to save the Makololo, Livingstone sought a readily accessible commercial trade route, either from Africa's west or east coasts. Only he could prevent this tragedy, making the treacherous walk across the continent and opening the route himself.

He first headed west, reasoning that if Portuguese slave traders could make the journey, then legitimate commercial traders could do so as well. The route grew more difficult than expected. On principle, Livingstone refused existing trails—trails the slavers had built.

"It is so undesirable to travel in a path once trodden by slave-traders," Livingstone told his spellbound audience, "I preferred to find out another line of march."

The long march west from his base in Linyanti to Loanda, the capital of Angola, took more than six months. Deathly ill, Livingstone rested for three months in Loanda before turning around to begin trekking east, backtracking over his westerly trail until reaching uncharted territory in Central Africa. For much of the expedition, he followed the Zambezi River—Africa's fourth largest river system. He tracked the Zambezi to its mouth on the Indian Ocean, only neglecting a short stretch of river. This three-year journey on foot completed his historic continental crossing.

Livingstone's search for an accessible trade route brought about an idea novel to African missionaries: the use of rivers. Rivers could be highways for Christianity, he reasoned, and they answered the geographic riddle of opening the African interior to commerce.

Commerce, however, had a vicious rival in the slave trade. Captured slaves served two purposes: they transported ivory to the coast and then they became goods for sale. Selling slaves at a journey's end proved far easier than returning them or reusing them. No significant trade went back into Africa. Exported ivory powered the slave trade; European demand for ivory-keyed pianos and ivory-decorated utensils showed no signs of slowing. To undercut slavery, Livingstone needed to undercut ivory. But, to undercut anything, he needed to establish his watery highway.

"It is therefore most desirable to . . . open a way for the consumption of free production, and the introduction of Christianity and commerce."

Livingstone ended his Cambridge speech abruptly. The audience waited with bated breath for his next words. Suddenly, he looked up, speaking directly and decisively to the massive crowd.

"I beg to direct your attention to Africa," he bellowed. "I know that in a few years I shall be cut off in that country, which is now open; do not let it be shut again! I go back to Africa to try to make an open path for commerce and Christianity; do you carry out the work which I have begun. I leave it with you."

Silence. The awestruck audience had clung to every word, and as the man's appeal settled upon them, it left a penetrating reticence. Moments later, the crowd rose to their feet, exploding into roaring applause. Livingstone's call to action—leaving the opening of Africa to his audience—would not fall on deaf ears.

Departing the stage, Cambridge officials ushered Livingstone into a reception in the Combination Room at Trinity College—far enough away to escape the adoring mobs. There, dignitaries and luminaries awaited him.

Round after round of cheers rained on Livingstone at the gathering. Professor Sedgwick, Vice Master of Trinity College, delivered the farewell speech thanking Dr. Livingstone. Sedgwick declared the evening "the most enthusiastic reception which he had ever witnessed there during the last half century."[4]

Cambridge culminated the Livingstone victory lap. As he retired for the evening, his life stood at a new crossroads. He could remain in England, basking in the glory of success and a life of quiet satisfaction with his wife and children, or he could return to Africa to continue his pursuits. Yet, along with the stories he carried back from Africa, he also carried heavy, soul-crushing burdens. Family tensions mounted. Professional relationships reached their breaking points. All of Britain awaited his next move.

And then the fame. Fame had its own challenges. While he embraced it, Livingstone did not seek prominence. In part, he resented it, perhaps because it came with a danger: his future work might not rise to the world's great expectations.

2 ✿ THE COST OF FAME

. . . some abuse me now, and say that I am no Christian.
—David Livingstone

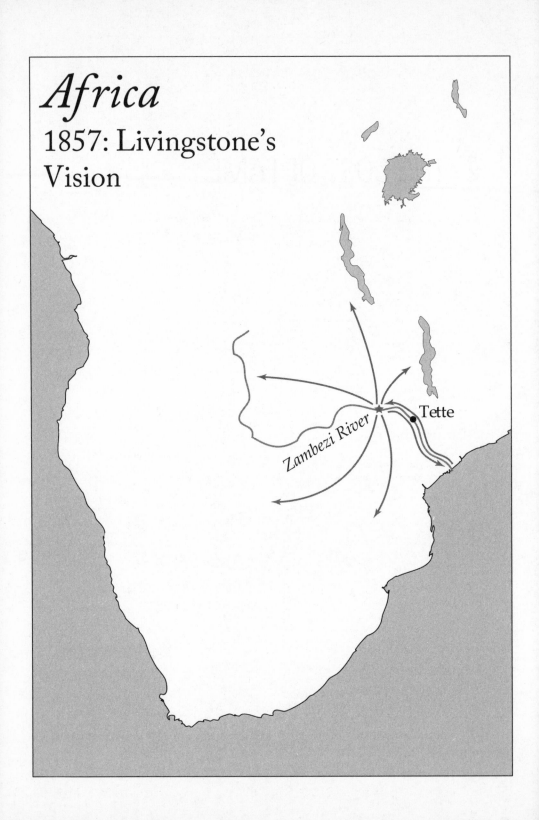

Africa
1857: Livingstone's
Vision

Tette

Zambezi River

November 1, 1857: Livingstone publishes *Missionary Travels and Researches in South Africa.*
15 years, 7 months, and 4 days until the end of the East African slave trade.

Slaves sold per annum: 15,000
Total victims of the slave trade: 225,000

The greatest triumph in geographical research which has been effected in our times," Sir Roderick Murchison had declared of Livingstone's African crossing.[1] The statement could come from no greater authority: Sir Roderick Murchison was the new president of the Royal Geographical Society.

His chiseled face between a broad forehead and a consummate high collar, Murchison presented himself as a stately man of high society. His work as a renowned Scottish geologist had led to his knighthood, and admirers honored him with Murchison-named geographic features the world over.

The Royal Geographical Society had fallen on hard financial times prior to Murchison's installation as president. With an onerous business model relying on membership fees and event proceeds, Murchison had to curry fresh interest in exploration and find marquee names to fill seats at RGS events. Livingstone could certainly draw a crowd.

Even before Livingstone returned to England's shores, Murchison had Livingstone in his sights. Murchison praised him, wrote about him, and awarded him the RGS Gold Medal. He had to make Livingstone synonymous with British exploration. He would make the man of science an icon.

The era of grandiose, seafaring exploration had passed. The triumphs of ocean-going heroes such as Polo, Columbus, Magellan, and

Cook could no longer be replicated. With all continents accounted for, nearly everything under the sun had been discovered. Exploration now turned to the most remote interiors of the world, with Africa in the fore. Deeming it the "Dark Continent," cartographers, knowing only Africa's coastlines, simply blotted the entire interior black with ink. The nickname did nothing to tame imagery of a hostile, terrifying world. To Europe, Africa presented an uncharted abyss.

The Royal Geographical Society needed a fresh spokesperson to champion a new generation of British exploration, and Murchison could not dream of a more perfect archetype than Livingstone, African explorer. Livingstone's rapid trajectory from poverty to graduation from medical school with a year of theological study was remarkable. Accomplishing this by the age of twenty-seven was perhaps unprecedented.

Murchison took notice.

But Livingstone also brought another important sphere of influence: the faith community. He was, first and foremost, a missionary. The title carried a charming image of piety and selfless determination in the pursuit of a higher calling. Unlike the RGS, he spoke the language of religious leaders—he was theologically trained with a message of freedom through Christ. His antislavery rhetoric revived the religious sentimentality of the antislavery fervor of Wilberforce and the Clapham Circle.

Even purely secular ends of the state admired his missionary work. Livingstone carried British ideals to lands beyond her arms and extended the Wilberforcean vision of abolition. Although British foreign policy had begun retreating from further imperialistic colonization, the thought of a global "moral empire" built upon British principles delighted the nation. Livingstone embodied it all, and Murchison sensed opportunity.

Yet, as long as Livingstone remained under the authority of his sending agency, the hero could not be notably repurposed for science. Murchison pursued him hard, and his timing could not have been better.

He sent Livingstone a letter before his arrival in England. Serendipitously, it reached Livingstone immediately after a stinging funding denial from the London Missionary Society, his missionary sending agency. Despite Livingstone's success and the celebration of his achievements, the LMS saw his achievements as too far removed from the call of a missionary.

"While yielding none to their appreciation of the objects upon which, for some years past, your energies have been concentrated," the letter from the LMS directors read, "[the directors] are nonetheless restricted in their power of aiding plans connected only remotely with the spread of the Gospel."[2]

In one short letter, the directors had ceased all of Livingstone's work, everything he had accomplished in the past twelve years. They cast the blame on the harsh African climate and poisonous insects—such a place could not be suitable for missionaries, Livingstone included. The directors would no longer support missionary efforts in remote and difficult locations. Livingstone was furious.

While his walk across Africa had had little to do with evangelism, he believed his work ultimately opened routes for the gospel. Yet he had little to show in way of converts to Christianity. The LMS wanted numbers, not narratives.

To Livingstone, the LMS letter contradicted his purpose in Africa and his understanding of the great commission: taking the gospel to uncharted portions of the country. He thrived on challenge, and corralling him into a developed mission community presented none. He longed for the wilds.

At the age of twenty-one, Livingstone had read *Journal of Three Voyages Along the Coast of China*. He set China, largely unreached by the gospel, as his target. But by the time Livingstone finished seminary, Britain and China found themselves at war over international trade, including poppies. The Opium Wars forced him to set his sights elsewhere.

During Livingstone's theological studies, Dr. Robert Moffat, a celebrated missionary in South Africa, returned to London and spoke to a group of young missionaries. Moffat addressed an eager crowd; Livingstone watched from the audience.

"I had sometimes seen in the morning sun the smoke of a thousand villages where no missionary had ever been."[3]

The imagery captivated Livingstone—he imagined himself standing in the morning sun; a vast African plain with the smoke of a thousand villages could be his new calling. After the presentation, Livingstone approached Moffat.

Livingstone asked Moffat what he could do for Africa.

"I believe [you] would not go to an old station, but would advance to unoccupied ground." Moffat suggested the vast plain of which he spoke—a thousand villages ready to receive the gospel.

Livingstone soon reported to the directors of the LMS.

"What is the use of my waiting for the end of this abominable opium war?" Livingstone bemoaned. "I will go to Africa."

The directors concurred; Livingstone would follow Moffat.

Much had changed since then.

The new letter from the LMS—the letter denying his return to the unreached African plains—showed a different side of the society. Tightening their belts or compressing their message, the LMS lacked the innovation and ingenuity to retain a man like Livingstone. For Murchison and the Royal Geographical Society, opportunity knocked.

For Livingstone, the allure of the RGS came with an obvious attraction: government funding. And it allowed more freedom to reach unexplored areas. But the RGS also struck a deeper chord with Livingstone: science.

Livingstone loved science. Its books had offered a means of escape from the bondage of the mill. He read extensively in his youth and found a fascination with the workings of the world. His studies left him convinced science and faith were not mutually exclusive, but complementary. Had he not felt a religious obligation to ministry, he might have chosen a career grounded in science.

Science, however, contradicted his upbringing. His family had entrenched Christian faith in him at an early age, almost fundamentally so. His father allegedly went so far as to drop the *e* from the family name for several years to avoid any connection between *Livingstone* and *living stone*, a talisman of witchcraft. The possibility of personal damnation terrified a young Livingstone, and he struggled to reconcile his family's fundamentalism with the world around him.

"I found neither peace nor happiness, which caused me (never having revealed my state of mind to anyone) often to bewail my sad estate with tears in secret," he wrote as an adult.[4]

Livingstone's anxieties and upbringing compelled him to search for a faith component to his vocation; his life calling would involve spreading the gospel to unreached parts of the world. Then he found medical missions. Medical missions answered to both science and faith. He could spread the gospel and study the world. Healing the sick offered the opportunity to practice science while gaining access to places potentially forbidden for missionaries. Above all, he saw his purpose in mirroring Jesus.

"My great object," Livingstone said, "was to be like Him to imitate Him as far as He could be imitated. We have not the power of working miracles, but we can do a little in the way of healing the sick, and I sought a medical education in order that I might be like Him."[5]

Livingstone approached Africa in a manner differing from his explorer and missionary contemporaries. Scientists and missionaries of the day largely explained the lag in development between Africa and Europe as a lack of intelligence among Africans. The supposition led to a broad predisposition of racial inferiority. Livingstone found it to be quite the opposite.

"[W]e have seen nothing to justify the notion that they are of a different 'breed' or 'species' from the most civilized," he wrote. "The African is a man with every attribute of human kind."[6]

The mutual understanding and respect Livingstone shared with the people of Africa came through time and attention. Villagers would often remark how he spent time getting to know them, unlike many of his contemporaries who would preach and leave. Livingstone relished his time in the presence of Africans, purposefully making long, meandering trips in their company.

No jugglery or sleight-of-hand, as was recommended to Napoleon III, would have any effect in the civilization of the Africans. They have too much good sense for that. Nothing brings them to place thorough confidence in Europeans but a long course of well-doing. They believe readily in the supernatural as effecting any new process or feat of skill, for it is part of their original faith to ascribe everything above human agency to unseen spirits. Goodness or unselfishness impresses their minds more than any kind of skill or power.[7]

Now, with the LMS rejection, Livingstone found himself again facing the question that plagued his youth: Could he reconcile science and faith? The LMS had taken him on the missionary path. He went on faith, but his work had gravitated toward science—an accidental explorer. He went in search of the unreached; he discovered new languages, insects, and points of geographic significance. But a missionary-scientist was an abomination in the eyes of the LMS. Such a person had no place in their organization.

"My views of what is *missionary* duty are not so contracted as those whose ideal is a dumpy sort of man with a Bible under his arm," Livingstone explained. "I have labored in bricks and mortar, at the forge and at the carpenter's bench, as well as in preaching and medical practice. I feel that I am 'not my own.' I am serving Christ when shooting a buffalo for my men, or taking an astronomical observation."[8]

The interest from the RGS presented Livingstone the opportunity to pursue science but use his scientific platform for matters of spiritual consequence, specifically the abolition of slavery. He wrote to Murchison confidentially: "I suspect I am to be sent somewhere else [by the London Missionary Society], but will prefer dissolving my connection with the Society and following my own plans as a private Christian."

Livingstone opened the door for an offer from Murchison by sharing the details of the paltry one-hundred-pound "subsistence" salary the LMS scarcely provided.

Murchison immediately approached the British government to

secure funding. He organized a fundraising event for Livingstone and appealed to Lord Clarendon, the British Foreign Secretary, zealously urging him to make use of "this extraordinary man."

The LMS knew nothing of any of this. The society even honored Livingstone at its own event, and he attended board meetings advocating for plans to push the society deeper into Africa. The LMS directors assumed Livingstone would remain financially dependent on them and dutifully return to the South African mission post they had assigned.

Meanwhile, Murchison arranged for a meeting between Livingstone and Lord Clarendon. After the meeting, Clarendon asked Livingstone to submit a formal statement of his aims for the next expedition. The government would entertain funding it.

The Zambezi River, Livingstone wrote to Clarendon, could be a path for commerce and Christianity into the center of Africa—"God's Highway," as he reportedly put it.[9] "I believe we can by legitimate commerce, in the course of a few years," he continued, "put an entire stop to the traffic of slaves over a large extent of territory."[10]

Livingstone had, in fact, a bolder vision, imagining a British colony deep in Central Africa. By providing lawful trade and legitimately employing Africans, Britain would starve out the slavers. Commerce would supplant slavery, and the model would replicate throughout Africa. Britain would directly benefit too: vast virgin land would provide England with a supply of unending natural resources.

Despite this ambitious vision, Livingstone proposed only a moderate fact-finding venture. He knew his dreams might be too bold for the government to support. With the British Empire reeling from discontent in its far-flung colonies—settled in overzealous imperialism—Livingstone thought perhaps he would delay suggesting a full-fledged colony.

Five proposals outlined the Zambezi expedition. Livingstone's first and foremost purpose was to eliminate the slave trade. His next propositions appealed to more than British public conscience. He tempted the government's appetite for resources with burgeoning prospects for trade in groundnut oil, sugarcane juice, and, most alluring, cotton. Britain desperately wanted to quit its reliance on American slave-grown cotton. The banks of the Zambezi, Livingstone asserted, could offer more plentiful land for cotton than even the southern United States. Britain salivated at the thought.

While Clarendon considered the proposal, Murchison campaigned for funding, and Livingstone wrote. Instead of immediately returning to Africa, friends persuaded him to stay and publish *Missionary Travels and Researches in South Africa*, a compilation of the adventures and discoveries of his past twelve years.

The public devoured *Missionary Travels*. Each page of his book described a world no European had ever laid eyes upon—vibrant people, extraordinary customs, mysterious diseases, and dangerous animals. Adding adventure to novelty, Livingstone had constantly brushed with death.

His most infamous narrow escape had come at the jaws of a lion. In an African village paralyzed by the beasts, terrified villagers ran to Livingstone seeking his hunting skill to kill the lion. Livingstone had encountered lions before—he once helplessly witnessed a woman "devoured in her garden."[11]

At the villagers' request, Livingstone set out, gun over his shoulder, to track the lion. As he walked alone across the valley to track the beast, the lion found him first. Livingstone lifted his gun, aimed, and fired both barrels. *Bang!*—a direct hit. But not a kill shot. Startled, the giant cat turned in defense. As Livingstone rushed to reload, the lion rushed him. Pouncing with a giant leap, the lion's teeth sank into Livingstone's left shoulder as it tackled him to the ground. Growling, the beast violently shook him "as a terrier dog shaking a rat."[12]

"It caused a sort of dreaminess," Livingstone recalled. He felt no pain or terror. "I was quite conscious of all that was happening . . . It was like what patients partially under the influence of chloroform describe, who see all the operation, but feel not the knife."[13]

Livingstone thought the moment would be his last as he painlessly watched his approaching death in slow motion.

Unexpectedly, an old African man appeared on the scene with a gun and fired both barrels. The gun jammed. Yet the noise distracted the lion from Livingstone, drawing its attention to the old man. The lion released Livingstone, leaping at the man and driving its teeth deep into his thigh. Then it turned to attack another native, biting him in the shoulder. Amidst the commotion, the lion succumbed to the wounds inflicted by Livingstone's initial gunshot.

The beast fell to the ground and Livingstone rose to his feet. Shattered and bearing eleven permanent tooth scars, his arm would never fully heal or again rise higher than his shoulder. Despite injury, the attack transcended the physical—Livingstone became fearless. Death no longer scared him.

"The shake annihilated fear," Livingstone reflected, "and allowed no sense of horror in looking round at the beast. This peculiar state is probably produced in all animals killed by the carnivore; and if so, is a merciful provision by our benevolent creator for lessening the pain of death."[14]

Punctuated by the lion encounter, *Missionary Travels* sold an astounding seventy thousand copies. Livingstone was not only famous, but fever gripped England.

A best-selling book now made Livingstone not only famous but rich as well. He set aside money to take care of his family, who had mostly lived in squalor while he was away. From rags to riches, Livingstone now possessed financial security, social respect, and modern comforts. He had it all; he had become an icon.

Yet, this new life was unfamiliar—uncomfortable in fact. He preferred the modesty and seclusion of Africa. He wished to be back on African soil as soon as possible.

But with paling LMS support and no reply from the government, Livingstone faced a crucial decision: Would he remain a missionary?

3 ❦ GREAT EXPECTATIONS

*Some of the brethren do not hesitate to tell the nativs that
my object is to obtain the applause of men. This bothers
me, for I sometimes suspect my own motives.*

—David Livingstone

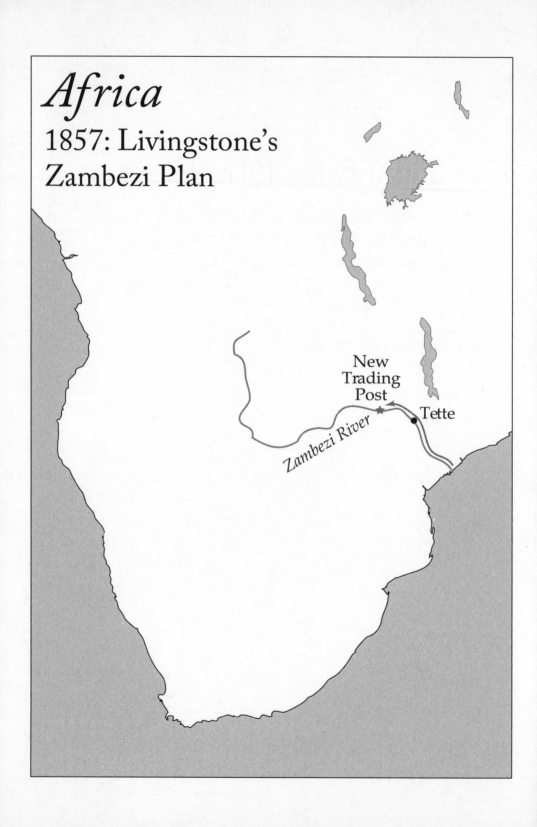

Africa

1857: Livingstone's
Zambezi Plan

New
Trading
Post

Tette

Zambezi River

February 15, 1858: Livingstone receives a farewell banquet.
15 years, 3 months, and 21 days until the end
of the East African slave trade.

Slaves sold per annum: 15,000
Total victims of the slave trade: 240,000

R esignation tendered.

Livingstone shocked the London Missionary Society with his declaration of departure in 1857. The directors were caught completely off guard. They did not want to lose Livingstone at the height of his popularity—and the peak of his earning power.

His colleagues confronted him at once. A trusted friend and counselor, J. B. Braithwaite, expressed concern over the prospect of Livingstone dissolving his connection with the missionary society.

"[M]y fear," Braithwaite wrote to him, "has been lest the severing of thy connection with a recognised religious body should lead any to suppose that thy Christian interests were in the least weakened; or that thou wast now going forth with any lower aim than the advancement of the Redeemer's kingdom."

His friends advised against making a public departure from the LMS. It might lead people to think he gave up missionary work, or even his Christian faith. With "missionary" as a foundational identity, Livingstone's resignation might indicate a major fracture in his faith, character, and the society.

"[The decision] would in a greater or less degree," Braithwaite continued, "and, perhaps, very gradually, and almost insensibly to thyself, turn the current of thy own thoughts and feelings away from those channels of usefulness and service, as a minster of the gospel."[1]

Livingstone ignored the advice.

Indeed, Livingstone's resignation raised public questions. Had he cast off the faith component of his work to pursue purely secular ends? Perhaps he sought fame and fortune? Livingstone vigorously refuted such remarks.

"Knowing that some persons do not believe that opening up a new country to the sympathies of Christendom was not a proper work for an agent of a Missionary Society to engage in," Livingstone wrote, "I now refrain from taking an salary from the Society with which I was connected; so no pecuniary loss sustained by any one."[2]

Privately, Livingstone's decision drifted against family currents. Robert Moffat, Livingstone's missionary-mentor turned father-in-law, responded with fury. Moffat unequivocally believed Livingstone should continue as a missionary and that his son-in-law's resignation deceived the society that had launched him. The decision rippled through the family. Livingstone soon persuaded Moffat's son, John, to follow suit, leaving their cherished society to go out independently as a private Christian.

"I never felt a single pang at having left the Missionary Society," Livingstone reflected. "I acted for my Master, and believe that all are to devote their special faculties to Him. I regretted that unconscientious men took occasion to prevent many from sympathizing with me."[3]

While he never looked back on the LMS, Livingstone would not proceed for long as the "private Christian" of whom he wistfully wrote to Murchison. Murchison's persuasion and the political weight of the RGS were not long ignored. Murchison convinced Clarendon to appoint Livingstone as British Consul with a roving commission throughout East Africa. Without hesitation, Livingstone accepted the government post—a powerful title and an open door for funding his next much-anticipated expedition.

Accompanying his new government post, Livingstone received Foreign Secretary Lord Clarendon's support for an expedition of the Zambezi River and a five-fold increase over his previous salary. On December 11, 1857, the government allocated five thousand pounds to underwrite the Zambezi expedition for the purpose of opening up the river to navigable travel and surveying the region's natural resources. The next day, Livingstone met with the prime minister, Lord Palmerston, who told him preparations for a full-scale expedition would begin immediately.

In the eyes of Palmerston and Clarendon, any investment in Livingstone was a political boon. They did not need significant results from the expedition. Supporting Livingstone—a national hero—and his expedition would boost their political popularity, capitalizing on England's Livingstone enthusiasm. Of course, any new geographic discoveries would further feather the hat of British exploration; a successful commercial venture would be a windfall.

Livingstone crafted a plan. No expedition to Africa remained free of obstacles—and the Zambezi imposed several imminent challenges. First and foremost, access to the Zambezi fell to the discretion of the Portuguese. Having established various settlements along the Zambezi, Portugal controlled the river, monopolized its trade, and claimed the entire Zambezi Valley. There could be no expedition without Portuguese permission.

Permission required careful diplomacy with Lisbon. Portugal opposed Britain establishing commercial ventures in its territory, no matter how innocently presented. Under the guise of a geographic expedition, Britain might lay claim to portions of land or resources. Portugal also had secrets to hide. She did not want Britain to witness her participation in the lucrative slave trade. But, despite Lisbon's trepidation, Britain's request could not be denied over a matter as trivial as a "scientific expedition"—it was a fight not worth the political capital. Lisbon nervously tolerated the expedition's request.

Expedition plans appeared modest: steam up the Zambezi and back. Anticipating minor rapids, the steamer would anchor in the shallows until seasonal rains arrived. When waters rose, they would pass through the rapids, proving the Zambezi navigable by boat. Upstream, the crew, along with a team of African recruits, would establish a trading center and begin agricultural experiments to prove that the land was suitable for growing cotton and sugar.

For Livingstone, the upper Zambezi offered more than a resource trove. He had broader, largely unrevealed, ambitions for the plateau. He suspected fertile land, perfect for farming and living—the right soil for cotton and elevation beyond the reach of mosquitos. He dreamed it would one day host a British colony—an outpost in Central Africa for trade and Christian missions. To him, a permanent colony justified his entire life's work opening up the continent.

On paper, the expedition looked flawless. Livingstone assembled a crew of six men with skills as diverse as the goals he planned to accomplish. He hired a geologist, a botanist, an engineer, an artist, a physician, and a chaplain.

In his search, several professors recommended John Kirk as the crew physician. At only twenty-five, Kirk was twenty years younger than Livingstone—a greenhorn, but competent and committed. He had earned a medical degree and, like Livingstone, Kirk was a Scot—an immediate amity between the men. Kirk's duties would be diverse, from doctor to botanist, and his appointment would begin a long, often rocky friendship between the men. Confiding in Kirk in a personal letter at the outset of the expedition, Livingstone admitted his commitment in advancing abolition and invited Kirk to "aid in the great work of supplanting by lawful commerce the odious traffic in slaves."[4] It would prove to be a prophetic charge.

Perhaps Livingstone knew the demands of African exploration to be a young man's calling. He hired nineteen-year-old Richard Thornton as the expedition's geologist. Despite his youth, Thornton brought intellectual horsepower to the challenge, underscored by references deeming him a prodigy of science.

The expedition received enthusiastic public support. Upon announcing it in Parliament, cheers rose up from both sides of the aisle. The English public favored the endeavor and eagerly awaited updates on plans and expectations.

To celebrate the soon-to-launch expedition, the RGS threw a grand banquet in the ornately colonnaded Freemason's Hall in London. Despite carefully controlled capacity, the audience swelled to more than three hundred, comprising the most illustrious names in art, politics, science, and theology. Among the most celebrated attendees were diplomats from Denmark, Norway, and Sweden, as well as the bishop of Oxford, Samuel Wilberforce, the son of William Wilberforce. Offers to buy an invitation soared to five times the face value of a ticket, and the RGS turned away many willing buyers.

At one end of the grand hall lay the buffet feast; at the other end sat the platform party chaired by Murchison, front and center. To Murchison's right sat Livingstone, accompanied by his wife, Mary Livingstone, and to the left the Duke of Argyll, the powerful Scottish nobleman. Behind them, the RGS exhibited a map marking Livingstone's discoveries, and before the table, unveiled for the first time, rose a bust of the explorer.

Before the raucously energetic crowd, the Grenadier Guards performed national songs followed by Scottish tunes from the duke's pipers dressed in full highland regalia.

"I now rise to propose the toast of the evening," Murchison bellowed as he stood to the crowd's applause.[5]

"A week ago, when this farewell dinner to my distinguished friend was first announced, I was told that there would be great difficulty in obtaining a sufficient number of persons to attend it. I replied at once that the name Livingstone was sufficient to attract an assembly larger than any room in London could hold."

The crowd let out a cheer.

"And that the only weak part of the proceeding was requesting me to take the chair."

"No, no!" retorted his listeners.

"A year and a-half ago it would perhaps have been necessary for me to make statement as to who Dr. Livingstone was, and what he had done, but now the 30,000 copies of his book have shown the public what is the character of the man, and what the nature of his deeds . . ."

The audience erupted in loud cheers.

". . . we all now know his character, and few words are necessary in treating of the actions of my distinguished friend. I will, however, call attention to one or two facts. My distinguished friend has not only made us acquainted with the character and disposition of the inhabitants of the interior of Africa, but he has accomplished that which no missionary has ever accomplished before, for with great perseverance and labour he has laid down the longitude and latitude of places hitherto unknown to us. This is a great claim upon our admiration as men of science; but great as this claim is, it falls far short of others which attach to the name of Livingstone . . ."

"Hear, hear!" rose voices around the crowd.

". . . who, by his fidelity to his world, by his conscientious regards for his engagements, has conciliated the natives of Africa by the example which he has shown them in his treatment of the poor people who followed him in researches through that great continent."

A roar of excitement filled the hall.

"Sitting by my side," Murchison pointed to Livingstone, "is one who, knowing what he had to encounter—who 20 or 30 times had struggled with the fever of Africa,—who, knowing that a ship was waiting to carry him to his native land, where his wife and children were anxiously awaiting his arrival, true to his plighted word, threw these considerations, which would have attracted any ordinary man, to the winds, and reconducted those poor natives who had accompanied him through the heart of the country back to their homes, and who by that noble conduct has left for himself in that country a glorious name, and has shown to the people of Africa [what] an English Christian is."

The audience gushed with loud and sustained cheering.

". . . and now a few words with regard to his future expedition, of which I may say that no expedition could have been better organized than this one has been . . . I would not, however, wish you to raise your hopes too high as to the immediate success of this expedition; it must be looked upon as an expedition of an exploratory character. It is, in fact, merely sowing seed, which, under God's Providence, may produce a great and abundant harvest. We must not expect a sudden inundation of crops of indigo, cotton, and those raw materials which we manufacture in this country, nor must we expect suddenly to light upon a new El Dorado. I believe, however that my distinguished friend may be able to find districts which abound in gold and copper. If, however these expectations should fail, if we gain nothing more than having in Africa that good name which Dr. Livingstone is sure to leave . . ."

Applause interrupted Murchison again.

". . . and that accession to our knowledge which the discoveries of our distinguished guest are certain to supply to us, even then I say that the Livingstone expedition will be a great and glorious one."

The crowd roared with excitement, taking a long time for Murchison to settle them.

"I propose, therefore, the health of my distinguished friend Dr. Livingstone, and success to his enterprise."

After the enthusiastic toast and cheering subsided, a gentleman in the room suggested an honor to Mary. The crowd gave her three cheers.

Livingstone rose to respond as the crowd held its breath for the words of the man whom the evening honored.

"When I was in Africa," Livingstone began, "I could not but look forward with joyous anticipation to my arrival in my native land; but when I remember how I have been received, and when I reflect that I am now again returning to the scene of my former labours, I am at a loss how to express in words the feelings in my heart.

"In former times," Livingstone continued in an uncharacteristically personal fashion, "which I was performing what I considered to be my duty in Africa, I felt great pleasure in the work; and now, when I perceive that all eyes are directed to my future conduct, I feel as if I were laid under a load of obligation to do better than I have ever done as yet."

Cheered on, he redirected his comments to the slave trade.

". . . I feel convinced," Livingstone spoke, "that if we can establish a system of free labour in Africa it will have a most decided influence upon slavery throughout the world."

The crowd roared wildly.

"Success, however, under Providence, depends upon us as Englishmen. I look upon Englishmen as perhaps the most freedom-loving people in the world, and I think that the kindly feeling which has been displayed towards me since my return to my native land has arisen from the belief that my efforts might at some future time put an end to the odious traffic in slaves."

Applause filled the room.

"England has, unfortunately, been compelled to obtain cotton and other raw material from slave States, and has thus been the mainstay and support of slavery in America. Surely, then, it follows that if we can succeed in obtaining the raw material from other sources than from the slave States of America we should strike a heavy blow at the system of slavery itself."

The crowd cheered.

"I do not wish to arouse expectations in connexion with this expedition which may never be realized," Livingstone concluded, "but what I want to do is to get in the thin end of the wedge, and then I leave it to be driven home by English energy and English spirit."

After extended applause subsided, Murchison rose again, proposing a toast to the British government for sponsoring the expedition. The duke of Argyll responded to accept the recognition.

"It was an honor for any Parliament or to any Government," the duke began, "to have it in their power in any way to aid so great a cause as that noble enterprise to which Dr. Livingstone had devoted his best energies, and to the further prosecution of which he was willing to devote his life.

"The main source, however, of the interest which was felt in the expedition," the duke continued, "was in the feeling of Englishmen that the principles advocated by Wilberforce on the subject of slavery should be carried into effect."

The duke affirmed the weight of Livingstone's obligation: "This

expedition was looked forward to with perhaps more inter\
expedition of modern times . . ."

After the launch dinner, as he prepared to cast off the bo\
Livingstone's "load of obligation" weighed heavy under the weight of public expectation. Privately, he bemoaned the continuous stream of events and recognition, wishing for an end to his "lionsing" and "public spouting." He feared going out in public—keeping his head down and covering his face with his hands. Yet the aggrandizing momentum of Murchison's propaganda and *Missionary Travels*'s success could not be contained. The Livingstone myth had already outpaced reality.

Africa, despite the dangers of disease and deadly animals, afforded him safety. Its remoteness insulated him from embellishment and scrutiny where he could continue his work with little oversight.

Still, as all Britain watched with "perhaps more interest than any expedition of modern times," they expected nothing short of success.

PART TWO

FALL

4 TURBULENCE

*I shall hold myself in readiness to go
anywhere, provided it be forward.*

—DAVID LIVINGSTONE

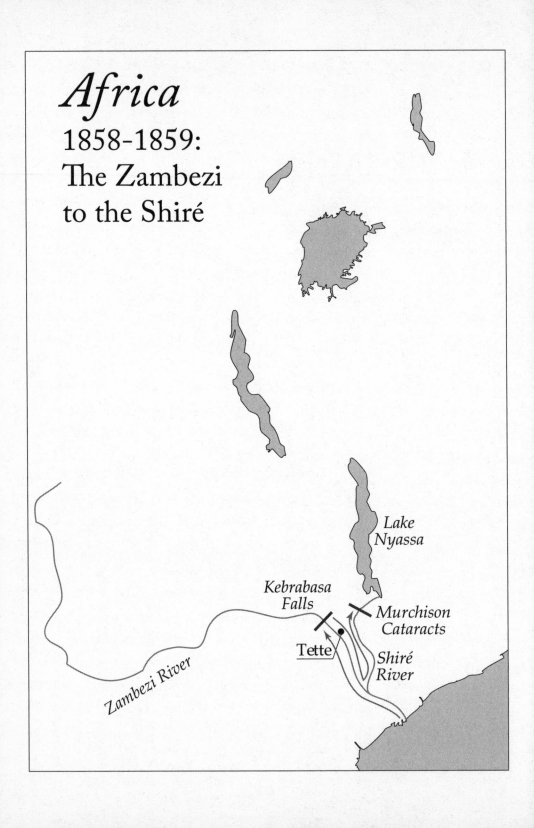

Africa

1858-1859:
The Zambezi
to the Shiré

Lake
Nyassa

Kebrabasa
Falls

Murchison
Cataracts

Tette

Shiré
River

Zambezi River

W e are off again," Livingstone wrote the day of departure, "and we trust that He who rules the waves will watch over us and remain with you, to bless us and make us blessings to our fellow-men."[1]

Beautiful spring weather spurred on the Zambezi expedition's celebrated departure from Liverpool on March 10, 1858. Her Majesty's colonial steamer, the *Pearl*, found favorable winds, carrying them rapidly across the English Channel and the Bay of Biscay.

With the *Pearl* under sail, Livingstone immediately began expedition business. Gathering all members of the party, he read the Foreign Office's instructions and delivered a written account of specific duties to each man.

"You will understand," Livingstone told the crew, "that Her Majesty's Government attach more importance to the moral influence which may be exerted on the minds of the natives by a well-regulated and orderly household of Europeans, setting an example of consistent moral conduct to all who may congregate around the settlement; treating the people with kindness, and relieving their wants; teaching them to make experiments in agriculture, explaining to them the more simple arts, imparting to them religious instruction, as far as they are capable of receiving it, and inculcating peace and good-will to each other."[2]

Livingstone felt optimistic, declaring all his men to be of "the right stamp." With his plan meticulously crafted and his team carefully selected, he anticipated a short, smooth expedition. In addition to Kirk, Livingstone's younger brother Charles joined the crew with the four other men. Livingstone had not seen his brother in eighteen years, as he had traveled to America to study theology. When he returned to England for a brief visit, Livingstone proposed the position and the peculiar title of "moral agent." Charles would serve as an assistant to Livingstone and act as the expedition chaplain, maintaining morale.

Two more stowed away for the voyage: Mary and Oswell, Livingstone's wife and youngest son.

The couple led a complicated life. As the daughter of Robert Moffat, Livingstone's missionary mentor, Mary had arrived in Africa at age four and lived there most of her life. They began their courtship after Livingstone returned to the mission base to recover from his lion attack. Until their meeting, he had rejected any thought of marriage, but Mary swept him away—and they wed in short order. They sometimes traveled into remote areas together as Livingstone went about his duties. Along the way, Mary gave birth to five children within six years. Livingstone referred to her as "the great Irish manufactury."[3] The young Livingstones joined the expeditions as well.

The Livingstones enjoyed a close relationship, but their work afforded no easy marriage. Mary faithfully joined her husband on his adventures far afield, crossing the Kalahari Desert herself and giving birth in the bush. In addition to Africa's lack of basic comforts, she endured hardship and early tragedy. Late in the pregnancy of her fourth child, the Livingstones, along with their three young children, made a treacherous expedition to the interior. Terrible heat, little food and water, and a wagon accident made for a dreadful journey.

Conditions worsened. Mosquitos grew so thick that not an inch of the children's bodies remained unbitten by night's end. The short supply of water occasionally forced them to go as long as two days without a drink. The children grew weak—unable even to stand—compelling the Livingstones to abandon the expedition. Mary gave birth to a daughter once they returned to the mission base. Tragically, the week-old child soon succumbed to a bronchial infection and died screaming. The loss haunted Livingstone. Yet, he reasoned, "[it was] just as likely to have happened if we had remained at home, but now we have one of our number in heaven."[4]

Mary soon became very ill herself. Improperly diagnosed as pain from a rotten tooth, the illness left the right side of her face paralyzed and deformed. She was likely afflicted by Bell's palsy.

"The affection causes considerable deformity," Livingstone described it, "especially when smiling."[5]

His myopic commitment to Africa began to tear his family apart in South Africa. Despite a deep bond with the Moffats, Livingstone's in-laws protested his practices. When the Livingstones learned they should expect another child, a scathing letter from Livingstone's mother-in-law implored him not to take his family back into the interior.

"O Livingstone, what do you mean?" she wrote. "Was it not enough that you lost one lovely babe, and scarcely save the other, while the mother came home threatened with Paralysis? And will you again expose her & them in those sickly regions on an exploring expedition? All the world will condemn the cruelty of the thing to say nothing of the indecorousness of it."[6]

Even on the trip home to Britain, family relations hardly improved. The family spent little time together. Off traveling and lecturing, Livingstone largely left his wife at home to raise their three children. She did not enjoy it.

An affable, vibrant woman while roughing it in Africa, Mary struggled to adjust to hectic, modern England. Growing up as a missionary in the African bush made assimilation to Europe later in life challenging, both physically and socially. Like her husband, she felt more comfortable in Africa than in Europe. She could handle nearly everything, but not London. Anxiety and depression plagued her in Britain.

When Livingstone planned the Zambezi expedition, Mary insisted on joining, and Livingstone factored her in to the equation. He reasoned she could be of constructive use to the team. All but one of the Livingstone children would remain with their grandparents in Europe.

Mary's presence quickly grew complicated. Her seasickness did not subside after the rest of the party gained their sea legs. Off the west coast of Africa, the Livingstones discovered it was not seasickness at all. Mary was pregnant again.

"This is of great trial to me," Livingstone admitted, "for had she come with us, she might have proved of essential service to the expedition in cases of sickness and otherwise."[7]

Shocked and embarrassed, Livingstone kept the news from his team as long as possible. Eventually, however, their speculation demanded verification. She could not continue on to Zambezi with its health risks and discomfort—the boy would also stay with his mother. As the expedition continued toward the Zambezi, it left Mary and Oswell in South Africa for the birth. It would be four years before she would see her husband again.

———

"The two colours did not intermingle," Livingstone noted as the *Pearl* steamed within six miles of land.[8] The water formed a sharp line of contrast between the yellow-green hue of the open ocean and the opaque, muddy outflow from the Zambezi River. The *Pearl* crossed into the murky wrack, the refuse of Africa's interior—debris, sticks, and plant matter.

Approaching new territory, Livingstone kept his notebook at the ready in the pocket of his dark overcoat. The scientist in him took note of everything from plant life to native dress. Later, he would transfer the notes and sketches to his fastidiously kept journal.

As they arrived at the mouth of the Zambezi, the river appeared impenetrable. High waves, heavy surf, and surreptitious rugged coastline made ramparts around the river. Conditions forced the team, which lacked accurate charts or local knowledge, to make experimental attempts to enter the mouth. For two weeks, attempts failed and tempers flared. The irritating delays after a long voyage lit an already short fuse.

Once the *Pearl* finally entered the river, Livingstone planned to steam a significant distance upstream to Tette, an outpost above the worst malarial areas of the lower Zambezi. From there, the expedition would launch a smaller vessel carried on the *Pearl*, the *Ma-Robert*, affectionately named in honor of Mrs. Livingstone. The *Ma-Robert* followed the native tradition of the mother taking the name of her eldest son, "the mother of Robert." The *Ma-Robert* could travel farther into Africa than the *Pearl*, through shallower parts of the river.

Along the Zambezi, native people assembled in astonishment on the banks to watch the ship lumber past. At more than two hundred feet long with three tall masts, the *Pearl* bewildered them. Its sheer size exceeded anything previously seen on the river. An old native man called it a floating village, but the construction perplexed him even more. "Was it made out of one tree?" he asked.

But the large vessel inspired little fear in the local people compared to another power in the region: Mariano. Mariano had made his name as the most notorious slave hunter in the region, earning a reputation for merciless violence. His name would become a wretched, evil word to the expedition. Born of mixed Portuguese and African blood, Mariano's reputation extended to the "half-castes." A native of Portugal expressed a common sentiment, "God made white men, and God made black men, but the devil made half-castes." Well armed with muskets and many men, Mariano had built a slave stockade at the tributary of the Zambezi and Shiré rivers. From there he gained control of the region north of the Zambezi.

In their own tongue the native people named him Matakenya—"trembling." Mariano's brand of slavery did not involve "harmlessly" buying and selling humans for labor, as many of Livingstone's contemporaries imagined the remaining vestiges of the African slave trade to be. Mariano himself had no work to offer his captives. His slaving involved violent raids—slave-hunting forays—among the more helpless tribes. Violently placing his captives in chains, he would march them to the coast for shipment to plantations on the island of Bourbon east of Madagascar in the Indian Ocean.

Initially, Portugal partnered with Mariano to act as its slave agent in exchange for the title to the lands he conquered. Unable to rein in the warlord or the instability caused by his terror, Portugal turned a blind eye to his violence. As long as the slave hunting happened far away, Portuguese authorities chose not to interfere. But Mariano's slaving soon drew attention from a growing audience. He gained more and more power, and his slaving closed in on Portuguese settlements.

As a gentleman of "the highest standing" told Livingstone, "while at dinner with his family, it was no uncommon event for a slave to rush into the room pursued by one of Mariano's men with spear in hand to murder him."[9] Mariano recognized no boundaries to his evil.

The Portuguese soon spoke of him as a "rare monster of inhumanity."[10] Mariano enjoyed living up to his name. To build his reputation of terror, he would spear his captives with his own hands and, according to Portuguese reports, once consecutively took forty lives placed in a row before him, simply to make a statement.

Mariano's growing reign of terror eventually began to disintegrate Portugal's own trade in the region, and the ensuing chaos finally broke its protectorate's stoicism. Portuguese authorities declared war against Mariano, sending an armed force to remove him from the field. Yet even after Mariano's arrest, his followers continued the fight for power, buoyed by the pursuit of their leader's freedom. In the six months leading up to the expedition's arrival, the war had halted all activity on the Zambezi. While it cost the expedition no delay, it left the *Pearl* alone on the water.

The quiet river made for easy sailing on the Zambezi for the first week. Then, only fifty miles upriver, the waterway became impassable to the large *Pearl*. She could steam no farther. Shallower than Livingstone had anticipated, the Zambezi's regularly shifting channels complicated their passage. They could find no one locally with the knowledge to navigate it. Forced to stop, the expedition dreadfully prepared to ferry all its supplies on the small *Ma-Robert*—an operation that would take months.

Even the nimble *Ma-Robert* faired little better steaming upstream than had the clumsy *Pearl*. Harsh conditions made sailing the *Ma-Robert* uncomfortable, and large loads continuously overcrowded the tiny boat, which provided little escape from the blazing heat, soaking rains, and stinging insects. Going upstream with as much as ten tons of weight, even canoes would pass her. The *Ma-Robert* quickly became an impediment to their progress. The boat consumed several tons of firewood a day to power the engine, which snorted so fiercely she earned the moniker "The Asthmatic." Worse yet, the *Ma-Robert* constantly ran aground and the steel hull began to rust and decay.

"A wretched, sham vessel," Livingstone declared her.[11]

Sluggish progress made Livingstone volatile and anxious. But his anxieties stemmed from more than just the boat. A detail gnawed at his mind: the "small rapid" he had overlooked in 1856.

When he followed the Zambezi during his easterly trek across Africa, he had departed from the river's course for one section. He later heard rumors suggesting it contained a small, easily passable rapid, but he had neither seen it nor probed local knowledge with any diligence. All his plans—his hopes for this expedition and his grand vision for opening up Africa's interior—rested on the *Ma-Robert* passing through this uncharted section of river. The question of what lay ahead would burn in him for another six months before he could lift the veil on the unknown stretch of the Zambezi.

To shuttle all the supplies up the river, the *Ma-Robert* made five trips to the *Pearl* through the mosquito-infested jungle. The men suffered from malaria, Livingstone's leadership waned, and near-constant conflict left the team divided. Morale plummeted.

Harsh conditions aboard the boat led to even harsher behavior. Captain Duncan, a mere officer in the Merchant Navy, clashed with Commander Norman Bedingfield, the second-in-command of the expedition. Duncan came with the *Pearl* as master of the ship, while

Bedingfield, a career naval officer accustomed to positions of senior authority, joined the Zambezi expedition after commanding a large warship crewed by several hundred men. Both men believed their instructions entitled them to make navigation decisions over the *Pearl*. Bedingfield resisted any form of subordination to a simple merchant officer—and struggled taking orders at all.

Two months up the Zambezi, an ugly shouting match broke out between Bedingfield and Duncan. Instead of settling the matter privately, Livingstone sided with Duncan in front of the crew. Livingstone and Duncan shared working-class origins, creating a natural amity between the men. His decision smacked of favoritism. The fallout further devastated morale and undermined Livingstone's authority as the impartial expedition leader. Bedingfield offered to resign and return to England as soon as he could be replaced. But until a replacement could be found, he continued to serve the expedition. Consequently, he became Livingstone's scapegoat for the woes of the *Ma-Robert*.

The unfair accusations broke Bedingfield. He left the expedition and waited for another boat to return him to Europe. The expedition gladly welcomed his departure.

———

Livingstone's men often found him standing silently on the deck in his dark overcoat and blue consular cap. He could go weeks without speaking a single word. The unwavering persistence that allowed him to rise above other explorers commandeered his personality under stress. He refused to answer his men's questions. He refused to laugh at a joke. Occasionally he would hum, but nothing more came from his mouth.

Livingstone's sphinxlike autonomy bred resentment. The longer his men went without encouragement from their leader, the deeper he entrenched bitterness. Yet Livingstone remained very much alive under the surface. His private journals overflowed with words, humor, and wit. The expedition received none of it.

Unaccustomed to working in teams, Livingstone lacked inter-personal leadership. The final four years of Livingstone's first expedition to Africa had left him practically alone as he crossed the continent by foot. In those years, he did not have the company of other Europeans. His teams were comprised primarily of Africans who knew only local languages and customs.

Livingstone's method of exploration was to travel fast and light—with the bare minimum of men and supplies. They would barter at villages, often relying on the customary generosity of feeding and hous-ing strangers. Traveling alone, Livingstone pressed ahead at a tenacious pace. This strategy made him a successful explorer—a leg up over other explorers of his day. His contemporaries would travel in large caravans with hundreds of porters carrying many months of supplies. These teams stopped frequently and required regular resupplying as they plod-ded slowly across Africa.

On the Zambezi, Livingstone found himself in close proximity with six European men unfamiliar with African travel. He frequently waited on them. He could no longer stop and start as he wished. Preparing to march or sail demanded additional prep time and tested his patience. The men expected conversation as they walked, which Livingstone had grown to dislike. Unless he had something to say, he proceeded in silence.

Livingstone's brother Charles added fuel to the fire. He would slack off and force the expedition to stop for frequent naps. Yet Charles's older brother refused to chastise him as he did other team members. Livingstone's perceived nepotism bred resentment toward them both.

Inner turmoil exacerbated Livingstone's tense silence. He knew that if the expedition failed, blame fell on him. He had played his entire hand on the Zambezi. He had given up the LMS and spent his political capital securing expedition approval, all the way up to the level of prime minister. All of England watched its hero, waiting for the grand results he promised—results that would liberate a continent, restore England as a major power broker in Africa, and add a jewel to its crown of global exploration.

So far, he had little good to show: abandonment of his wife and son, defection of a high profile colleague, and growing team contention. Overshadowing everything, the rapid loomed: Livingstone's small, overlooked detail now became an imminent, menacing monolith of obsession.

———

After six months of shuttling supplies, the *Ma-Robert* finally rested at the village of Tette on September 8, 1858. Built on a succession of standing ridges on the banks of the Zambezi, Tette formed the final staging ground before entering uncharted water. When they landed, Livingstone celebrated a joyous reunion with the Makololo—a tribe to whom he had grown close during his first expedition. Their chief had ordered them to guide Livingstone along his walk across Africa, and they promised to continue their service after his brief trip to Britain. The Makololo had waited in Tette two years for his return and would accompany the Zambezi expedition as porters.

The expedition would not wait long in Tette. A month after their arrival, they pulled anchor and continued north. Ever so slowly, the *Ma-Robert* steamed upriver against an increasingly strong current. The expedition had optimistically set sail from Tette, but now it barely moved against the intense current.

Despite painfully slow progress, the men found themselves surrounded by magnificence. Cloaked in all her splendor, the Kebrabasa Valley carved deep, narrow ravines dissecting ranges of lofty, tree-covered mountains. Gigantic trees, one measuring eighty-four feet in circumference, shadowed the river and dwarfed the *Ma-Robert*. Brilliant greens, yellows, and reds stood out in relief against the grey bark of their trunks.

"No bottom at ten fathoms," the man running the chains called out.[12] The *Ma-Robert* sailed smoothly in deep, fast water.

The Kebrabasa Rapid—the "small rapid"—preoccupied Livingstone's mind as they approached the narrowing gorge. He imagined it with fear and hope. The *Ma-Robert* would need to sail through it, up the rapid, in order to reach the high plateaus where the expedition promised to establish a commercial outpost. Future trading rested on the expedition's assessment of regional agricultural and mineral resources. As a must-pass barrier, Livingstone would, if necessary, take extreme measures to get through the Kebrabasa. Occasionally, his teammates overheard him mumble about dynamite.

Arriving at the first set of lesser rapids, the *Ma-Robert* steamed quickly through. Prospects increased for the effort, but more cascades lay ahead. Reaching the second series of rapids, the boat lurched violently in the current. With a painful crunch, the bow swung into a rock, breaching her hull. The *Ma-Robert* sustained a hole—above the waterline of the boat, but below the belt of morale. The *Ma-Robert* could proceed no farther—at least not at those water levels.

Livingstone refused to retreat. He demanded they explore the river farther—on foot. The next day, he and Kirk set off to trek up the Zambezi. The rock ramparts protecting the river turned the Zambezi gorge into an oven. A viciously hot day made for strenuous hiking in the blazing sun. When the river split, so did Kirk and Livingstone. Both encountered steep rapids with visibly worse prospects upstream.

For Livingstone, this "obstruction to navigation" meant the unspeakable: the expedition could not ascend the Zambezi.[13] But, while the river made herself impenetrable in the dry season, an unknown variable still remained: Would the Kebrabasa be passable in the wet season when the Zambezi swelled?

Kirk calculated an answer. Due to the elevation drop, width of the river, and volume of water, he concluded the currents at high water would become too quick for a steamer. Livingstone disagreed. Livingstone believed the water would crest over the banks at flood, slowing down the pace enough to allow the steamer to pass.

The men sought knowledge from native tribes. Stories of the river in high-water season sided with Kirk's hypothesis. Natives even spoke of larger rapids yet to come upriver. And, in flood, the natives told

Livingstone, the river only became more dangerous. No man attempting to descend the rapids in canoe survived the torrents.

"Things look dark for our enterprise," Livingstone confided in his journal. "This Kebrabasa is what I never expected. No hint of it ever reached my ears." He continued, prayerfully. "What we shall do if this is to be the end of the navigation I cannot now divine, but here I am, and I am trusting Him who never made ashamed those who did so."[14]

The final blow for the Zambezi plan came as Livingstone and Kirk ventured farther upriver. Following the guidance of a native who spoke of a much larger waterfall, they searched for the impediment that could, beyond a doubt, prevent a steamer in all seasons.

The thundering of water in the distance hinted at the answer. Kirk and Livingstone followed the roar to a ledge where the Zambezi cascaded over a thirty-foot-high drop. The men were stunned. The waterfall confirmed to Kirk that the Zambezi would remain unnavigable. Then, to Kirk's disbelief, Livingstone offered a desperate suggestion: if the water rose eighty feet with the rains, they might steam through.

Privately, Livingstone grappled with his own oversight and the reality of failure. He would have explaining to do in England. At first, he excused his mismanagement: How could failure be attributed to him if he knew nothing of the rapid? Blame could also be placed on the boat maker, he reasoned. The *Ma-Robert*, the "sham vessel," sailed too slowly, steamed too inefficiently, and proved too heavy for such an expedition. Had Livingstone received the proper tools—a lighter, faster boat—he could plow through the rapids in the rainy season.

Though he struggled to admit it, Livingstone knew responsibility for the expedition's mistakes ultimately rested with him.

"I look back on all that has happened to me. The honours heaped on me were not of my seeking. They came unbidden. . . . I never expected the fame which followed me. It was Thy hand that gave it all . . ."[15] Everyone—England, his government, Murchison—expected too much of him and the expedition.

"I expected snarling after I was gone," Livingstone wrote to his brother-in-law of the bitterness in Britain from his LMS decision and the bitterness aboard the *Ma-Robert*. "I did not seek their praise, nor do I much care for their frowns. All came unsought. I have had abuse before, and whatever our Father in heaven wills I mean to submit to it and learn his lessons. . . . If I were to begin again as a missionary I should most certainly choose to be alone with my wife."[16]

Meanwhile, he concealed the trials and troubles of the expedition from the British government. In his letters to the British Foreign Office, he also neglected to include the expedition's interpersonal conflict, obfuscating his reports in a discourse of harmony. Livingstone continued to present the Zambezi expedition optimistically, perhaps misleadingly so.

"We are all of the opinion that a steamer of light draught would pass the rapids without difficulty when the river is in full flood," he wrote to the Foreign Secretary.[17]

Nonetheless, word of the expedition's failures began to leak. Bedingfield—the dismissed and aggrieved commander—led the charge of tarnishing Livingstone's reputation. As he made his way back to England through various ports, he shared his version of events and his opinion of Livingstone's character.

If Livingstone were to remain in Africa continuing his career as either consul or explorer, he would need more time. Time to regroup, save the expedition, and save his reputation. A new steamer ranked chief among his needs—the bruised and rusting *Ma-Robert* would not float much longer.

He would be unable to contain the chaos forever.

———

Livingstone pondered three options: the expedition could wait for the river to miraculously rise high enough for the unfit ship to pass; the expedition could disband and return to England; or the expedition could search for alternate routes into Africa's interior. Although he would not admit it, the Zambezi plan had failed, and if he did try to push his team to wait, he risked mutiny. Equally unappealing, the option of returning to England would concede Livingstone's failure and his ineptitude as a leader. It could cost him his reputation and, quite likely, any chance of forming a future expedition. The third option, finding another river, had one distinct advantage: he was already in Africa with a funded venture. If he could repurpose his trip, he might salvage the expedition.

Early on their course up the Zambezi, they had sailed past another river: the Shiré. The Shiré flowed into the Zambezi approximately one hundred miles from the Indian Ocean. Livingstone knew little of the Shiré or its navigability. He had, however, heard a rumor that the Shiré began in a large lake in Central Africa. For Livingstone, even a rumor and a hunch warranted a search.

A large inland lake would alone make an important geographic discovery—a discovery that might resurrect his expedition. Perhaps the expedition's goals—establishing trade and destroying slavery—could be accomplished along the Shiré. Personally, it might add another geographic discovery to his résumé.

Livingstone's religious faith left little room for coincidence. The waterfalls and rapids of the Zambezi, he believed, existed to redirect him. Livingstone concluded the expedition had not failed but hit a turning point toward its divine purpose. Perhaps God had guided them to the Shiré.

The Zambezi expedition officially abandoned its namesake river and lifted anchor to drift seaward with the current. The *Ma-Robert* coasted two hundred miles south to the tributary mouth of the Shiré. On New Year's Day, they entered uncharted waters and found conditions perfect for steaming. Livingstone brimmed with optimism.

"The delight of threading out the meanderings of upwards of 200 miles of a hitherto unexplored river must be felt to be appreciated," Livingstone wrote.[18]

The Shiré presented the team with unfamiliar territory, but the presence of white men seemed chillingly familiar to the indigenous peoples along its banks. While natives along the Zambezi had gazed upon the passing *Pearl* as if stunned to see such an outlandish object traversing the river, those along the Shiré fled with wailing fright or displayed aggressive hostility.

As the *Ma-Robert* progressed, hostile tribes protested or attacked. The men occasionally had to run for cover to escape a maelstrom of poison darts. Livingstone sometimes ordered Kirk to return fire with a warning shot. Often, near protesting villages, the natives ran along the riverbank next to the boat, demanding payment to pass through their territories. Livingstone refused; he wanted to make a statement that rivers were free.

The expedition team grew more optimistic with each passing mile. For two weeks, they meandered north on the winding Shiré, which, though growing steadily shallower, still remained navigable for the *Ma-Robert*. Although it had lower water levels, it lacked the shifting sandbars that had plagued them in the Zambezi. Livingstone could see a mountain range in the distance, which, to him, signaled a mosquito-free home for his colony. The Shiré profferred to be Livingstone's promised land.

A few more bends and the expedition heard an ominous thundering sound upriver, reminiscent of its adversary on the Zambezi. Soon, the expedition found itself facing more rapids. The *Ma-Robert* ground to a halt. The crew looked out upon a series of cascading waterfalls covering a distance of thirty miles. It brought back painful memories. Although it had no thirty-foot drop, the length of these rapids would be too much for the vessel to consider ascending. The expedition, and Livingstone in particular, became deeply discouraged.

"If we dedicate ourselves to God unreservedly," Livingstone lamented, "He will make use of whatever peculiarities of constitution He has imparted for His own glory, and He will in answer to prayer give wisdom to guide. He will so guide as to make useful. O how far am I from that hearty devotion to God I read of in others! The Lord have mercy on me a sinner!"[19]

Livingstone believed God's guidance had turned them from the Zambezi to the Shiré. Now he questioned God and his own faith. Perhaps the expedition had finally met its end.

"I have prayed for this," Livingstone wrote, "and Jesus himself said, 'Ask, and ye shall receive,' . . . yet this heart is sometimes fearfully guilty of distrust. I am ashamed to think of it."[20]

After several days of disappointment, Livingstone grew decidedly more confident that he had to reach the Shiré region. Natives spoke of fertile hills farther upriver—a plateau—near the alleged large lake. Livingstone again imagined the perfect setting for his fields of cotton, trading post, and British colony. Indeed, the Shiré sounded as though it possessed all the opportunity he had sought in the Zambezi, and more. He needed no further convincing: the Shiré was his river. The expedition had to find a way.

Livingstone christened the rapids the "Murchison Cataracts" after their expedition's champion and began pondering solutions to pass through them. He started dreaming of a new ship—a vessel to be sailed upriver, disassembled, carried overland, and reassembled again. This nimble boat, he imagined, could traverse the Shiré. But he had no such portable boat, and no proof of the Shiré highlands' value. To legitimately request the boat, he would need to see what lay beyond the rapids— perhaps his lake. The expedition would proceed up the Shiré on foot.

Livingstone and company stepped off the *Ma-Robert* and beyond the Murchison Cataracts. With those steps, they entered the land of the Ajawa.

5 SATAN'S SEAT

The day of Africa is yet to come.
                                    —DAVID LIVINGSTONE

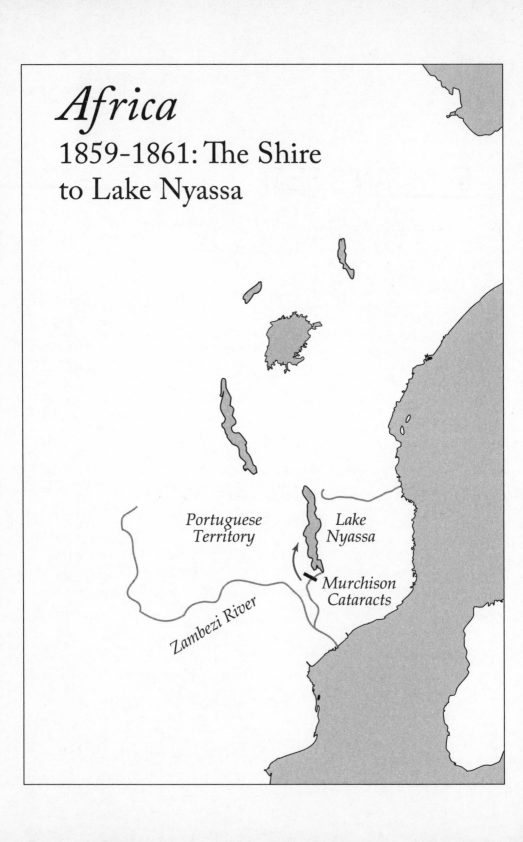

Africa

1859-1861: The Shire
to Lake Nyassa

Portuguese
Territory

Lake
Nyassa

Murchison
Cataracts

Zambezi River

August 28, 1859: Expedition begins its walk to Lake Nyassa.
13 years, 9 months, and 8 days until the end
of the East African slave trade.

Slaves sold per annum: 16,000
Total victims of the slave trade: 288,000

nglish do not buy slaves, they buy food!" the men yelled as they entered villages.[1]

At the sight of the Europeans, children screamed and villagers fled in terror.

"[E]ven the hens would fly away and leave their chickens," Livingstone remarked.[2]

At first they found the villagers' fearful reaction puzzling—dramatically different from their spellbound welcome on the Zambezi. The explanation soon became clear: The slave trade had preceded the expedition to the Shiré highlands. The natives presumed they came to join in the raiding. The Shiré tribes feared them.

As they walked between terrified villages, Livingstone and crew passed piles of dozens upon dozens of slave-taming sticks. The heavy, wishbone-shaped logs forced onto the shoulders of a slave placed a heavy burden on its captive as the slave teams crossed the continent. Locked with an iron rod across the throat and riveted at both ends, the slave-taming stick made for an excruciating yoke. To keep a slave from escaping in his stick, the slavers bound together the trunks of two sticks.

Soon enough, the expedition came upon its first slave-raiding party. Lines of men in taming sticks and women bound in chains passed the expedition. The sight shocked everyone, including the Makololo porters.

"Why won't you let us choke them?" the Makololo asked.

Livingstone restrained his native porters from attacking the slave drivers.

"We might have released these slaves," Livingstone explained, "but did not know what to do with them afterwards."[3]

The men watched solemnly as the coffle of slaves marched past. Livingstone had neither the capacity for rehabilitation, nor the ability to incorporate freed slaves into his team. Freeing them far away from their homes and tribes, he knew they would only be seized and sold again by people in the surrounding villages. Above all, Livingstone wanted to remain ostensibly a scientific expedition exploring rivers, while quietly gathering evidence of the slave trade.

Privately, Livingstone burned with anger. The slavery he had witnessed in South Africa paled in comparison to its brutal offspring emerging in the Shiré highlands. The Africa he loved and his hopes for a civilized society seemed to deteriorate before his very eyes.

As the expedition proceeded north, the violence increased. The confluence of the Shiré and Lake Nyassa formed the heart of the greatest slave trading route in East Africa. From here, the trade forked southwest through the Shiré valley to Portuguese ports and northwest to Arab ports near Zanzibar. Slavers, like the notorious Mariano, made their way up from the south; raiding parties from Zanzibar penetrated Central Africa beyond Lake Nyassa.

In villages welcoming to the expedition, Livingstone inquired into the specifics of the trade. Some chiefs felt ashamed, admitting to selling their own people—but only selling those who committed crimes. The chiefs, as they saw it, sold their people out of necessity. They wanted to trade or needed food, but had nothing else for barter.

All trade centered around ivory—Arab traders from the east wanted elephant tusks but quickly depleted the closest resources. Scarcity pushed traders deeper into the interior. The caravans required for their ambitious hunts demanded more capacity to port the loads and support convoys numbering, at times, into the hundreds. With plentiful human populations near the best ivory harvesting grounds, slavery brought the ivory traders efficiency and added profit. Arriving with a skeleton Arab troop, the traders could enslave a seemingly unlimited number of porters and sell them at the end of the journey. They would profit from both ivory and people. Unlike its West African cousin, the East African slave trade initially engaged slavery as a marketable by-product, not the target resource.

African tribes faced few alternatives. Ivory became the dominant currency, and if a chief possessed none, he only had one other item of value for barter: human flesh. A man brought four yards of cotton, a woman brought three, and a boy or girl brought two.

"It is only by cutting off the supplies in the interior, that we can crush the slave-trade on the Coast," Livingstone calculated.[4]

As it functioned in 1859, Livingstone reasoned, the slave trade in East Africa could not stand on its own. Without ivory, slaving would be unprofitable. Livingstone imagined commerce removing the human element, and doing so by means of his rivers. A ship could purchase all the ivory at the price the traders received after carrying the ivory three hundred miles to the coast. Traders would lose all incentive to exploit human labor.

The expedition crew found the Ajawa, into whose tribal lands they had wandered, deeply entangled with slavery. With guns and black powder gifted by the traders, the Ajawa had become slave agents— mercenaries not just for the Portuguese but now Arab traders from Zanzibar as well—stealing men and women from rival tribes. Slavery gave the Ajawa currency, as well as musket-wielding foreign allies in the power struggle for tribal control of the region.

"Thousands perish in internecine war waged for slaves with their own clansmen and neighbours, slain by the lust of gain," Livingstone noted.[5]

The growing complicity of African tribes in the slave trade made Livingstone evermore anxious to find a solution. It pained him to see Africans involved. He recognized the best in native cultures and agonized over the untapped potential for good commerce. But foreign slave traders from the coast had preceded him and his commercial dreams.

Supplanting the evil enterprise obsessed him. Slavery was no longer a nuisance, but a force in fierce competition with good.

———

Livingstone finally reached the shores of Lake Nyassa on September 16, 1859.[6] At 210 miles long by 26 miles wide, only the masses of people eclipsed the enormous body of water.

"Never before in Africa have we seen anything like the dense population on the shores of Lake Nyassa," Livingstone wrote. Everywhere they went along Nyassa, hundreds of villagers surrounded the expedition for a closer look at what they called "wild animals."[7]

The achievement proved bittersweet. Livingstone wanted to be the first European to discover the lake; he was not. A Portuguese trader, Candido José da Costa Cardoso, had reached Nyassa thirteen years earlier. The men had once met briefly, and Livingstone had learned of the lake from Cardoso then, even logging the trader's crude directions in his journal.

Livingstone could record no new discoveries at Nyassa, and he did not want seconds—he wanted firsts. Coming in second to anyone, much less the Portuguese, infuriated him. Knowing the glory belongs to the discoverer, Livingstone attempted to show that Cardoso mistakenly identified a different lake as Nyassa. If he continued to be the runner-up in African exploration, Portuguese success would chip away at his reputation.

Open, bloody devastation at Nyassa quickly stole his attention from geography. The men had not merely stumbled upon a lake; they had marched into hell. Nyassa formed slavery's epicenter—the gateway to a region plentiful in both ivory and humans.

"We never realized the atrocious nature of the traffic, until we saw it at the fountain-head," said Livingstone. "There truly 'Satan has his seat.' "[8]

They walked through a land littered with butchered bodies.

"The many skeletons we have seen, amongst rocks and woods, by the little pools, and along the paths of the wilderness, attest the awful sacrifice of human life, which must be attributed, directly or indirectly, to this trade of hell."

Livingstone wanted to describe the horrors of Nyassa to the world, but struggled to find words to describe it. ". . . we feel sure that were even half the truth told and recognized, the feelings of men would be so thoroughly roused, that this devilish traffic in human flesh would be put down at all risks."

The expedition set out to quantify the size and scope of the trade to report to Britain. Such data, they hoped, would move the British government more swiftly to decisive action.

Thousands of victims of the trade ended up in Portuguese slave ports farther south. Countless more never made it to the coast alive. With a cheap and limitless source of human life, slavers found it easier to kill sluggish slaves than to struggle with them.

"[A]n awful waste of human life," Livingstone decried. "From what we know and have seen, that not one-fifth of the victims of the slave-trade ever become slaves. Taking the Shiré Valley as an average, we should say not even one-tenth arrive at their destination.

"Besides those actually captured, thousands are killed and die of their wounds and famine, driven from their villages by the slave raid proper," Livingstone explained.[9]

If Satan held a stronghold at Nyassa, men like Mariano did his handiwork. Since the expedition departed Tette in 1858, the Portuguese had released Mariano from jail. Perhaps in a desperate attempt to end the war, Portuguese authorities declared his sentence served and sent him out with fines to pay. Mariano promptly absconded, returning to the protection of his forces and resuming his slave raids.

"It was not long before we came upon the ravages of the notorious Mariano," Livingstone wrote.[10]

Mariano and his band unreservedly slayed villagers and burned villages, destroying entire valleys. The expedition found few survivors of

Mariano's raiding forays. Occasionally, they happened upon those who had dodged Mariano's blade—frightened, starved, and robbed of everything, including their clothes.

Mariano embraced his notorious reputation as a feared merchant of death. His path of destruction could be traced throughout East Africa, symbolizing the anarchy and lawlessness of Portugal's African colonies, as well as the ignorance of apathetic Lisbon. Openly violent and unrestrained, Mariano embodied evil in Livingstone's eyes and became Livingstone's mascot for the slave trade.

Slave traders like Mariano did more than raid and murder; they implanted conflict. Intentionally fueling wars between tribes, the slave traders conditioned the Ajawa and other peoples to capture rival clansmen in the act of tribal domination, and profit. In return, the traders gave their new proxy militias the tools they craved: guns.

In the few years Livingstone spent exploring East and Central Africa, he had witnessed a fundamental shift: slavery began to surpass ivory as the primary African export. Demand for human labor on plantations in Arabia and around the Indian Ocean found a cheap supply in the Zanzibari traders eager to sell their human ivory-haulers. As the slave trade changed, so did the mind-set of African tribes. The people now showed little interest in bartering and traditional commerce, challenging Livingstone's hypothesis that legitimate trade could wipe out slavery. If legitimate trade no longer had incentive in Nyassa, it would take other, more forceful, means to eradicate slavery. Perhaps East Africa needed determined British intervention.

Indeed, British battles against the slave trade happened the world over—and largely victoriously. Britain's strategy, however, remained confined to the seas. Now the most important battlefield lay in the interior—the heart of the fight would be a terrestrial one.

Britain's military might and abolitionist history made her the obvious potential enforcer. Until abolition in 1808, Britain had led the global slave trade. After shipping more than 2.5 million Africans across the Atlantic—roughly 40 percent of the entire 6-million-head global trade in humans—British parliamentarian William Wilberforce and his Committee for the Abolition of the Slave Trade dealt a decisive blow to slavery. Wilberforce's Act for the Abolition of the Slave Trade brought this terrible era to a close.

Effective January 1, 1808, the Act suppressed the trade throughout the British Empire by imposing a fine of one hundred pounds for every slave found aboard a British ship. To enforce the law, the British Royal Navy established the West African Squadron, which between 1807 and 1860 seized approximately 1,600 ships and freed 150,000 Africans aboard those vessels.

On his first journey to South Africa, Livingstone had witnessed the Squadron's success. Harbors once filled with slaving ships sat empty due to the Squadron's efforts. Britain's naval power inspired Livingstone and filled him with optimism.

He imagined a parallel with Lake Nyassa. Not simply the geographic epicenter of slavery, Lake Nyassa afforded the slavers with economies of scale unreached by purely migratory means. Nyassa had become an instrument of the trade. Two Arab traders had built a dhow—an Arab-style sailboat—to traffic slaves regularly across the lake. Livingstone hoped to investigate it, but news of the English party's arrival forced the dhow to sail the day before the expedition reached its dock.

The expedition's stay at Nyassa was short. To avoid suspicion that they might be there to acquire slaves, the men returned to the *Ma-Robert* moored below Murchison Falls. As they steamed south on the Shiré, dead bodies floated past the *Ma-Robert* daily, and in the mornings, the crew cleared the paddles of corpses caught during the night. Despite its gory revelations, the excursion inspired Livingstone.

"A small armed steamer on Lake Nyassa," Livingstone surmised, "could easily, by exercising a control, and furnishing goods in exchange for ivory and other products, break the neck of this infamous traffic in that quarter; for nearly all must cross the Lake or the Upper Shiré."

He envisioned the British Royal Navy patrolling Lake Nyassa, bringing the battle against the slave trade inland.

"[B]y judicious operations . . . one small vessel would have decidedly more influence, and do more good in suppressing the slave trade, than half a dozen men-of-war on the ocean."

A bold solution. Even Livingstone admitted to his audacity: "This reasoning, if not the result of ignorance, may be of maudlin philanthropy."[11]

———

One tiny island controlled nearly half of the African continent: Zanzibar. Despite its small, one-thousand-square-mile footprint, Zanzibar sustained the Arab slave trade as its mastermind and encouraging protectorate.

More than two hundred years before Livingstone's arrival, Portugal gained substantial control of the East African coast, including the island of Zanzibar, a mere twenty miles from shore. Nearly 150 years later, the Arab conquests ousted the Portuguese as they advanced on Oman, the easternmost cape of the Arabian Peninsula, then down the African coast. Britain eventually took an interest in the future of the Arabian Peninsula—not in Oman specifically, but in its station as a gateway to Asia. Across the Arabian Sea, beyond Omani shores, lay India. Arab conquerors lusting after India's vast wealth and resources would not have far to sail, while Britain with its Indian empire had everything to lose.

If the Omani sultanate could be lured in to British favor, Oman would provide a western buffer against further Arab advances. Britain had a powerful incentive to offer: military strength. Britain's military power could help protect the sultan's territories, including the critical but vulnerable island of Zanzibar. Britain signed a treaty with Sultan Said of Muscat to provide protection for Zanzibar in exchange for the sultan's cooperation in shielding advances toward India.

With British military protection, the sultan of Muscat could confidently encourage trading between Zanzibar and mainland Africa. Given Zanzibar's strategic location between Africa, Arabia, Asia, and the Indian Ocean, the island became a commercial hub and the sultan's empire flourished. With Zanzibar's growing wealth and prominence, the sultan relocated his capital from Oman's Muscat to his blossoming archipelago.

The slave trade quickly became a leading industry on Zanzibar. Slave agents soon came from India, Persia, and islands in the Indian Ocean to acquire labor for sugar and clove industries. But the largest demand came from Arabia to accommodate its date plantations. The slave trade soon grew domestically on Zanzibar as clove plantations sprung up on the island. Conclusive evidence that the slave trade had become a fully institutionalized pillar of Zanzibari commerce came in 1811: the great Zanzibar slave market opened its doors.

Slave traders arriving in Zanzibar found that the island itself offered nothing in terms of labor. All slaves came from coastal ports along mainland Africa with Zanzibar serving as the hub for exchange. When demand increased and available human labor near the coast dwindled, slave agents went greater distances to gather slaves. From Zanzibar, they organized and launched raiding caravans into the African interior.

Chaotic control of the sultanate in Zanzibar put Britain in a position of powerful influence, but also allowed the slave traders to gain a larger foothold in Zanzibar. The death of Sultan Said in 1856 resulted in a succession dispute between his sons. Britain stepped in to arbitrate. By 1861, they had reached a settlement creating separate sultanates of Oman and Zanzibar. Sultan Majid received Zanzibar, at a great financial loss to his brother in Oman. To compensate, Britain required Sultan Majid to pay a large annual subsidy to his sibling in Muscat.

The new sultan in Zanzibar did not possess free and unrestrained reign over the interior. Much of East Africa fell under the control of the Portuguese, particularly the Zambezi and Shiré rivers. With Portugal's West African slave trade decimated by the British navy, East Africa served Lisbon's interests—and it fell far out of the watchful eye of other European nations, particularly the British, who might condemn their actions. Although Portugal outlawed slavery throughout its territories, it for the most part overlooked its colonies in East Africa—scant accountability afforded Portugal high profitability.

Livingstone had already made life difficult for Portugal. In *Missionary Travels* and on his British speaking tour, he railed against Portuguese complicity in the West African slave trade. Livingstone's fiery censures irritated Lisbon, eroding any goodwill remaining between the explorer and the Zambezi's guardian nation.

Livingstone's hostility perhaps had more to do with a rivalry than the truth about the slave trade. Portugal published maps and articles showing that its explorers had reached or identified many sites before Livingstone's arrival. For a man of Livingstone's constitution, insecurity and preservation of reputation overwhelmed reason. He developed a personal vendetta against the Portuguese.

While the Portuguese had diplomatically accepted Livingstone's Zambezi expedition, they feared it foreshadowed British colonization in Africa—on land to which Portugal lay claim. As Livingstone sailed the Zambezi, Portugal made its flag known, erecting a fort at the river's mouth and a customs house at its tributary with the Shiré.

Livingstone's criticism of the nation grew stronger. He scolded Portugal for lacking morality in its colonies, calling the Portuguese "worse than Sodom," "abominable," and "a worn-out, used-up syphilitic race."[12] His charges all contained elements of truth.

But Livingstone and his expedition posed a greater threat to Portugal than name-calling. As the East African slave trade grew at Portugal's behest, so did the risk that Livingstone would become an effective whistleblower.

———

Livingstone's thoughts turned again to the royal crown and a permanent presence in the African interior: a British colony. A colony offered much more than his trading outpost; it signified a profound commitment to Africa, and it heralded the modernity of Europe. In Livingstone's lexicon, it foreshadowed rapid civilization.

For Livingstone, watching the carnage around Nyassa, a permanent presence of justice and progress could not arrive soon enough. Abandoning the Shiré highlands and leaving the region to chaos, he believed, would leave all his work in Africa—his entire career—for nothing. Success on the Shiré became essential.

Livingstone opened correspondence with the British foreign secretary to cast his vision. Although it ran directly against popular anti-imperialist foreign policy, Livingstone recommended colonizing the Shiré highlands. Moreover, his party could establish it, but at no small cost. The expedition needed a new vessel—one to be disassembled into sections and transported on land around the Shiré's Murchison Cataracts. The task would cover thirty miles on land. They would need to build roads; in addition to the boat, he requested a British construction team and carts.

With each passing day, Livingstone became more convinced of his plan and the inevitable success of a British colony in Africa's interior. Knowing the foreign secretary's decision would not be easy, he enlisted the lobbying prowess of his champion, Sir Roderick Murchison, and tempted England's zeal for resources: cotton, sugar, and indigo, asserting they would all grow rampantly. Finally, he appealed to the nation's sense of social justice. If England had its own cotton fields, it could free itself from the guilt of buying slave-produced cotton from the United States.

Livingstone's letters walked a fine line between presenting ideal conditions for a colony and calling for intervention in a humanitarian crisis. If he focused too strongly on resources, he risked sounding imperialistic—conquering territory for the sake of monopolistic growth. But if he overemphasized the humanitarian crisis and violence of the slave trade, Britain would recoil at the notion of starting a colony in a war zone.

Letters moved mind-numbingly slow. The British navy collected mail at the mouth of the Zambezi every three months. When Livingstone had letters too important to entrust to the hands of unreliable Portuguese traders, he made the trip down the river himself. The letters could take a year to arrive in England.

As he anxiously awaited a response in Nyassa, his ambitions grew and his imagination went forth boldly. He no longer envisioned small trading colonies, but vast cities. The Shiré highlands "could support millions of people where now there are just thousands or hundreds." He imagined it could solve other social ills, specifically the plight of England's urban poor. The poor and destitute, transplanted to his colonies, would get a fresh start and their presence would benefit Africa, a "double blessing—to Africa and to England."[13] The migration of Christian European influence would create the massive social change necessary for Christianity to take root among the African natives.

Despite his bold plan, he still had his doubts. Such a society would need substantial leadership and education to bring the right skill sets for a robust society.

Paralleling the chaos they found in Nyassa, chaos seized the expedition crew, with Livingstone as its tumultuous epicenter. His mood swung violently, provoked by his own wavering health. At times, he would say nothing for days—or even weeks. He would only silently stare straight ahead.

Livingstone had acquired obstinacy as a way to cope with a boyhood of child labor. He would try to read and study while spinning cotton, positioning his books on the loom, but always to the consternation of the other boys. They would torment him and knock over his books. "When I was a piecer," Livingstone reflected, "the fellows used to try to turn me off from the path I had chosen and always began with, 'I think you ought, etc., till I snapped them up with a mild 'You think! I can think and act for myself; don't need anybody to think for me, I assure you.' This must, according to my experience, be the way all through. I never followed another's views in preference to my own judgment i.e. did a thing out of deference to another when I myself thought it wrong but I had reason to repent of it."[14]

Livingstone's social distance from his men cut deep into morale. He never encouraged them. When he spoke, he only complained or criticized. Under the surface, Livingstone held little respect for them. He secretly wanted to cast them aside and return to his past rituals of traveling solo.

"All exploration effected would have been better done alone or with my brother," he confided.[15]

Kirk could not stand to be near him, fleeing to the cabins below when Livingstone's mood deteriorated. Despite their close proximity, Kirk felt emotionally deserted, "alone in the cabin for four months with millions of cockroaches and not a single companion to speak to."[16]

With the men on edge, the cockroaches compounded their irritations. The pests bred everywhere and ate everything, including the men, who suffered annoying bites at night. Livingstone captured two cockroaches in a bottle and, to his horror, found the two multiplied to seventy-eight. He introduced potential solutions, from spiders to a mongoose. Nothing worked. Despite eating thousands of cockroaches, the mongoose lost weight. In his journal, Livingstone made light of the cockroach diet, quipping, "This would be invaluable to fat young ladies."[17]

Livingstone knew he was causing much of the turmoil and knew he should do better. In his journals, he admitted to his awful mood and his constant frown. He confessed to battling depression and to his lack of sympathy toward the crew. Even in a letter to his eldest child, Robert, he advised him not to follow his father's course: "Let your smile be pleasant and easy," Livingstone wrote. "Seldom show that you are displeased for very often the cause of displeasure may be a mistake you have made yourself."[18] Still, he continued down his destructive path.

A bigger challenge soon threatened the team: Charles Livingstone grew increasingly troublesome with members of the team, and the allegiance between the Livingstone brothers strengthened. As bickering between Charles and the crew swelled, Charles found opportunities to strike behind the scenes. He planted discontent in his older brother and encouraged the dismissal of teammates.

Charles drew a line in the sand between himself and all others on the expedition, luring his brother into his court. Livingstone trustingly listened to Charles and made important decisions, in part, upon his brother's advice. Acting on his sibling's counsel, Livingstone sent away two more members, including Thornton, halving the British expedition crew. Of Livingstone's six, only Charles, Kirk, and George Rae, the engineer, remained. Rae, too, now spoke of departing.

The turmoil spread to the native crew enlisted as porters. Livingstone typically remained calm and diplomatic around the Africans—but even that tolerance faded. When one of the native crew attacked Kirk with an iron bar, Livingstone lost his temper. Beating the native with a cooking ladle, the clash sent both Livingstone and the porter overboard. After a separate altercation occurred, Livingstone shocked Kirk with an order to "break their heads if they do not do as I told them."[19]

Morale bottomed out. With the expedition failing to find a navigable river and the crew almost disbanding, the three remaining teammates neared mutiny. The terribly leaking *Ma-Robert* could only last a matter of months and no mail had arrived from the foreign office about a replacement boat. After a year of biding his time, Livingstone still had no response to his proposals for Lake Nyassa and the Shiré colony.

Tired of waiting on the British government, Livingstone set a plan in motion. Rae would go back to England to supervise the construction of Livingstone's proposed portable boat. If the British government would not pay for it, he would—out of his remaining profits from *Missionary Travels*. Rae left for England on the next British naval ship.

With only Kirk remaining, Charles directed his antagonism toward his older brother. Fights between the brothers came to blows, followed by spitting criticism. As Charles turned on him, Livingstone began to see how his brother had undermined the team all along, playing a contentious and self-interested role in removing his adversaries.

Finally, Charles imploded. He snapped, denouncing Livingstone and exclaiming that he worked "in the service of the Devil."[20] Losing his temper one afternoon, he kicked a native leader with iron-nailed boots. Charles quickly found himself on the ground, and a spear mere inches from his heart. Had it not been for the porters' respect for the elder Livingstone, the spear likely would have ended Charles's life.

The expedition had reached the brink of collapse.

6 ❧ INTERFERENCE

Our duty is to go forward . . . I have observed that people who have sat long waiting have sat long enough before they saw any indication to go.

—DAVID LIVINGSTONE

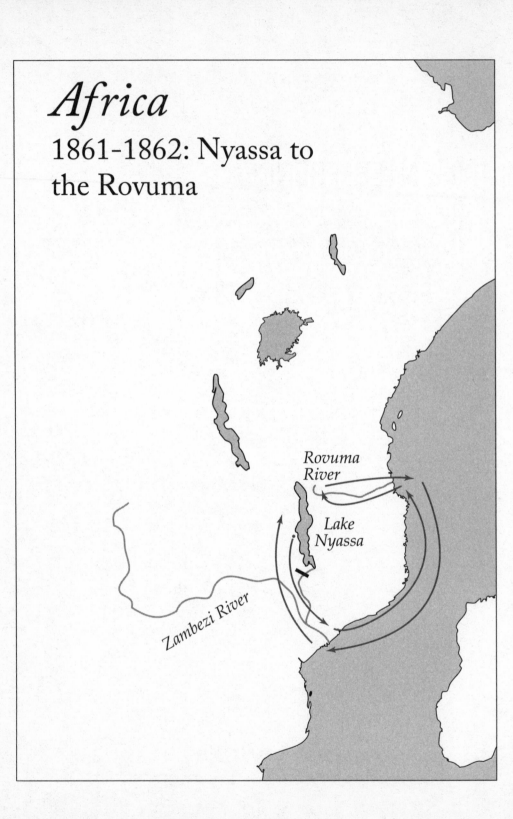

Africa

1861-1862: Nyassa to
the Rovuma

Rovuma
River

Lake
Nyassa

Zambezi River

With nervous trepidation, Livingstone's fingers worked to open his freshly arrived mail. Returning to the mouth of the Zambezi to restock supplies and rendezvous with the British navy, Livingstone found that November 8, 1861, brought renewed hope in sealed envelopes. His eyes darted across the pages for his long-awaited answers.

No—a clear message from the foreign secretary swiftly rejected his proposal for a colony and government-funded boat to patrol Nyassa. Even Murchison, Livingstone's tireless champion, could not garner support for the plan. Still, Britain had taken it seriously. Livingstone's Shiré colony proposal had moved all the way up to Prime Minister Palmerston, who outright rejected it.

"I am very unwilling to embark on schemes of British possessions," Palmerston wrote to the new foreign secretary, Lord John Russell. "Dr L's information is valuable, but he must not be allowed to tempt us to form colonies only to be reachable by forcing steamers up cataracts."[1]

Despite the disappointment, the expedition received some promising news: an extension. The foreign office granted the Zambezi expedition another three years to turn the venture into a success. More good news followed. Livingstone's new steamer built to replace the *Ma-Robert* had set sail and would arrive soon. The foreign office, however, had granted only one vessel—a standard steamer, the *Pioneer*—and had rejected his portable boat for Lake Nyassa. Livingstone would have to pay for the custom vessel on his own.

He also received a slap on the wrist. Livingstone's blunt criticisms of the Portuguese had roused the ire of Lisbon. To quell diplomatic tension, the British government asked Livingstone to temper his future remarks.

———

As the *Ma-Robert* made her final push down the Zambezi, she finally expired. The crew could no longer patch the rusted holes and constant leaks. The men made it out with most of their supplies before she came to rest at the bottom of the river. The loss mattered little; the *Pioneer* arrived a few days later.

Under the command of E. D. Young, the *Pioneer* arrived with a joint investigative party from the universities of Oxford, Cambridge, Durham, and Dublin. University leaders had listened to Livingstone's plea that wintery night in the Cambridge Senate House: "Carry out the work which I have begun."[2] Answering Livingstone's call to action, they had formed the Universities' Mission to Central Africa. The first order of the Universities' Mission involved establishing a missionary post in Africa's interior.

Bishop Charles Mackenzie led the Universities' Mission. Behind a short, dark beard, Bishop Mackenzie hid a youthful face and zealous passion. At thirty-six, the energetic bishop had already served as a missionary in South Africa and taught theology at Cambridge. He had a fight in him, enjoyed a good theological debate, and spent nights on the *Pioneer* in long discussions over Darwin's recently released *On the Origin of Species*. The Universities' Mission planned to settle in the highlands above the Shiré.

Livingstone now took command of the *Pioneer*. His first orders did not entail a new attempt on the Murchison Cataracts or the Kebrabasa Rapids. Livingstone had a new river in mind: the Rovuma. The Rovuma solved the growing dilemma of tightening Portuguese authority. The

Zambezi could be blocked at any time by Portugal's control of the river mouth, barring all Livingstone's work. With his vocal accusations against Portugal, such measures grew increasingly likely. He needed an alternate river to access the African interior. The Rovuma began in the Nyassa region, flowing directly to the Indian Ocean as it formed the northern border of Portuguese territory. He suspected Lake Nyassa to be the Rovuma's source.

The expedition steamed out of the Zambezi, onto the Indian Ocean, and six hundred miles north along the African coast. Arriving at the mouth of the Rovuma, Livingstone delighted in the river's great promise. Its bay offered a safe harbor, and the river produced a deep channel. Even more attractive, geography suggested it might make a speedier passage to higher, malaria-free land.

A week up the river, the *Pioneer* suddenly ran aground. The Rovuma proved shallower than he had anticipated, and the *Pioneer* performed below expectations. Livingstone had requested a vessel with a draft of three feet, but due to the ballast necessary for its open-ocean sail from England, the *Pioneer* drew five. Facing an impassable river and quickly approaching the dry season, Livingstone saw no option but to prematurely abandon the Rovuma.

"Had the Expedition been alone, we would have pushed up in boats, or afoot, and done what [we] could toward the exploration of the river and the upper end of the lake," an irritated Livingstone wrote.[3]

To make matters worse, malaria began infecting the crew. By the time they returned to the mouth of the Rovuma, only four of the seventeen on board were free of fever. With most of his crew sick, including Young, Livingstone took the helm to pilot the *Pioneer* over open seas and back up the Zambezi to the Shiré. A voyage he had planned to accomplish in three weeks lingered into ten. For the final two months of the journey, they frequently, and painstakingly, dragged the *Pioneer* with ropes over successive sandbars as they moved up the Shiré.

"It caused us a great deal of hard an[d] vexatious work, in laying out anchors, and toiling at the capstan to get her off sandbanks . . ."

Livingstone described the ordeal. "Once we were a fortnight on a back of yielding sand . . ."[4]

Finally, the *Pioneer* came to a halt at the foot of the Murchison Cataracts. Livingstone's team, along with the university party and native crew, set off on foot for a seventy-mile journey in search of a suitable site for the Universities' Mission base.

Bishop Mackenzie's theological debates soon turned to an un-concealed irony: Livingstone's guns. How could missionaries carry weapons? Mackenzie asked. Livingstone and his men always carried guns, which Mackenzie objected to on principle. It sent the wrong message to the African people, he protested.

". . . having been sent out to this country to bring blessing and peace to people," Mackenzie reflected, "I could not reconcile it to myself to kill them even in self-defense: and I still think that if by any possibility the people of this land should attack us, to drive us away or to rob us, we ought not to kill our own sheep."[5]

The debate remained unsettled as they came to rest in mid-July at a small village. Not long after arriving, the group learned that a large slave caravan would soon pass through on its way to Tette—the first direct contact with the slave trade for the Universities' Mission. They antici-pated the interaction with apprehension and curiosity.

"Shall we interfere?" asked a member of the Universities' Mission. Discussion led to a decision, with Livingstone's team coalescing: they would impede the caravan, if possible.

Minutes later, eighty-four men, women, and children rounded a hill—hands bound and necks locked in taming sticks. The slavers proudly drove their catch, marching triumphantly with their muskets in parade position. The sound of horns rose up from the procession, announcing their arrival to the village.

Then the slavers saw the European men. Their proud ranks broke in all directions, fleeing into the forest with cowardly fear. In their scat-tered departure, they disregarded the slaves, who now stood before the expedition, bound and abandoned.

The eighty-four began kneeling to the ground, then vigorously clapped their hands as a show of thanks. The expedition rushed forward with knives to slash the ropes binding the women and children. The taming sticks proved more difficult. They found a saw and, one by one, cut each man to freedom.

"An act of God," the Universities' Mission leaders declared, when they finally paused to offer an explanation. Livingstone felt otherwise— the slavers had feared their fierce Makololo guards. But with eighty-four lives newly under their care, they had little time to debate the source of liberation.

An expedition member immediately gave instructions: take the meal you are carrying and cook breakfast for yourselves and the children.[6]

Their suspicious disbelief required coaxing, but jubilant enthusiasm quickly overwhelmed hesitation. The newly freed men and women turned their former taming sticks into a hearty fire and began preparing a meal.

As food and freedom set in, the victims began to tell of the tragedies they had witnessed. The day before, the slavers had shot two women after they attempted to untie themselves. Another woman could not carry her load, so a slaver "had her infant's brains knocked out."[7] They murdered another man with an axe simply because he fell down in fatigue.

Soon, a young boy approached Livingstone and the men.

"The others tied and starved us, you cut the ropes and tell us to eat; what sort of people are you?" the boy asked Livingstone. "Where did you come from?"[8]

"[We are] English," Livingstone always liked to say, "and the English neither bought, sold, nor held black people as slaves, but wished to put a stop to the slave-trade altogether."[9]

Although he spoke of ending slavery, Livingstone had largely avoided personally liberating slaves in the past. Always on the move, he had no resources for aftercare. The slaves often needed medical attention, transport, and, most importantly, protection. Freed slaves left to their own devices would shortly be recaptured in the nearest village and sold back to the same slave raiders.

With the Universities' Mission present, the equation changed. The Universities' Mission had resources to care for victims, and they wanted a project to begin their permanent settlement. The expedition gave those liberated a choice: freely go where they pleased or stay to join the Universities' Mission's Christian community. All chose to stay. The mission instantly had a membership.

"Logic is out of place when the question with a true-hearted man is, whether his brother man is to be saved or not," Livingstone wrote after the incident.[10]

Perhaps liberating the eighty-four inspired him. On Livingstone's orders, the expedition split up to search out the other captives of nearby Ajawa raids.

They freed dozens more slaves from neighboring villages and detained some of the Ajawa raiders. As they continued, Manganja survivors began following to form a resistance. But the worst of the raids, they learned, lay ahead—an onslaught on the Manganja tribe was in progress. Livingstone resolved to intercede and confront the Ajawa using his honed African diplomacy.

They traced the destructive trail of the Ajawa, walking through charred, deserted villages and passing throngs of terrified Manganja fleeing the slaughter. The Manganja had left everything behind, taking only what they could carry on their heads. Field upon field of unharvested corn, ripe for picking, had been abandoned. Anything harvested, the Ajawa toppled and poured across the trail to prevent consumption. It pained Livingstone to enter a village where he had breakfasted two years before. "Paisley of the hills," as he then nicknamed the tranquil hamlet known for its weaving.[11] Now, it had been burned to the ground.

By midafternoon, they could see fires looming on the hills ahead. As they closed in on the latest Ajawa raids, the cries of women wailing in grief mingled with the celebratory voices of victory. The bishop implored the expedition to stop and ask for God's blessing. They knelt to the ground and bowed their heads in fervent prayer.

When the men rose, a long line of Ajawa warriors rounded a bend in the hill below them. Returning to their village, the warriors were escorting newly enslaved prisoners of war. When the Ajawa headman spotted the Europeans up the hill, he climbed a tall anthill for a better view.

Livingstone stepped forward to de-escalate the standoff.

"We come to have an interview," Livingstone shouted.

Before the Ajawa could respond, the trailing Manganja began taunting their Ajawa conquerors.

"Our [savior] is come!" the Manganja yelled.[12]

"War! War!" the Ajawa screamed in retort, charging up the hillside in chaotic fury while their captives fled into the bushes. Within seconds, the Ajawa had surrounded the expedition, taking positions in the tall grass and behind large rocks. The Ajawa assumed a formation for attack.

"We have not come to fight but to talk," Livingstone's men yelled in vain.[13]

Their protests fell on deaf ears among the belligerent Ajawa, flushed with victory over three Manganja villages. The small expedition party presented little intimidation and the Ajawa closed to within one hundred yards.

"Whoosh!" the sound of blowguns preceded a barrage of poison arrows. Narrowly missing Livingstone and the bishop, a dart lodged in the arm of one of the expedition's native companions. They turned and ran farther up the hillside.

The Ajawa gave chase, with warriors advancing "in bloodthirsty fury" to within fifty yards.[14]

"Fire!" Livingstone yelled to his men with guns. Unwilling to pull the trigger, Bishop Mackenzie handed his gun to Livingstone, who proceeded to fire away. When the Ajawa saw their adversary's rifle power, they retreated. The expedition drove them out of the village and into the forest.

"We will follow, and kill you where you sleep!" Ajawa voices shouted from the hills.[15]

When the commotion settled, six Ajawa and one of the expedition's native crew lay dead on the ground. The European men suffered no injuries but showed little sympathy in their attackers' retreat. To keep the Ajawa from returning, the men lit the village ablaze.

"Though we could not blame ourselves for the course we had followed, we felt sorry for what had happened," Livingstone reflected. "It was the first time we had ever been attacked by the natives or come into collision with them; though we had always taken it for granted that we might be called upon to act in self-defence [sic], we were on this occasion less prepared than usual, no game having been expected here."[16]

Livingstone had not come to pick a fight. His men carried only a single round each, and Livingstone himself had brought no gun. Since he did not plan to hunt game, he left the rifle he usually carried on the ship to save it from the rains.

"Had we known better the effect of slavery and murder on the temper of these bloodthirsty marauders," Livingstone lamented, "we should have tried messages and presents before going near them."[17]

The altercation immediately converted Bishop Mackenzie to arms.

". . . this is a different case," Mackenzie wrote. "These are strangers . . . coming to make war on our people and carry them off as slaves. This we must help them resist by every means. . . . [W]e are right, though clergymen and preachers of the Gospel to go with him, and by our presence, and the sight of our guns, and their use, if necessary (which God may avert), to strengthen his hands in procuring the liberation of these people."[18]

The bishop proposed an aggressive response to the Ajawa: drive them out of the country. With the Manganja now in his mission, he felt a duty to its people. Only Livingstone opposed the plan, suggesting the bishop wait to see how the Ajawa reacted. Perhaps, he reasoned, it would put a check on Ajawa slaving to know a superior force now existed.

But what if the Manganja asked for the mission to intercede on their behalf? the bishop probed Livingstone.

"No," Livingstone replied, "you will be oppressed by their importunities, but do not interfere in native quarrels."

The fight with the Ajawa weighed on him, and he feared they would be "enemies to the English forever."[19] He never wanted to kill Africans. He wanted the natives to see missionaries as peaceful people, not a polarizing force, and especially not a group upon whom to exact revenge.

Livingstone gathered Manganja chiefs at the village of Magomera.

"You have hitherto only seen us as fighting men," Livingstone told the Manganja chiefs, "but it is not in such a character we wish you to know us. My brothers who will remain at Magomera, wish to teach you about the great God—the good father of us all—and they will make Magomera a strong place, to which those who are afraid may fly. I do not think the Ajawa will trouble you; the lesson we have given them will keep them quiet; but should they do as they have done, I shall be up here again soon, and then they must be looked after once more."[20]

Now in the Shiré highlands, and occupied with their Manganja membership, the Universities' Mission planned to settle at Magomera, a seventy-mile walk from the river. Accompanied by Kirk, Charles, and their team of porters, Livingstone parted ways with the Universities' Mission to continue their geographic research. Their eager departure purposefully distanced the Livingstone expedition from the Universities' Mission's shifting objectives. The bishop did not want to heed Livingstone's advised neutrality, but rather continued forcibly driving the Ajawas from the region.

"People will not approve of men coming out to convert people, shooting them," Livingstone wrote in his journal. With the expedition's public estimation eroding, Livingstone grew increasingly conscious of potential critics. "I am sorry that I am mixed up with it, as they will not care what view of my character is given at home."[21]

Somberly, Livingstone continued on toward Nyassa to make a more thorough survey of the lake. Unable to sail up the Rovuma, they would reverse course. Livingstone would attempt to find the exit from Lake Nyassa and drift down the Rovuma to the Indian Ocean. With the help of their native porters, Kirk and the Livingstone brothers hoisted a small four-oared gig from the *Pioneer* and carried it around the Murchison Cataracts. They rowed it optimistically up the rest of the Shiré and into the waters of Lake Nyassa.

The notorious lake brought no new hope. Since his last visit, the region had descended into further violence and chaos. More dhows ferrying slaves, more burned villages, more bloodshed. With Nyassa's havoc, he could not finish the geographic survey and determined that the Rovuma did not begin at Nyassa as he had expected—it started forty miles east. Livingstone left Nyassa with nothing to encourage him.

The clock continued ticking away on Livingstone's Zambezi expedition. He had a year to show measurable progress to the British Foreign Office. With no new rivers to explore, he focused his attention on receiving his custom-built portable steamer. George Rae had followed the instructions to build the boat from Livingstone's own fortune, and now the explorer wanted to introduce the *Lady Nyassa* to her namesake.

The team rendezvoused at the *Pioneer*, anchored below the Murchison Cataracts, and steamed back toward the mouth of the Zambezi.

7 RETURNING TO RAGS

*I still prefer poverty and mission-service to
riches and ease. It's my choice.*
                              —David Livingstone

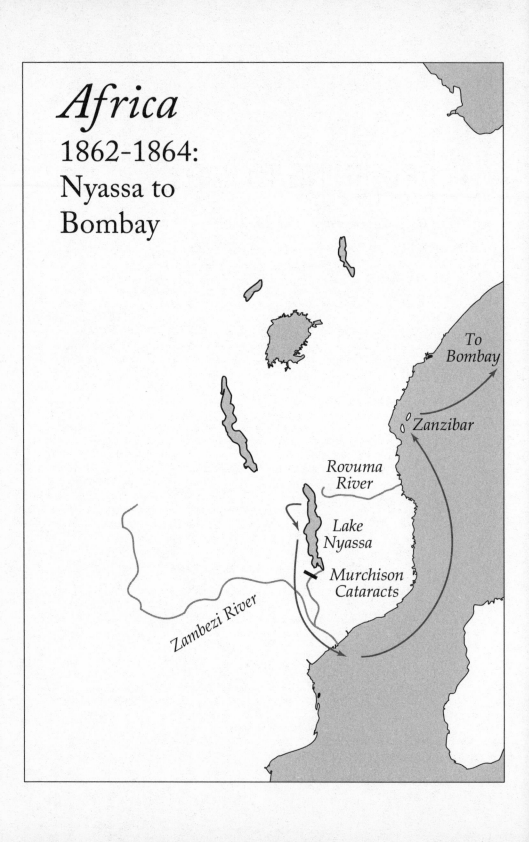

Africa

1862-1864:
Nyassa to
Bombay

To
Bombay

Zanzibar

Rovuma
River

Lake
Nyassa

Murchison
Cataracts

Zambezi River

ivingstone peered through his telescope, carefully scanning the long line of the horizon. Two objects appeared: ships. Perhaps the very ships he eagerly wanted to see steaming toward the Zambezi. Already the last day of January 1862, he had expected their arrival at any time. Looking back through his telescope, he saw the ship's crew signal: his wife and his portable steamer were arriving.

His long-anticipated *Lady Nyassa* was not yet seaworthy and would not sail anytime soon. She came in crates aboard a British frigate and would require months of assembly. George Rae, the expedition's original engineer, accompanied the *Lady Nyassa* to Africa and received instructions from Livingstone to begin construction at once. With the aid of a young native named Susi, and additional local labor, Rae began bolting together the pieces of the new steamer. For Livingstone, an urgent personal matter demanded his attention: Mary.

Mary Livingstone had changed dramatically during her three-year abandonment in South Africa. The dowdy, quiet housewife became a coarse, vulgar woman and an alcoholic. She now resented her husband's sense of religious call to Africa. She resented missionaries—those she lived among the last years in South Africa had insinuated that her marital seclusion branded her an unwanted spouse. Above all, she believed faith in Providence had destroyed her life, and for that, she resented God too.

Mary's condition shocked Livingstone and brought the expedition trouble. Her frequent bouts of hysteria stole his attention and worsened when Mary drank. Gossip swirled, albeit unlikely, that she had an affair with another missionary onboard the boat. But most troubling to Livingstone, he feared Mary had given up her Christian faith. Africa, it seemed, had completely devastated her.

Privately, Mary appeared very much herself. Livingstone and Mary put aside their public troubles to recover the years lost in their relationship. In Livingstone's words, "There was more than would be thought by some a decorous amount of merriment and play."

"We old bodies ought now to be more sober and not play so much," Livingstone told his wife.

"O, no," Mary replied, "you must just be as playful as you have always been. I would not like you to be so grave as some folks I have seen."

Livingstone saw Mary as his vivacity, as he reflected on her in his journal, "[She] led me to feel what I have always believed to be the true way—to let the head grow wise, but keep the heart always young and playful."[1]

New tragedies soon overshadowed Livingstone's anxieties about Mary. In his dark cabin on the *Pioneer*, Livingstone received dreadful news from the Universities' Mission.

Bishop Mackenzie was dead. The missionary leader had succumbed to dysentery on his way to rendezvous with the Livingstone expedition. The loss would not only change the course of the Universities' Mission, but it would send shockwaves throughout England. Livingstone knew when word got back to London, it would affect his expedition and the government's assessment of his judgment.

"This will hurt us all," Livingstone mumbled, head buried in his hands.[2]

Immediately, he wrote to the foreign secretary to share the sad account himself and place the responsibility on the Universities' Mission. He had justification for this, as the bishop and his mission had acted recklessly after they parted ways with Livingstone's crew. Attempting to restore order to regional anarchy, the mission group had conducted a series of attacks against the Ajawa, in spite of Livingstone's clear advice not to make offensive actions in Africa.

Finally, against the will of his fellow missionaries, the bishop had started out on a trek to convene with Livingstone and the *Pioneer*. Beginning his trek during heavy rains and in declining health, Mackenzie soon found himself with severe diarrhea, which quickly took his life.

But despite his attempts to deflect attention, Livingstone bore the burden of accountability. He had misled Britain, and consequently the Universities' Mission, by overselling the suitability of the Shiré highlands. He had diminished its dangers, particularly the lawlessness overrunning the region. With the bishop's death, little cover remained for Livingstone to hide the realities of Africa.

A month later, when it seemed nothing could get worse, it did. As the expedition restocked and prepared to move the *Lady Nyassa* up the Shiré, Mary Livingstone came down with a fever. Her condition quickly grew serious—terrible nausea with no apparent remedies proving effective. Her moaning grew constant until she became unresponsive and unable to speak.

"My dearie, my dearie you are going to leave me?" Livingstone asked, wrapping his arms around his wife at her bedside. "Are you resting on Jesus?"[3]

He wept like a child. Even more than losing his companion, Livingstone feared she might pass away rejecting God. He waited by Mary's bedside until her final moment. As he bent over to kiss her, she took her final breath.

"It is the first heartstroke I have suffered and quite takes away my strength," Livingstone confided in his journal.

> I wept over her who well deserved many tears. I loved when I married her and the longer I lived with her I loved her the more. God pity the poor children who were all tenderly attached to her, and I am left alone in the world by one whom I felt to a part of myself. I hope it may by Divine grace lead me to realize Heaven as my home and that she has

but preceded me in the journey. Oh, my Mary, my Mary, how often we have longed for a quiet home since you and I were cast adrift at Kolobeng [South Africa]. Surely the removal by a kind Father who knoweth our frame means that he rewarded you by taking you to the best home, the eternal one in the Heavens.[4]

"There are many regrets which will follow me to my dying day," he wrote to his mother.[5] He would regret not exploring Mary's doubts and questions about faith. As he sorted through Mary's papers, he found a little note, a prayer to God she had written not long before her death: "Accept me Lord as I am, and Make me such as thou wouldst have me to be."[6] The note brought Livingstone a little comfort.

———

"Dr L. particularly communicative and agreeable," noted James Stewart, a Scottish missionary who had arrived with the *Pioneer*. "His recent loss seems to have had some effect of a softening kind on him."[7]

The loss of Mary brought a noticeable change to the gruff, demanding expedition leader. Perhaps his regrets extended beyond his wife, or perhaps the loss tore down walls he had built between himself and others. Livingstone began showing more compassion, conversing more often with his team, and became generally more congenial. His crew took notice.

Although outwardly he seemed to be adjusting to life as a widower, internally remorse agonized him. The thought of death crept frequently into Livingstone's mind.

"For the first time in my life I feel willing to die," he confided in his journal.[8] "Since the death of Mary I often feel that I have not long to live, but I will do my duty for all that."[9]

The loss completely cured him of his interest in returning to Britain permanently. With the *Lady Nyassa* still under construction, Livingstone distracted himself with exploration. He focused myopically on finding a navigable river until he could join Mary.

"I suppose that I shall die in the uplands and that somebody else will carry out the plans I have longed to put into practice," he wrote. "I have been thinking a great deal since the departure of my beloved one about the region whither she has gone . . . I work with as much vigor as I can until the change comes, but the prospect of a home is all dispelled."[10]

Even doubts about God's intentions entered his mind.

Livingstone's providential plan had encountered so many road-blocks: obstructing rapids on the Zambezi and Shiré, dissension among the expedition team, rejection by the British government for his new boat, and now blood on his hands—the deaths of the bishop and his own wife. Perhaps God did not want him in Africa after all.

If God had another path, Livingstone could not discern it.

"There is something I have to do or be; such I take to be the meaning of dispensation," he told James Stewart. "I wish I could find out."[11]

While his temperament softened, Livingstone's steadfast resolve grew still more determined. Finding a river into Africa's interior took his mind off tragedy, but even more, he needed vindication. He would prove that God had ordained him and the expedition for this purpose.

Livingstone turned, yet again, to the Rovuma. Perhaps recognizing that the Murchison Cataracts on the Shiré would present too formidable a foe, Livingstone saw the Rovuma as a last-ditch attempt at reaching Nyassa. Livingstone cast away obvious navigational and geographic doubts, unwaveringly pushing the expedition forward. They sailed the long distance back to the Rovuma.

Once again, the *Pioneer* constantly ran aground in the Rovuma's shallow waters. The expedition struggled to make progress. Livingstone knew the attempt to be nearly impossible. Yet he would not call off the mission, pressing his men to continue their tedious slog north. With little left to live for, he would ascend the river or die trying.

"Am I to be a martyr to my own cause?" Livingstone confided. "I begin to think that I may not live to see success. Am I to experience that this cause is to be founded on my sacrifice and cemented by my suffering?

Every covenant was ratified with sacrifice . . . I hope this may be compensated if I die by my death."

He resigned himself not only to death but to impending failure.

"It is probable that I may fail in establishing a new system on that great centre of slaving, Lake Nyassa," Livingstone confessed in a letter to family.

His team knew nothing of Livingstone's mounting fatalistic disposition, they simply thought he had grown obsessive, bordering on insane.

"I can come to no other conclusion than that Dr L. is out of his mind," Kirk declared in his journals.[12] Kirk and the few men who remained with the expedition saw no worthwhile purpose in exploring the Rovuma again. Kirk believed Livingstone simply desired "geographical glory."[13]

They knew many miles of the river to be too shallow for boats, while unknown miles of uncharted river still lay ahead. Yet Livingstone could not be convinced of a contrary course. When they reached an imposing series of cataracts on the Rovuma, Livingstone ordered the cumbersome *Pioneer* carried around the rapids. Mentally and physically, they began preparations for a grueling portage.

Suddenly, Livingstone changed his mind. With an about-face the day after the portage order, the expedition reversed course for a return trip down the river. The reason for Livingstone's abrupt departure: the *Lady Nyassa*. Her assembly would finish soon, and Livingstone did not want another rainy season to pass before putting her under sail.

Although the team welcomed the abrupt change, it appeared reckless.

"Dr. L is a most unsafe leader," Kirk concluded.[14]

The return felt even more perilous than previous journeys. Native tribes attacked regularly, increasing their hostility likely due to the aggression of the Universities' Mission and the expedition's role in attacking the Ajawa. The crew worked desperately to avoid sandbars. If they ran aground, they expected a battle. Even from their floating fortress, they routinely traded bullets for poison arrows. Livingstone's men killed at least two natives.

After the treacherous journey down the Rovuma, the *Pioneer* finally returned to the assembly rendezvous point to find the *Lady Nyassa* afloat. Livingstone eagerly wanted to steam toward Lake Nyassa with his new boat, turning his crew begrudgingly back toward the Shiré.

The men found the Shiré region enveloped in the worst famine anyone, including the native tribes, could remember. Due to two years of drought and failed crops, ecological conditions had deteriorated to the brink of environmental collapse. For the expedition, the environmental disaster created unexpected setbacks. The drought lowered river levels, slowing their pace to an agonizing crawl and often leaving the *Lady Nyassa* stuck on sandbars.

Worse yet, the pitiful human condition cast a heavy shadow of doubt and hesitation. The Shiré's hearty men, women, and children who once watched from the riverbanks had become mere skeletons, ghosts of the former riverside inhabitants. Famine gripped the region and stole effort from anything beyond survival. The bloated stomachs of the children verified that little food could be found.

Ajawa warriors exploited the tragedy, pushing farther into the Shiré region with their terrifying and ruthless slave raids. The dead accumulated so quickly that natives dumped bodies into the river to avoid the terrors of the evil spirits that superstition led them to believe followed an unburied corpse. Bodies floated past the *Lady Nyassa* regularly—thirty-four counted in one day.

Conditions among the crew deteriorated as well. Discontent and division ran rampant, accompanied by fever.

"The officers are all but in rebellion, and the Dr daily becomes more incapable of self-control," wrote one of the UMCA missionaries. "A catastrophe, or tragedy, I fear is not far off."[15]

Tragedy, indeed, soon found them. Thornton, the brilliant young geologist, reluctantly returned to the expedition at Livingstone's invitation. After withdrawing from the Zambezi expedition in 1861, he had fallen in with a German expedition to continue exploring the Zambezi region north of Tette, then joined the first European survey of Mount Kilimanjaro. Soon after reuniting with Livingstone's team, fever and

97

exhaustion from his journey caught up with him. Thornton's storied but short career ended at age twenty-five.

But the wave of tragedy had not yet crested. Suffering severely from the drought, the Universities' Mission lost two more men to ulcers and fever.

"This will be another blow to our work," Livingstone responded to the news.[16]

He knew more deaths would compound the government's frustration with his failing expedition. Nonetheless, Livingstone chalked it up, again, to the Universities' Mission's foolishness and inexperience.

Kirk had remained by Livingstone's side since the beginning. Astonishingly, he had stayed out of the line of Livingstone's fire and never irked Charles into a forced removal. Kirk rarely spoke up. He found it better not to cross Livingstone, although he often objected to his decisions. His moderation left him frequently alone, but solitude had kept him on the team.

Now plagued by death and devastation, the expedition reached complete disintegration. Kirk and Charles finally both quit.

For six years, Kirk had stood at Livingstone's side through disappointment, death, and despair. Now Kirk departed disillusioned with Livingstone's leadership and angry at his decisions. "He is one of the sanguine enthusiasts wrapped up in their own schemes," Kirk wrote, "whose reason and better judgment is blinded by headstrong passion."[17]

Kirk admired Livingstone's capacity and determination but abhorred many traits of his leadership. By the end of five arduous years of exploring, little tolerance remained. Kirk hardly trusted Livingstone—"as ungrateful and slippery a mortal as I ever came in contact with."[18] Despite the bitter parting, it would not leave their devotion beyond repair.

Livingstone did not object to Kirk's departure. He objected to no one's departure. Only George Rae remained from the original cast while adding a sailor from a government ship and twenty natives.

Livingstone longed for the days in South Africa left to work alone at his own devices.

"It would be well to get rid of them all and have no more," he wrote.[19]

Livingstone expected the government to withdraw him at any moment. Until then, he continued to push forward. If he worked until the end, he could place the responsibility for termination of the expedition on his orders, not his own ineptitude.

As the *Lady Nyassa* steamed deeper into the interior, Livingstone's heart broke for the Shiré Valley.

"It made the heart ache to see the wide-spread desolation," Livingstone wrote, "the river-banks, once so populous, all silent; the villages burned down, and an oppressive stillness reigning where formerly crowds of eager sellers appeared with the various products of their industry."[20]

The devastation was catastrophic.

"People had been killed, kidnapped, and forced to flee from their villages . . . The sight and smell of dead bodies was everywhere. Many skeletons lay beside the path, where in their weaknesses they had fallen and expired. Ghastly living forms of boys and girls with dull dead eyes were crouching beside some of the huts."[21]

Of all Livingstone's failures, perhaps this realization hurt the most. He had done nothing to slow the slave trade. It had only increased.

———

Arriving at the Murchison Cataracts, Livingstone ordered the *Lady Nyassa* to be sectioned for overland transport up the thirty-mile stretch of rapids. Estimating a year of work to construct suitable roads, his native porters began felling trees.

Knowing he had few resources remaining and limited money, Livingstone issued an invitation for the foreign secretary to finally order a recall. With newfound honesty, he shared word of the Shiré's destruction with the British government. In a letter published in the *Times*, he wrote about the misgivings of the Rovuma journey. He finally began admitting to the unfit conditions of the Shiré and the famine's recipe for the failure of any colony.

As his list of failures grew, so did public grievances. The British tide turned against Livingstone, and gave the government more reasons to bring him home. The *Times* spoke out, thus:

> [Livingstone's letter] described the approaching fall, if there really ever was a rise, to the East African Mission . . . Dr Livingstone is unquestionably a traveller of talents, enterprise, and excellent constitution, but it is now plain enough that his zeal and imagination much surpass his judgement, we must come to the conclusion that the time has arrived when the hopeless enterprise undertaken on his advice ought to be relinquished.[22]

A letter from Lord Russell finally reached Livingstone in Africa on July 2, 1863. Livingstone read the news he had anticipated but hated to hear: the Zambezi expedition was over. Government pay would end after December, Lord Russell wrote, citing the deaths of so many people as the most persuasive reason to conclude the five-year undertaking.

Before he could sail home, Livingstone received one more black eye: the recall of the Universities' Mission. A new bishop arrived to replace the late Bishop Mackenzie and determine the future of the mission. Given the conditions he found in the Shiré highlands, coupled with the failure of Livingstone's expedition, his decision to close the mission met with little dispute.

The Universities' Mission—a refuge of Christianity deep in the African interior—had remained the sole successful product of Livingstone's Zambezi career, and the only intimation of his colonial fantasy. Now, he had nothing at all to show for the last half decade. Everything he had worked for had failed. The Zambezi expedition would leave neither a significant legacy nor a meaningful contribution to Africa.

With five more months of pay to wrap up the expedition, Livingstone's friends and family pleaded for his return to England.

"Earnestly hoping that the great South African explorer may now come home to his motherless children and numerous friends," Murchison publicly pleaded in the *Times*, "and not expose his valuable life to further risks . . ."[23]

Livingstone, however, refused to retreat.

———

The *Times* broke the news: ". . . a report reached this country that Dr. Livingstone had met with an untimely end on his expedition up the Zambezi."[24]

When Livingstone did not return immediately after the recall, rumors swirled suggesting the explorer had been murdered. Perhaps Murchison foretold it, knowing death would eventually catch even the most determined explorer. Many in England held their breath for confirmation about whether a final tragedy had befallen the disgraced expedition.

Then, in early April, the dilapidated husk of a man appeared on foot at the mouth of the Zambezi. In lieu of an immediate return, Livingstone had concluded his expedition in the same fashion as his South African expedition—a final overland journey. He walked seven hundred miles along Lake Nyassa, then back to the Murchison Cataracts, marrying physical depletion to his bankrupt reputation.

A British steamer relayed the news to London: Livingstone "alive and well."[25] A flurry of editorials in London followed.

Livingstone bid farewell to the *Pioneer*, which sailed to the cape, and turned his attention to the future of the *Lady Nyassa*. Lest the *Lady Nyassa* fall into the hands of the slavers, Livingstone knew it must be sailed away from the slave ports and sold in a broader market. Zanzibar offered the closest trade in vessels.

Only lakes and rivers suited the *Lady Nyassa* with its small stature and short draft. Open ocean waves could quickly capsize it or rip apart its ambulatory sections. Still, his fear that it could be used to expand the slave trade outweighed the risks.

Livingstone dismissed his porters and gathered a new crew. Among them was Chuma, one of the boys freed during their 1861 raids on the Ajawa. Captured and orphaned at a young age, the slave trade had separated Chuma from his family. He now considered Livingstone his only family. Susi, an African man who helped assemble the pieces of the *Lady Nyassa*, also agreed to join. Both young men were Muslim but felt a deep devotion to Livingstone and his cause. They would follow him wherever he went.

Livingstone threw off the bowlines for the thousand-mile voyage from Mozambique to Zanzibar. Sailing with an undersized crew on his inadequate vessel, he arrived in Zanzibar in a week.

In Zanzibar's markets, Livingstone found no buyer. Outlandishly, he looked east toward India. At nearly three thousand miles across the Indian Ocean, Bombay provided a more robust boat market. But the Bombay option presented severe danger—a long voyage on a small craft with monsoon season arriving in just three weeks. Once the "break of the monsoon" arrived, most mariners believed no boat could survive. This, as Livingstone put it, "made us sometimes think our epitaph would be 'Left Zanzibar on 30th April, 1864, and never more heard of.'"[26]

Despite the odds, Livingstone set off with a mere five days of coal for steaming. For weeks, the *Lady Nyassa* cruised toward Bombay, mostly under sail. The prolonged trip offered considerable time for reflection. Chiefly, he pondered his life in England and his future—if any—in Africa.

"I shall have nothing to do at home," Livingstone wrote in his journal. "By the failure of the Universities['] Mission my work seems vain. Am I to be cut off before I can do anything to affect permanent improvement in Africa? I have been unprofitable enough . . ."[27]

Livingstone knew the criticism awaiting him in England, and he knew it would be no easy task to mount a return expedition to Africa. He had burned his bridges with the missionary society, exhausted his savings on the *Lady Nyassa*, and depleted his goodwill with the British government. With the loss of Mary, he felt no desire for a permanent home, nor to remarry. He had not functioned well in close proximity with Europeans, so the notion of joining the working masses in England gave him little consolation.

Livingstone pondered escaping back to the comfortable wilds of Africa, surrounded by natives who never challenged his autocratic leadership. But, even if he did return, where would he go? He had made enemies with the Portuguese who, without political pressure, would undoubtedly cut him off from all areas he had previously explored. He had no funds to sustain his own expedition. The future presented no clear answers.

On a hazy morning, forty-five days after leaving Zanzibar, Livingstone finally spotted the forest of masts looming over Bombay's harbor. The *Lady Nyassa* floated into port, unnoticed among the much larger oceangoing vessels. She took a slip—and not a moment too soon. The gale winds of the monsoons arrived the next day.

In Bombay, no crowd awaited Livingstone. No missionary societies or explorers' clubs greeted him. He received no welcome party in the harbor. He appeared to be just another sailor arriving at port.

Livingstone walked into the courthouse and listened to cases. He thought about the work he had to do over the next few days: mooring the *Lady Nyassa* until he could sell her, placing Chuma in school, and finding work in the docks for Susi. And so, the heralded Zambezi expedition came to a sobering, anticlimatic end.

As Livingstone boarded a ship bound for London in the ensuing days, Africa had not drifted from his mind.

"I don't know whether I am to go on the shelf or not," he wrote from the boat to a missionary friend. "If I do, I make Africa the shelf."[28]

———

The *Times* again condemned Livingstone in a bitter editorial:

> We were promised cotton, sugar, and indigo, commodities which sav-
> ages never produced, and of course we got none. We were promised
> trade and there is no trade. We were promised converts and not one
> has been made. We were promised that the climate was salubrious,
> and some of the best missionaries and their wives and children have
> died in the malarious swamps of the Zambezi.[29]

As Livingstone arrived back in London in July 1864, the grace proffered to him at his 1858 farewell dinner was conspicuously absent. The
public condemned him for his many unfulfilled promises, from assur-
ing a navigable Zambezi River to missionaries living safely in Central
Africa. Watchdogs at London's newspapers even noticed his "failure of
the efforts . . . to check the slave trade on the east coast of Africa."[30]

His critics overlooked the value of Livingstone's expedition.
Geographically, he had explored the Zambezi, usefully determining
it to be an unnavigable waterway. He had also explored the Shiré and
Rovuma rivers more thoroughly than any previous European. These
objectives alone might have warranted a sponsored expedition. In addition to these findings, the expedition precisely positioned and mapped
Lake Nyassa, which, while previously reached by Portuguese traders,
lacked accurate documentation. On humanitarian grounds, the expedition had also uncovered the immense and devastating Arab slave
trade and its routes through the Nyassa region to Zanzibar. These findings were new, informing the world and the British Foreign Office of
unresolved horrors.

At the 1858 outset of the Zambezi expedition, Her Majesty's
government and its citizenry needed little justification for funding
Livingstone's foray—simply knowing his efforts advanced British exploration brought glory enough. But Livingstone had gone further, building
the expedition's foundation on great expectations, overpromising and
underperforming. Perhaps if Livingstone had tendered a humble survey

of the Zambezi and returned in 1864 armed with even his meager successes, the expedition would have been deemed a triumph.

On the heels of grossly unfulfilled promises, Livingstone's private champions and government sponsors preferred to disassociate from him. Prime Minister Lord Palmerston granted him a dinner invitation, but it became clear to Livingstone the evening amounted to a mere courtesy. The foreign secretary, Lord Russell, spared him a few unfriendly minutes. Worse yet, he had lost the favor of the British people—they rarely recognized him in public. On the streets, crowds no longer rushed to him as they once did.

Despite his discouraging reception, Livingstone still believed in his cause. His first conversations with Lord Palmerston focused on stopping the slave trade. He believed the misery in Africa's interior needed to end, and that it would only end by a stronger British presence on the continent.

For this purpose, he would continue to press.

Of the next expedition, or how he might return to Africa, Livingstone had no clear idea. He only knew he had not finished his work. Sitting down at his journal, Livingstone resolved to see his life not vilified, but vindicated. Putting pen to paper, he summarized his deepest emotions.

"The future," he wrote, "will justify my words and hopes."[31]

8 ✦ THE SOURCE

I have always found that the art of successful travel
consisted in taking as few impediments as possible,
and not forgetting to carry my wits about me.

—DAVID LIVINGSTONE

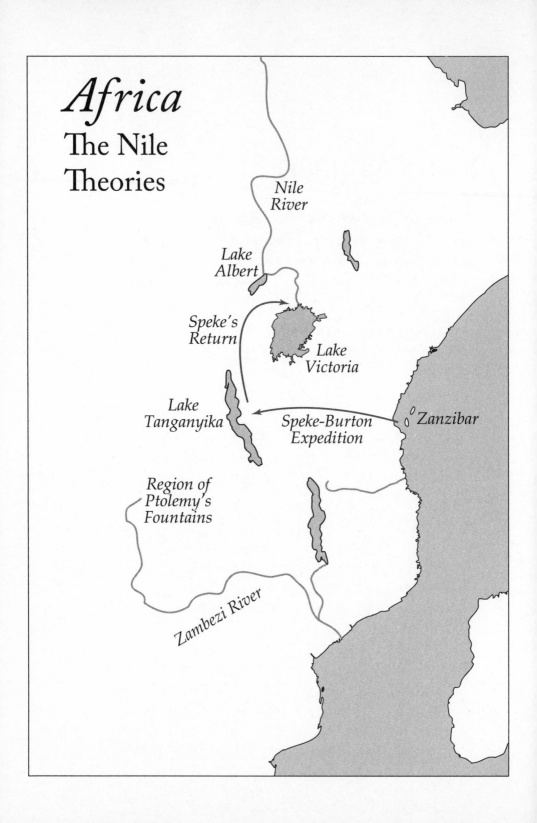

Africa
The Nile
Theories

Nile
River

Lake
Albert

Speke's
Return

Lake
Victoria

Lake
Tanganyika

Speke-Burton
Expedition

Zanzibar

Region of
Ptolemy's
Fountains

Zambezi River

July 20, 1864: Livingstone arrives in London.
8 years, 9 months, and 13 days until the end
of the East African slave trade.

Slaves sold per annum: 20,000
Total victims of the slave trade: 376,000

R eturning to England in 1864 was like arriving at a new era. Seven years had passed since Livingstone last saw European shores. His children had grown considerably in his absence and the world had changed immensely. Science united continents and war divided nations. Europe and America had connected via transatlantic telegraph, presaging a day when an overseas letter might no longer take months to arrive. The issue of slavery split the United States.

London life offered Livingstone little. With no banquets and few speaking engagements, Livingstone spent his time working to mend his broken home. He had much to learn about his own children, so he returned to Scotland to reconnect with a family who had mostly grown up in his absence. The loss of Mary had left a distinct hole in their lives and, to add more grief and sorrow to his return, Livingstone's mother passed away not long after his arrival.

The eldest child, Robert, struggled at home—and broke his father's heart. Born in the wilds of the African mission field, Robert never fit in well in Britain. Struck with wanderlust, he bounced around boarding schools, often running away, and never continued his education, much to his father's chastising chagrin. Soon after arriving in Britain, Livingstone learned that Robert had drifted to the United States where he enlisted in the American Civil War. Livingstone woefully anticipated that Robert would die in the bloodbath of a foreign battle. And he did so that year.

Livingstone had never met Anna Mary, now five, the child who had unexpectedly changed their plans en route to the Zambezi. Born in South Africa, she had been sent back to England before her mother went on to meet Livingstone on the river. Livingstone scarcely mentioned his sons Oswell or Thomas in his writing, aside from his concern for Thomas's health, which had the fifteen-year-old falling behind in school. Oswell, who had turned twelve in the intervening years since off-loading in South Africa, largely fell between the cracks of more demanding siblings. Livingstone felt the strongest bond to Agnes, his now seventeen-year-old daughter. Despite only six years in each other's company, they spent considerable time together at home.

When not with his children, Livingstone put pen to paper. *A Narrative of an Expedition to the Zambezi and Its Tributaries* would need to be a success on the scale of *Missionary Travels*. He had spent his entire fortune on the *Lady Nyassa*, leaving the book his only practical hope of salvation from financial ruin.

Content for the book proved delicate. Livingstone debated whether to include his harsh criticisms of the UMCA and the Portuguese. In Murchison, Livingstone found a provocateur.

"I think that the truth ought to be known," Murchison told him, "if only in vindication of your own conduct, and to account for the little success attending your last mission."[1]

As Livingstone wrote, he avoided documenting the constant conflict and mistakes of the Zambezi expedition. He focused on the adventure, the expedition's few successes, and most notably, his account of the slave trade. In *Missionary Travels*, Livingstone had written only mildly against slavery. On the Zambezi expedition, he had witnessed hell on earth, and now he spoke about the "curse of Africa" with passionate outrage.

"It has been my object," began the first words of his preface, ". . . to bring before my countrymen, and all others interested in the cause of humanity, the misery entailed by the slave-trade in its inland phases . . ."[2]

Livingstone charged European nations with the "shame" of allowing slavery to continue unrestrained in the nineteenth century. Anticipating the public shame he would bear for the failed Zambezi expedition, perhaps Livingstone knew he needed to steer attention to a scapegoat. Portugal, with her unaccountable endeavors in East Africa, provided the perfect cover. He could blame the chaos and violence at the hands of the Portuguese for the collapse of the expedition.

He vigorously directed his wrath at the Portuguese. In *Missionary Travels*, Livingstone had applauded Portuguese anti-slavery efforts on Africa's west coast. In a blistering rebuke, he explained that he now saw matters differently; he vehemently indicted Portugal for complicity and fraud, much to the consternation of Lisbon—and British diplomacy:

> The credit which I was fain to award to the Lisbon statesmen for a sincere desire to put an end to the slave trade, is, I regret to find, totally undeserved. Portugal's claim that she was taking civilization to the untutored and her talk about spreading Christianity and putting down cruelty and slavery were mere shams.
>
> But the main object of the Portuguese Government is not geographical. It is to bolster up that pretence [sic] to power which has been the only obstacle to the establishment of lawful commerce and friendly relations with the native inhabitants of Eastern Africa. . . . they completely shut out the natives from any trade, except that in slaves.[3]

Livingstone's fight bent the sympathetic public ear in Britain. Riding on a wave of anti-slavery successes throughout its empire and along Africa's west coast, new movements against the slave trade inherited spirited momentum. Antislavery rhetoric still captured passionate British minds.

Yet, when it came to East Africa, devotion to abolition sagged. Britain had not directly participated in the East African trade as it had along the west coast. The British people just could not garner the same zealous rage and sense of moral obligation toward East Africa; Britain had never been involved there.

Furthermore, if Britain intervened in East Africa, her actions would undoubtedly come at a cost. Any enforcement along East African shores would interfere with the sovereignty of Zanzibar. British diplomatic relations suggested that pushing the sultan of Zanzibar would harm their friendship and create a political opening for other European nations vying for a piece of Africa. France and Germany eagerly awaited any opportunity to gain political power in Zanzibar to Britain's detriment.

Livingstone saw moral obligation differently and cast responsibility for the slave trade on the British government. In his view, Britain aided the Portuguese by recognizing and respecting their East African territorial claims: ". . . by our acquiescence in the sham sovereignty of the Portuguese, we effect only a partial suppression of the slave-trade, and none of the commercial benefits which have followed direct dealing with the natives on the West Coast."[4]

But if shame would not move Her Majesty's government to action, perhaps competition would. Livingstone cited, "[T]he great fact that the Americans have rid themselves of the incubus of slavery . . ." He then continued his censure of British inaction.

Livingstone stoked a rivalry with America, crowning the younger nation as the leading abolitionist champion. The United States likely would "not tolerate the continuance of the murderous slave-trade by the Portuguese nation," he said.[5] More than two years had passed since President Lincoln issued the Emancipation Proclamation, the Thirteenth Amendment had been enacted to formally outlaw slavery, and America was growing in global stature. If Britain refused to act, Livingstone suggested American goodwill might soon surpass her.

Although his remarks embarrassed the British government, she listened. To popular approval, Britain responded with increased restrictions on the sultan of Zanzibar—but only restrictions. The government remained reluctant to take resolute action.[6]

Britain's restrictions made precipitated changes, persuading Sultan Majid to issue a decree forbidding all transport of slaves from January to

April—the period just before the southwest monsoon. The timing was strategic. Slave traders exporting from East Africa into the Middle East could only sail their dhows conveniently during the restricted period. Further British pressure on the sultan prevented the Zanzibari people from trading or cooperating with Arab slave traders altogether.

"[E]very northern dhow reaching Zanzibar," the sultan decreed to his citizens, "shall be burned forthwith, as their sole business here is to steal the children of the inhabitants of Zanzibar and their slaves."[7]

To enforce the new law of January 1, 1864, the British navy ran patrols over Zanzibar's waters. The British slave squadron captured any slaving ship caught during this period and set its captives free.

But despite British patrols, the slave trade barely contracted. Zanzibar's vast waters proved a large jurisdiction for the shrinking British navy. Downsizing for economic purposes had mandated the recall of many British forces and made the East African squadron a low priority for military spending. Zanzibar contributed little to the enforcement of the law. Its much smaller, more timid navy struggled to effectively influence the slavers.

The sultan's restrictions had weaknesses, and the slave traders worked to exploit them. The new restrictions only applied to seafaring trade; it did not prohibit the overland export of slaves. Despite physical challenges, the slave traders extended their land routes to avoid sailing in the sultan's territories.

On the island of Zanzibar, little had changed. No restrictions affected the great slave market; its doors remained open for the buying and selling of human lives. Slaves could still be imported under the non-export auspices of domestic servitude and labor.

As many as twenty thousand slaves continued to be exported through Zanzibar every year with less than nine hundred intercepted and freed. In England, public perception of the Zanzibar policies concluded that restrictions on the slave trade in East Africa had failed. England needed new leadership in Zanzibar to reinvigorate the fight and go head-to-head with the sultan.

———

Of the few speaking invitations extended to Livingstone, one came from the British Association for the Advancement of Science. He was asked to deliver a plenary speech in Bath at its annual event before an audience of twenty-five hundred. Although Livingstone disliked such large events, the British Association requested a topic he felt passionately about: the African slave trade. He accepted.

The meeting on September 16, 1864, did not constitute his first appearance at the British Association for the Advancement of Science. He had headlined its annual meeting eight years before on his celebratory first visit home. But this time it relegated him to a sideshow, an opening act for the main event: a debate between Richard Francis Burton and John Hanning Speke about the source of the Nile River, billed famously as the Nile Duel.

In 1856, while Livingstone had prepped for the Zambezi expedition, the British Foreign Office and Royal Geographical Society had dispatched Burton and Speke to the remote interior of Africa north of the Zambezi. The Burton-Speke expedition sought a route to a large inland body of water, Lake Tanganyika. They reached the lake together, but the explorers split up on the return. Burton continued directly to Zanzibar while Speke went north, becoming the first European to lay eyes on Lake Victoria. With the discovery of such a "vast expanse of open water," he declared Lake Victoria the apparent source of the Nile.

Not one to be left out, Burton vehemently disagreed, demanding better evidence. A public quarrel ensued, capturing the imagination of the lay and scientific communities alike. The men fiercely engaged in what became more than a mere geographic problem, the Nile question became a race for first. The world's leading explorers all had their eyes on discovering the prized source of the Nile and the glory to follow. The Nile controversy grew into the foremost public attraction in exploration.

Although Nile fascination had just reached Victorian vogue, the question of the source had perplexed geographers for millennia. The longest and arguably the most important river in history, the Nile held an unsolved riddle: no one knew where it began. Legend whispered that the source of the Nile bubbled up in great fountains from the ground. Yet no one had documented this fabled wellspring.

The earliest Nile rumors began with Herodotus, the Greek historian. In *History*, Herodotus wrote about his fifth century BC trip to Egypt, upon which he inquired extensively about the source of the Nile. Only a scribe of the treasury had any knowledge of the matter and he had a detailed account. Originating midway between two conical hills, said the scribe, half the water ran north to Egypt and half to the south.

In the second century AD, Ptolemy, the Greco-Roman astronomer and geographer, compiled all he could ascertain about the world into his work, *Geography*. Ptolemy's eighteen-hundred-year-old maps provided the best available charts of non-coastal Africa in Livingstone's time. Livingstone and his contemporaries pored over them. Ptolemy's work supported Herodotus's anecdotes. According to Ptolemy, the Nile originated from two springs located in a range he called the Mountains of the Moon. Until an expedition could confirm Ptolemy's theories, it was all they had.

Publicity surrounding the matter soon attracted other opportunistic explorers looking to make a name. In 1864, Samuel Baker set out to test the Nile theories, discovering Lake Albert farther north of Lake Victoria and subsequently declaring it to be the true source of the Nile. The debate intensified.

Burton put forth other plausible alternatives. The true source might be the more southerly Lake Tanganyika. Should water flow north from Tanganyika to Victoria, then Tanganyika would be the true origin of the river. Or, another river may flow from Tanganyika, joining with the Nile farther north. Speke's theory had enough holes for the matter to remain unsettled. None of the theories directly fit Ptolemy's suggestion, which might place each body of water in a long chain of lakes leading to the source.

The great Nile debate between Burton and Speke at the British Association never took place. The day before the event, a hunting accident outside Bath claimed Speke's life. The British Association would not solve the mystery, and the loss of the explorer only intensified public interest in the Nile.

Britain wanted to claim the answer. Her explorers had reached lakes Victoria, Albert, and Tanganyika. England could not let another nation solve the Nile riddle they had invested so much time and effort in answering. To be outdone would remove British exploration from prominence.

The Royal Geographical Society spearheaded the quest for the source, but it needed a high-profile figurehead to answer the question. He needed to be British, with the experience and tenacity to reach deeper into Africa than any man had previously traveled. From the outset, this limited the pool to only a few with the experience and ability. Burton and Baker would not do. They were too invested in the matter to assert neutrality and would only explore answers supporting their publicly stated theories. The RGS needed someone who had not yet pursued the source.

On January 5, 1865, Murchison's letter began:

> MY DEAR LIVINGSTONE,
>
> As to *your future*, I am anxious to know what *your own wish is* as respects a renewal of African exploration. Quite irrespective of missionaries or political affairs, there is at this moment a question of intense geographical interest to be settled . . . How, if you would really like to be the person to finish off your remarkable career by completing such a survey, unshackled by other avocations than those of the geographical explorer, I should be delighted to consult my friends of the Society, and take the best steps to promote such an enterprise.[8]

Murchison stressed "the purely geographical work" and said that if Livingstone could not rise to the undertaking, perhaps Kirk would accept the challenge.

"I have heard you so often talk of the enjoyment you feel when in Africa," Murchison concluded his letter, "that I cannot believe you now think of anchoring for the rest of your life on the mud and sand-banks of England."

Livingstone was the obvious candidate to Murchison. The Nile challenge played to his strengths: he had intimate knowledge of African interior travel, an undying persistence, and an uncompromising attention to detail in solving such a question. Despite his tainted image, he posed few risks. A Nile expedition was a small investment. Livingstone would not be leading a large team of Europeans, with colonial investment plans and custom-constructed vessels riding on his success. Unlike the unfocused, unrestrained Zambezi debacle, this expedition would give Livingstone clearly defined goals, budgets, and timelines.

Above all, the Nile venture offered the opportunity for redemption. If he found the source, it would be Livingstone's greatest discovery—the greatest geographic discovery of his day—and professional redemption after the failed Zambezi expedition.

"I should like the exploration you propose very much," Livingstone replied to Murchison, "and had already made up my mind to go up the Rovuma, pass by the head of Lake Nyassa, and away west or north-west as might be found practicable."[9]

Naturally, the prospect of the Nile dilemma intrigued him. Livingstone longed to return to Africa, and a competition for geographic firsts always enthralled him. Livingstone even had his own theory, and it differed from his peers'. He placed the Nile's origins farther south, believing Burton, Speke, and Baker had missed the target substantially. Livingstone took his guidance from the maps of Ptolemy and Herodotus, predicting the river originated at several great fountains.

The Nile question also stirred Livingstone's ego. Burton and Speke, before his death, became Livingstone's adversaries during the intermission in England. Speke criticized Livingstone in praise of Portuguese exploration—opening a painful wound. Then Burton and Livingstone found themselves at odds on ideological matters. Burton did not think Christianity could help Africa, challenging the bedrock of Livingstone's principles. Burton actually despised missionaries, arguing they caused more harm than good. His message undercut Livingstone's pleas for mission posts and colonies in Africa.

The winner of the Nile question would have more than bragging rights, he would have publicity—the loudest voice in the shaping of Africa. More than anything, Livingstone wanted his voice back. The risk of giving that voice to Baker, or worse Burton, Livingstone could not bear. If he failed again, it likely meant he would fade into obscurity as a washed up, destitute, widowed missionary.

"To return unsuccessful [would mean] going abroad to an unhealthy consulate to which no public sympathy would ever be drawn," Livingstone wrote to Agnes.[10]

The Nile quest also presented another opportunity for Livingstone to cut the slave trade off at its origin. His outrage while in England had focused primarily on the Portuguese slave routes south of Lake Nyassa, along the Shiré and Zambezi rivers. But the Nile would bring Livingstone into the heart of the Arab slave trade—the Nyassa region.

". . . a purely geographical question has no interest for me," Livingstone confided to his friend, James Young.[11] "I would not consent to go simply as a geographer, but as a missionary, and do geography by the way, because I feel I am in the way of duty when trying either to enlighten these poor people, or open their land to lawful commerce."[12]

"What my inclination leads me to prefer," Livingstone told Murchison, "is to have intercourse with the people, and do what I can by talking, to enlighten them on the slave-trade, and give them some idea of our religion. It may not be much that I can do, but I feel when doing that I am not living in vain."[13]

"I have promised to go out as soon as I can get through with this work but not purely geographical as they want me," Livingstone declared to Young, "I must be a missionary."[14]

The prospect of reporting on the slave trade tipped the scales. Livingstone was no longer mounting a Nile expedition, but a grand publicity stunt. The Nile quest provided the platform he needed to campaign against the slave trade.

But he would first and foremost need to succeed at finding the source of the Nile—or die trying.

———

"The slave trade must be suppressed as the first step to any mission that baffles every good effort," Livingstone wrote to his past comrade, John Kirk.[15]

Livingstone knew the success of a Nile expedition would rest on a strong diplomatic mission—the British Foreign Office in Zanzibar. Pragmatically, an ally in Zanzibar would reduce delays and keep his supply stores full. But beyond accommodating his expedition, consul leadership could craft the future of East Africa. Philosophically, Livingstone wanted to see effective leadership placed there—leadership that knew Africa and Christian missions and would fight the slave trade.

Despite their differences on the Zambezi expedition and a painful departure, John Kirk and Livingstone shared a mutual respect. Kirk had often found himself at odds with Livingstone, and on more than one occasion questioned his sanity, but he still admired Livingstone's tenacity to push forward. Time had healed some wounds.

Livingstone, likewise, respected Kirk. Kirk had stood by him on the Zambezi, the only expedition member not to show open hostility toward him. Most important, Kirk had seen the worst of the slave trade. He had witnessed everything Livingstone had witnessed and hated it too. He needed no educating or convincing to join the battle, and Kirk had a fight in him.

When the government vetted Kirk for the consulate, they turned to Livingstone as his reference. "I knew no defect of character or temper," Livingstone replied of Kirk.[16] "I felt certain that from [Kirk's] hatred to the slave trade and knowledge of the whole subject [he] would be invaluable at Zanzibar."

Livingstone's recommendation proved influential in pressing the British government to station Kirk in Zanzibar.[17] But not, initially, as the head of its diplomatic mission. Kirk would go to Zanzibar as the mission's surgeon. With time and experience, the placement positioned Kirk in line for upward mobility.

———

Looking across the Atlantic in 1865 raised Livingstone's hopes. With the American Civil War drawn to a close and the Thirteenth Amendment to the Constitution adopted, the United States shone as a beacon of hope for the end of slavery. Livingstone admired President Abraham Lincoln and his steadfastness for the cause of abolition despite fierce opposition. The news of Lincoln's assassination hit Livingstone particularly hard.

"'If every drop of blood shed by the lash must be atoned for by an equal number of white men's vital fluid,—righteous, O Lord, are Thy judgments!'" Livingstone quoted Lincoln's second inaugural address in his journal. "The assassination has awakened universal sympathy and indignation, and will lead to more cordiality between the countries."[18]

Livingstone's vision for ending the slave trade expanded after further reflection on the Zambezi expedition. Slavery, he decided, had to be abolished in Africa before European interests could arrive. His dreams of English colonies in the heart of Africa ultimately rested on the removal of slavery. The need for decisive government action—for justice—now overshadowed his dream that commerce alone could undercut the slave trade. Perhaps Lincoln's leadership and the ensuing war influenced Livingstone's thinking. Slavery no longer involved simple economics— though the commerce factor still informed a later phase of the equation. Livingstone now saw ending slavery as a matter of enforcement. With the ferocity of the slave traders, ending it would take an army.

Livingstone envisioned a new purpose for himself on the upcoming Nile expedition. He no longer imagined himself as the planter of missions throughout Africa, but as a mouthpiece who could "let it be known to the public."[19] With the Nile discovery as his megaphone, Livingstone could speak—he could report from the center of the Arab slave trade to move the British government toward abolition.

"I am going out again," Livingstone wrote to a friend, "to try and get an opening in by way of Rovuma . . . It is only by holding on bulldog fashion one can succeed in doing any thing against that gigantic evil the slavetrade."[20]

Although he had a new role and the company of his colleague Kirk in Zanzibar, he still faced obstacles with the British government related to abolition. The government felt it had gone above and beyond the call of duty by pressing the sultan of Zanzibar to restrict the trade seasonally and logistically. Any further action, Britain reasoned, might damage its key stronghold in Zanzibar and its good relationship with the sultan.

Livingstone also had funding obstacles to overcome before he could set sail. The Royal Geographical Society, even as expedition sponsor, could contribute only five hundred pounds. A hesitant British government chipped in another five hundred. A tiny offer, but while the RGS had chosen Livingstone for the challenge, the government still felt the need to insulate itself from his toxic image. They risked embarrassment by publicly investing in Livingstone and opening the floodgates for grant requests; government sources asked Livingstone not to share the news of the grant. To prevent scrutiny, they gave him the formal charge of Consul to the African Chiefs, but no consular salary.

By Livingstone's estimates, he needed two thousand pounds for the Nile expedition. The remaining one thousand pounds would not come easily. Money did not flow as freely as it had before the Zambezi expedition, and now Livingstone's personal coffers had run dry. A wealthy friend, James "Paraffin" Young, the inventor of paraffin, came through with a generous gift to fund the remaining deficit.

———

With giddy excitement, Livingstone boarded a steamer on August 13, 1865, and stepped off British shores.

"The mere animal pleasure of traveling in a wild unexplored country is very great," he wrote of his return to Africa.[21]

He estimated it would be two years before he sailed back into the protected harbors of England—not a long journey, particularly compared to his last two. He would savor every moment.

Livingstone backtracked his previous voyage from Africa, traveling via Bombay and Zanzibar. The *Lady Nyassa* was still moored in the docks at Bombay. When he finally sold her, he only received thirty-five hundred pounds, far short of the six thousand pounds he had invested. He placed the money in a local bank until it could be transferred home. He had other business to begin in Bombay as well, including outfitting much of his crew before sailing for Africa. In India he had left his loyal companions Chuma and Susi, who had journeyed with him across the Indian Ocean. Now he needed them again.

9 ❧ DESPERATION

We don't know how bad some people are until they are tried, nor how good others are till put to the test.

—David Livingstone

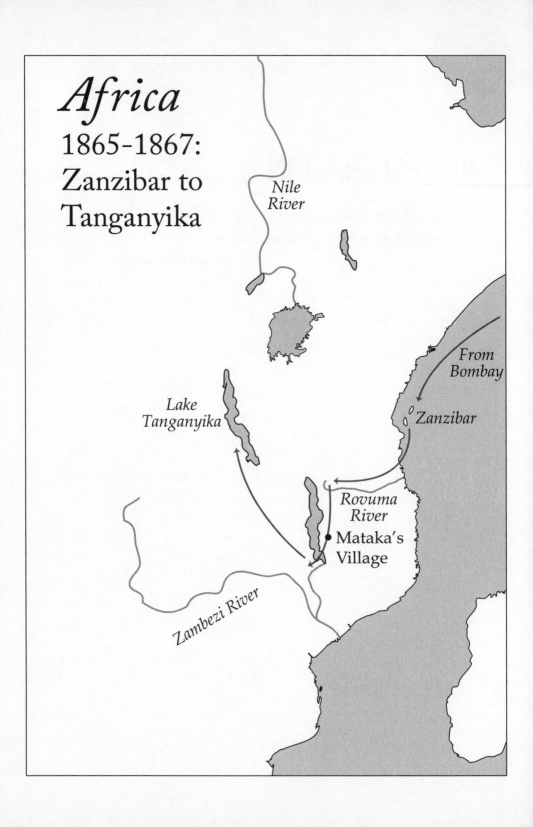

Africa

1865-1867:
Zanzibar to
Tanganyika

Nile
River

Lake
Tanganyika

From
Bombay

Zanzibar

Rovuma
River

Mataka's
Village

Zambezi River

The man across the desk from Livingstone personified British diplomacy. With hair perfectly swooped to the right and a long mustache framing his narrow chin, Henry Bartle Frere looked the part of imperial governor.

Frere had made himself a rising star in British diplomacy and, as governor of Bombay, sat as gatekeeper for British development in East Africa. Frere had excelled in his previous post as chief commissioner to the Sindh region of India. He shined in his efforts to quell the Indian Mutiny of 1857, an uprising against the East India Corporation and western influence. Most important for Livingstone, Frere believed deeply in the abolition of slavery—he fiercely opposed the East African trade and wanted to aid the fight.

Livingstone had met with Frere while returning from the Zambezi expedition via Bombay in 1864. That meeting had sparked a friendship; a visit to Frere on Livingstone's latest journey was not only strategic but also welcomed. Frere would help immensely in arranging logistics and support for the trip.

Livingstone wanted the expedition to proceed with surgical precision: light, nimble, and succinct. He would take no Europeans with him, only Africans—he worked best with Africans. He could speak their language; being conversant in Swahili and various tribal tongues gave him both authority and an ear to the ground. He would bring a variety of animals—buffalo, camels, and donkeys—to test their hardiness and resistance to the tsetse fly. While Burton and Speke traveled with teams of 130 men or more, mostly porters to carry supplies, Livingstone could travel with 60. The larger the caravan, the more attention it attracted, the slower it moved, and the more stops it required. His team would remain small and agile. He needed to move rapidly. Livingstone would make his discovery and promptly return to England to stake his claim in solving the great Nile debate.

Livingstone found Chuma, the boy he had freed five years before in the Ajawa raids. Loyal Chuma had remained at Livingstone's side through their death-defying sail across the Indian Ocean. Chuma became the expedition's first employee and Susi, who still worked in the Bombay docks, became one of his next.

At Frere's suggestion, Livingstone employed more freed slaves from a school organized for their education, as well as soldiers from the Bombay Marine Battalion. He also requested the British consul in Johanna, one of the Comoros Islands, to organize a team of porters to meet him in Zanzibar. In total, Livingstone readied thirty-five men. He would hire more when he reached mainland Africa.

Frere provided more than support, he opened doors. His government planned to gift the steamer *Thule* to Sultan Majid of Zanzibar. Frere asked Livingstone to travel to Zanzibar in the steamer and formally present the *Thule* on Britain's behalf.

With his team and equipment, Livingstone sailed into Zanzibar's dhow-lined harbor on January 28, 1866. The *Thule* docked in front of the mass of white, flat-roofed houses overshadowed by the immense palace, flying the blood-red flag of the sultan. Stretching down the harbor, the flags of the American, English, German, and French consulates flapped in the wind.

The breezes off Zanzibar and its white sandy beaches smelled of spices from the island's plantations of cloves, vanilla, and cinnamon, but they also reeked with the stench of death. Corpses of dead slaves washed up on the island's shores after being thrown overboard at sea. Rubbish off-loaded by ships and the island's own waste littered its shore. Disease was widespread.

"It is the old, old way of living," Livingstone bemoaned of Zanzibar, "—eating, drinking, sleeping; sleeping, drinking, eating. Getting fat; slaving-dhows coming and slaving-dhows going away; bad smells; and kindly looks from English folks to each other."[1]

Despite a population of three hundred thousand, only sixty Europeans lived in the main city. Black Africans made up more than two-thirds of the population, mostly slaves for domestic and plantation labor. Arab plantation owners and Indian merchants, the Banyans, controlled Zanzibar's power. All commerce was connected to the slave trade. The Arab plantation owners purchased slaves along with the international market. Banyan merchants financed and outfitted the Arab caravans to accommodate Arab adherence to Islamic religious code prohibiting credit. The Banyans would take a portion of the proceeds from the sale of slaves and ivory when the caravans returned to Zanzibar.

Joined by the captain of the *Thule*, Livingstone visited the sultan's palace to deliver Frere's official letter and formally present the steamer. Livingstone knew the sultan to be intertwined with the slave trade, as much of the coast of East Africa fell within his jurisdiction, but he also needed to maintain the sultan's good graces. Access to the interior and his personal safety rested on the sultan's disposition. Only fear of the sultan's retribution would protect him from the most violent slave traders.

The sultan met Livingstone at the bottom of the palace stairs. As they shook hands, a brass band from Bombay blared "God Save the Queen." They drank coffee and ate sherbet, listening to songs by, in Livingstone's words, the "wretched band."

Livingstone felt no shame in directly asking the sultan to give up slaving.

"Everything [you] could send to Bombay for sale would find a ready market there. We needed grain of all sorts as rice—dura—in fact everything but slaves."[2]

The sultan laughed out loud at Livingstone's bold appeal.

"I will help you as much as I can now and at all future times," the sultan replied.

Livingstone placed little faith in the sultan's offer, but he could not come face-to-face with the sultan without directly questioning him on the slave trade. For Livingstone, the entire event was superfluous. He disliked fanfare generally, but especially when he should be exploring. Still, he had consular duties to observe.

Soon, Livingstone had had enough of the sultan's pomp and circumstance. "Ready to explode," Livingstone thanked the sultan and anxiously rose from the table. He left the palace as quickly as possible.

"This was excessively ludicrous," Livingstone wrote of the event to Agnes, "but I maintained sufficient official gravity."

The sultan made good on some promises. From the window of the consulate, Livingstone watched as a dhow burned to ashes in Zanzibar's harbor. It had arrived with slaves, and when the sultan received notice, he ordered it destroyed. Beyond destroying slave ships, however, the sultan had little power over the trade. And in places where he did wield considerable power, such as Zanzibar's infamous slave market, he apparently refused to act.

Spending a month and a half in Zanzibar, Livingstone learned all he could about the complexities of the East African slave trade. It became clear to him that everything in Zanzibar was intertwined with slavery—the sultan could not cut ties with it easily. The island resupplied slave caravans, and the great slave market thrived at the crossroads of Africa, Arabia, and Asia. Zanzibar's economy rested on the back of the slave. Even more, the sultan's personal income depended on it—twenty thousand pounds annually.

"On visiting the slave-market I found about 300 slaves exposed for sale," Livingstone wrote, "the greater part of whom came from Lake Nyassa and the Shiré River."[3]

Underground holding pens surrounded the outdoor market. The slavers divided the captives who survived the journey from mainland

Africa into male and female, funneling the genders into the twenty-by-thirty-foot pens. Four-foot-high ceilings prevented the captives from standing or attacking. In the pens, they waited for their auction.

When it came time for auction, the slave traders would adorn them with dress clothes and line them up from shortest to tallest. They would parade through the market while their owners called out the auction prices. A tree in the center of the market acted as the whipping post to show the strength of a slave. Those who did not cry from the lashing, often with a stingray's tail, fetched a higher price.

"I am so familiar with the peculiar faces and markings or tattooings, that I expect them to recognize me," Livingstone remarked. "Indeed one woman said that she had heard of our passing up Lake Nyassa in a boat . . ."[4]

"The slave owners go about in the slave market here with a woman or a child held by the hand calling out 'seven dollars' 'seven dollars.'"

Livingstone described the scene to a friend:

The highest was 20 dollars. They sit in rows looking dejected and ashamed. An Arab or a Persian comes forward and raises up a girl—opens her mouth and examines her teeth—then her limbs and enquires how any scar was got. A wound from the lash decreases the value because it shews that she has been obstinate or disobedient. He usually ends by throwing his stick 20 yards or so and makes her walk for it to see as a horse dealer would say "her paces."[5]

Zanzibar forced Livingstone to live in close proximity to many of the slave traders, and despite his hatred for them, he acted cordially out of necessity for his own safety. Traders would be his only means by which to relay messages to the coast. He might need them. But the sight of slavery haunted him with memories of the Zambezi expedition.

"It makes me sick at heart to think of it," Livingstone wrote to Frere, "and raises bitter regret that we did not work out our experiment of cutting up slaving at its source."[6]

———

Livingstone set sail from Zanzibar on March 19, 1866. Not only had he learned much on the island, he had made arrangements to restock supplies. With his friend Kirk in the consulate, Livingstone felt confident he would be supported. A resupply would be delivered to the Arab trading town of Ujiji to wait for him. He planned to be in Africa for only two years—he expected this restock to sufficiently sustain the expedition.

The expedition had a clear primary objective: head due west to Lake Nyassa. At Nyassa, they would turn northwest in search of Lake Bangweolo. While Livingstone had not visited Lake Bangweolo, his study of maps and geography convinced him Bangweolo held the source of the Nile. Livingstone had heard about the existence of this lake while surveying Nyassa. At Bangweolo, he expected to find a river flowing north to Lake Tanganyika. He would follow this river north to Tanganyika, then from Tanganyika north to Lake Albert, where Baker had traced the Nile. In sum, he would start where he expected the source then backtrack the hypothesized Nile watershed to disprove Baker, Burton, and Speke. When he reached Lake Albert, there would be no doubt he had found the source of the Nile.

With his thirty-five men, Livingstone landed on mainland Africa just north of the Rovuma River. They planned to march west, intersecting the Rovuma to ascend the river as far inland as possible. They would carry one primary, and precious, cargo: cloth. Cloth was currency—it had value he could trade anywhere, for anything. Without it, he was a dead man. Beyond provisions, Livingstone's plan rested firmly on the loyalty of his team. He had to trust that his porters would not pilfer or run off. Based on his years with the Makololo, Livingstone felt confident around Africans and trusted them, perhaps to a fault. These men were not Makololo acting under orders of a Makololo chief.

On the mainland, he felt the fearful grip of slavery immediately. He began soliciting local porters to accompany them to the interior—he hoped to round out his team to sixty, but none would go in fear of being captured in slave raids. He had to push ahead with just thirty-five, a team about half the size he had anticipated.

From the start, the going was tough. They could barely tread through the thick jungle north of the Rovuma. The size of the expedition's animals, particularly the camels, added to the challenge of blazing a trail. The expedition inched ahead at a mere four miles a day.

As progress slowed to a crawl, discontent ravaged morale. The porters stole from the expedition's supplies, from Livingstone, and from villages along the way. They treated the animals cruelly and disrespected one another. Livingstone's authority crumbled, and the African porters grew impossible to lead.

As they sluggishly moved inland, they returned to the lingering famine Livingstone had witnessed on the Zambezi expedition. Dry, scorched, and empty, the country had become a wasteland. Between droughts and slaving raids, the region was terrified and hungry.

The scenes of slaving instilled no confidence in Livingstone or his team. Piles of taming sticks lined the trails, and Livingstone witnessed more traces of brutality than he had seen even toward the end of his Shiré River explorations.

"We passed a woman tied by the neck to a tree and dead," Livingstone wrote. "The people of that country explained that she had been unable to keep up with the other slaves in a gang, and her master had determined that she should not become the property of anyone else if she recovered after resting for a time."[7]

The continuous, guiltless murder shocked Livingstone, who thought he had seen the worst of humanity on his previous expedition. Unimaginably, the slave trade had become even more deprecated. Compelled to tell Britain, Livingstone wrote two letters to the foreign secretary, proposing a total prohibition of the slave trade by sea. His request required convincing the British government that such measures would not create anarchy in Zanzibar or force new slave markets to open on Africa's mainland.

Livingstone argued that Zanzibar would remain stable—his proposal would only end the *export* of slaves; domestic slavery would remain legal. While he vehemently disagreed with the practice, domestic slavery on Zanzibar seemed relatively mild compared with the brutal export of humans away from Africa. Further, he reasoned, should the export of slaves be ended, domestic slavery would slowly but peacefully come to an end.

Small slave markets on mainland Africa, Livingstone argued, would be impractical. Zanzibar hosted the great slave market due solely to geography—it was a natural prison fortified by sea. Its location on an island prevented slaves from escaping and tribes from attacking. On mainland Africa, it would be impossible to contain or protect a slaving operation.

In the meantime, Livingstone did what he could to convince the African chiefs to oppose the slave raids. At the village of Chief Chenjewala, Livingstone gathered the chief and his people to tell them of the murder he had witnessed. The number of dead slaves startled them. If you sell your fellow man, Livingstone told them, you are "like the man who holds the victim while the [perpetrator] performs the murder."[8]

Chenjewala blamed another chief, Machemba, upriver on the Rovuma, for encouraging the slave trade.

"It would be better if you kept your people and cultivated more largely," Livingstone explained.

"Oh, Machemba sends his men and robs our gardens after we have cultivated," Chenjewala replied.

"The Arabs who come and tempt [us] with fine clothes are the cause of [our] selling," a villager added.

"[You will] very soon have none to sell," Livingstone retorted, ". . . all [your] people who did not die in the road would be making gardens for Arabs at Kilwa and elsewhere."

Indeed, in many places people no longer existed to be sold. Bodies lay in the roads, and everywhere the toll of fear could be felt.

Livingstone had yet to come upon a slave-raiding party. It disappointed him. He wanted to report observations on their size and the amount of ivory they transported. The slaving parties, however, often caught wind of Livingstone's position first, choosing to march around him rather than cross his path. Knowing the white man in the jungle carried a British flag and aware of Britain's antislavery treaties, they presumed him to be a spy.

Although this spy would have been easy to kill—remorselessly—the slave traders left him alone. Despite its expansiveness, the jungle retained few secrets. Word of an assassination would travel quickly. British blood on anyone's hands would be severely punished by the sultan who, evidenced by his newly minted steamer, relied upon Her Majesty's protection and kindness.

In reality, Livingstone could do little spying—he and his men were starving. Based on past dealings in the African interior, Livingstone had brought little more than cloth to trade for food. Since then, Zanzibari trading caravans had flooded the cloth market. Coupled with the famine, his cloth now purchased almost nothing, and he otherwise possessed no liquid currency.

By mid-July, word of the British-flagged expedition's precarious situation reached the slave traders. One intrepid trader intentionally made a detour to meet Livingstone.

With a large caravan of slaves in tow, the trader "most kindly came forward and presented an ox, bag of flour, and some cooked meat."[9] Livingstone and his famished men welcomed the gift, and the generosity surprised Livingstone. The man had peacefully sought him out to offer assistance and share intimate details of their operations. This slave trader was no Mariano. Livingstone entrusted his letters to him.

This slave merchant offered a great deal of information about the trade. Known as the Kilwa route, the trail connected Lake Nyassa to the coast, ending at Kilwa for a dhow crossing to Zanzibar. The route held risks for the Arabs too—one hundred Arabs had died on the Kilwa route in the past year.

Only briefly nourished by the trader, the expedition finally reached a friendly community—Mataka's village. Reddish clay roads wound through gardens of English peas to a village of more than one thousand, square, Arab-inspired houses. In the village, Livingstone found shelter. They stayed two weeks. Mataka, the village chief, gave Livingstone a house while his team rested and rejuvenated. Livingstone, as he usually did in villages, spent time with Mataka and his people, observing and studying their culture.

One day, a group of Mataka's warriors returned from Nyassa and, without the chief's knowledge, conducted a slave-raiding foray. When the warriors returned to the village, Mataka ordered all the slaves to be sent back immediately.

"[Your] decision was the best piece of news I had heard in the country," Livingstone told the chief.

The chief looked pleased. He turned to his people, asked if they heard Livingstone clearly, and repeated his remark.

"You silly fellows think me wrong in returning the captives," Mataka said, "but all wise men will approve it."[10]

Livingstone gave Mataka a gift to be kept in remembrance of freeing the captives. He typically left gifts for people he stayed with or to commemorate an occasion—sometimes gifts as small as a fork or a knife. In Mataka's village, a strategic town along the Kilwa slave route, he left a grander gift: his coat.

After leaving Mataka's village, the hills turned green and the trees grew full, but Livingstone's party shrank. By his arrival at Lake Nyassa in August 1866, discontent and desertion had whittled the original thirty-five down to twenty-three.

The expedition's path to Lake Bangweolo had a clear obstruction: Lake Nyassa. He could either cross the lake or spend many weeks walking around it. As much as he hated them, the most efficient plan involved hiring Arab dhows to sail across. Nyassa now had many dhows aiding the slave trade. Unfortunately, Livingstone's reputation had preceded him. The Arab slave traders on the shores of Nyassa had heard about Livingstone freeing slaves and attacking the Ajawa in the Shiré highlands. Fearing that Livingstone intended to destroy their ships, no dhow would take him.

Livingstone turned the expedition south for a long walk around Nyassa. The change of course would add significant delays—a month to reach the southern tip alone. Worse, it would require Livingstone to cross his old foe, the Shiré River.

————

Three weeks later, Livingstone painfully arrived back on the banks of the Shiré.

"Many hopes have been disappointed here," Livingstone confided in the pages of his journal. "Far down on the right bank of the Zambesi lies the dust of her whose death changed all my future prospects; and now, instead of a restraint being given to the slave trade by lawful commerce on the Lake, slave dhows prosper."[11]

At the southern end of Lake Nyassa, news from the land lying before them gave the men pause. A passing Arab trader spoke of a country ravaged by a war of the Mazitu tribe. Fear spread further dissension through the expedition's ranks, and the Johanna men in particular declared they would go no farther.

"I want to see my father, my mother, my child at Johanna," insisted Musa, the leader of the Johanna men. "I no want to be killed by Mazitu."[12]

Livingstone dashed the protest and resolved to press forward, relying on contrary reports from a local chief. But the Johanna men gave their departure no second thought. They set off back to the coast as the expedition continued west. With the latest desertion, a mere eleven men continued on toward Bangweolo.

"Too wet to march," Livingstone wrote on December 6, 1866.

He could write nothing more. Massive thunderstorms set in, turning everything to mud and grinding the expedition to a halt. The trails they had once followed now lay hidden under a thick blanket of water. The men slept in wet clothes and dysentery returned.

Banking on the word of the chief, Livingstone had expected safe trails. Instead, the Mazitu rumors proved true. The raids made villagers cautious and unwelcoming to unfamiliar visitors—food once again grew scarce.

For two months, it stormed. The unrelenting rains and the solemn return to the Shiré gave Livingstone a chance to reflect. He found himself in a place not unlike the end of the Zambezi expedition four years before: leading a deteriorating team on a fledgling expedition. With no Europeans to blame, he could only blame himself.

"We now end 1866," Livingstone journaled on New Year's Eve. "It has not been so fruitful or useful as I intended. Will try to do better in 1867, and be better—more gentle and loving; and may the Almighty, to whom I commit my way, bring my desire to pass, and prosper me! Let all the sins of '66 be blotted out for Jesus' sake."[13]

———

"Every step I take jars in the chest, and I am very weak; I can scarcely keep up the march, though formerly I was always first . . . I have constant singing in my ears and can scarcely hear the loud tick of the chronometer."[14]

Illness had caught up with Livingstone. A spate of dysentery and malaria seized many of his men. To make matters worse, the porter in charge of Livingstone's medicine chest had defected, carrying off his most precious cargo—including the quinine. Livingstone had never imagined he would be without his malarial prophylactic.

"I felt as if I had now received the sentence of death," Livingstone wrote, "like poor Bishop Mackenzie."[15]

But illness only increased his persistence to push forward to his destination.

"Ground at present all sloppy . . . feet constantly wet," Livingstone lamented on the conditions of his march. The rains continued for two months, and the land spread out before them appeared to be a giant, unending swamp. Despite the rain, nothing edible grew. "Nothing but famine . . . the people living on mushrooms and leaves."

His small team of men did what they could to survive and wait out the weather. The men pretended they drank coffee by boiling roasted grain in water.

With no food to eat, the pack animals died and Livingstone wasted away.

"Don't think, please, that I make moan over nothing but a little sharpness of appetite," Livingstone wrote in a letter to the British consul. "I am a mere ruckle of bones, did all the hunting myself, and wet, hunger, and fatigue took away the flesh."[16]

Hobbling to his tent, Livingstone collapsed. Helpless and confused from rheumatic fever, he floundered on the ground, unable to crawl inside. Grabbing hold of two poles at the entrance, Livingstone pulled himself up from the ground but remained too weak to stand. He fell hard, hitting his head on a box.

Livingstone's ruckle of bones lay motionless on the ground.

10 ❦ LOST

*Man is a complex being and we greatly need our
motives to be purified from all that is evil.*

—David Livingstone

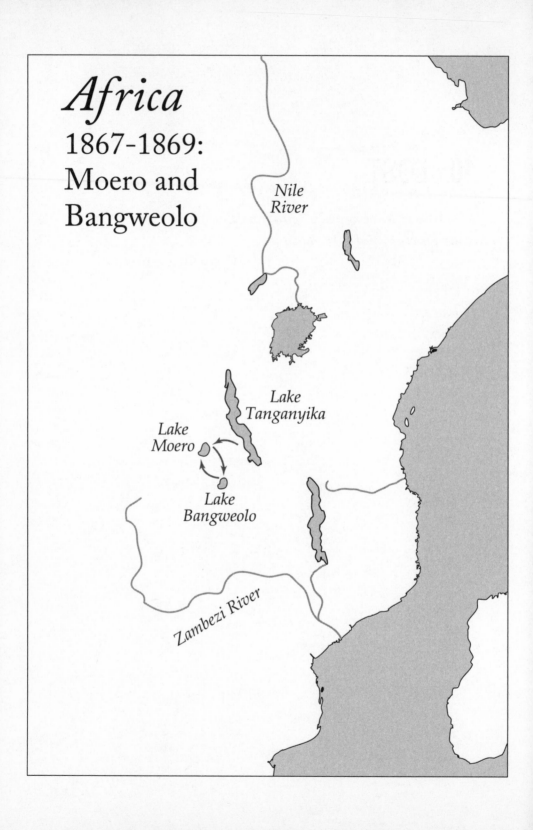

Africa
1867–1869:
Moero and
Bangweolo

Nile
River

Lake
Tanganyika

Lake
Moero

Lake
Bangweolo

Zambezi River

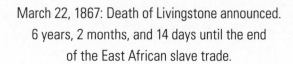

March 22, 1867: Death of Livingstone announced.
6 years, 2 months, and 14 days until the end
of the East African slave trade.

Slaves sold per annum: 20,000
Total victims of the slave trade: 456,000

D eath of Dr. Livingstone."
Headlining the *New York Times* and papers around the world,
startling news from Africa shocked the world. Livingstone was
dead. This time it had credibility.

The news came from the Johanna porters. Returning to Zanzibar
after leaving the Livingstone expedition less than four months before,
they carried the news of their former leader's death to John Kirk and the
British consulate. The loss was unimaginable.

From the pen of Edward D. Ropes, United States consul in Zanzibar,
came an official account of the death of Dr. Livingstone.

"It becomes my painful duty to report the death of Dr. David
Livingstone, the celebrated African explorer . . ." the *New York Times*
quoted Ropes mournfully. "The sad intelligence received here [. . .] by
the arrival of several native members of the expedition."

Consul Ropes relayed further details from John Kirk:

> The return of several of the Johanna men, who accompanied
> Dr. Livingstone, has made it certain that that distinguished traveler
> has fallen, and with him half of his native followers.
>
> His present expedition may be briefly stated to have been an
> attempt to unite the magnificent discoveries of late years, and deter-
> mine the limits and connections of the three great lakes . . . flowing

to the sea by the Zambesi and Nile at the two extremities, but with an intermediate space as yet unknown. Such was the geographical problem.

But Dr. Livingstone had in view to affect the present enormous East Africa slave trade, through pioneering the way which might lead to lawful commerce . . . these hopes have been wrecked by his untimely death.[1]

Britain had lost her hero. And the world had lost a legend.

Zanzibar felt Livingstone's death. The consulates of European nations flew at half-mast, and the sultan of Zanzibar ordered his ships to do the same. Soon, all the ships in his harbor followed suit.

"The news will cause deep regret among all classes," wrote the *Illustrated London News*. "Dr. Livingstone had won the admiration of the civilized [sic] world by his undaunted perseverance and the simple faith in which he went about his great work of opening the continent of Africa to commerce and Christianity."[2]

The "Death of Livingstone" news flash caught media attention across the globe, dominating headlines from India to the United States and Australia. The report led to public mourning and intense interest in how Livingstone met his fate. The RGS noted an unusually large attendance at its next meeting, with people clamoring to know more about Livingstone.

The press release from Zanzibar followed interrogations of the Johanna porters by British Consul Edwin Seward and John Kirk. Knowing the Nyassa region, Kirk cross-examined the men about the country—could they recount its environment, region, and geography? They had, indeed, walked in the Nyassa region alongside Livingstone, Kirk determined. And their version of unfolding events appeared consistent.

Musa, the leader of the Johanna porters, detailed the harrowing story of Livingstone's senseless murder. Not long after rounding the southern tip of Lake Nyassa, the expedition entered the territory of the

Mafites, a wandering tribe plundering caravans passing through the region. Despite warnings about the Mafites, Livingstone pushed ahead.

As usual, Livingstone marched in front of his caravan with a handful of attendants close behind, including Musa. Suddenly, three armed Mafites appeared on the trail in the path of the expedition.

"The Mafites are out, after all," Livingstone called out to Musa.[3]

Armed with bows and arrows, the Mafites attacked without provocation. Unprepared for a fight, Livingstone's men scrambled for their muskets and took cover behind the nearest trees. Livingstone drew his revolver and shot two of the Mafites. A third assailant flanked the party to ambush Livingstone from behind. When the musket smoke cleared from the barrage of firing, Livingstone lay on the ground with a battle-axe lodged in his back. He died instantly.

Hiding behind a tree, Musa watched as his compatriots, one by one, shared the same fate as their leader. Quietly, Musa took aim, firing his musket at Livingstone's murderer. The ball pierced through the attacker's body, and he fell beside Livingstone's corpse.

Musa fled the scene. He met the remaining caravan coming up the trail and told them to follow him. The party abandoned its baggage and ran until sunset, seeking shelter in the deep jungle. The Johanna survivors regrouped and discussed what to do next. Musa pleaded with the group to circle back to Livingstone's body and retrieve personal items. His family and admirers would cherish any keepsake. With trepidation, they returned.

Livingstone's body still lay where it fell. But it had not gone untouched. The Mafites had looted him of personal items, including his watch and clothes. Only Livingstone's trousers remained. Musa could find no memento to bring to Zanzibar.

The porters hurriedly dug a shallow grave and buried their leader. The bodies of the three natives lay not far away.

For Musa and the porters, the return to the coast proved as difficult as the journey inland. Traversing back across famine-stricken regions, the Johanna men starved again, living solely on what wild berries they could gather. Eventually, they arrived back at Lake Nyassa where they attached themselves to an Arab caravan bound for the coast.

But despite the consistencies in their story, Seward and Kirk remained unsatisfied. Kirk had worked with the Johanna men on the Zambezi expedition—and he didn't trust them. Casting doubt on the story, the Johanna men could not account for everyone from the expedition. Only the Johannas had returned to Zanzibar, yet other surviving porters and aids had not. What happened to Chuma and Susi? Surely they would return to Zanzibar too. Adding to Kirk's suspicion, the Johanna men had a motive for fabricating the story: they demanded nine months wages for their unpaid service.

Kirk and Seward sailed to mainland Africa to investigate. Consul Seward made inquiries among the trading caravans returning from Nyassa. Undoubtedly they would have heard rumor of a white man killed in the region. The traders knew of no death, and the inquiries brought no further evidence of a murder.

Seward immediately sent a letter to the Bombay government intended for the press:

> I have personally made inquiries amongst the traders of Keelwa Koiriga, and have gathered information there which tends to throw discredit on the statement of the Johanna men who allege that they saw their leader dead. The evidence of the Nyassa traders strengthens the suspicion that these men abandoned the traveller when he was about to traverse the Mazite-haunted district, and, for aught they know to the contrary, Dr Livingstone may yet be alive.[4]

As quickly as the news of his death had rung around the world, suspicion of Livingstone's possible survival displaced his obituary. Mystery, scandal, and an international manhunt provided fodder for public fascination. As the British consul's investigation played out in headlines around the globe, no one knew who to believe or the true fate of Livingstone.

After resolutely announcing his death, the *Times of India* printed an inconclusive retraction:

> We are very glad to learn, from later news received from Zanzibar, that there is a possibility of the apparently circumstantial account of Dr Livingstone's death, as narrated by his follower Moosa, and published in our issue of yesterday, turning out to be incorrect. . . . [W]e are sorry that we cannot attach great weight to Dr Seaward's opinion; but it is sufficient, in the meantime, to keep alive the hope that Dr Livingstone may yet return to give to the world his valuable discoveries, and to reap the reward of his philanthropic labours.[5]

Roderick Murchison, Livingstone's champion and promoter at the Royal Geographical Society, led public discourse, waging a campaign to ignite British longing for their hero. Independently, he began his own investigation, recovering government dispatches and reports to try to piece together the story. Letters from Murchison soon flooded the pages of the *Times of London*.

" . . . I felt it my duty to throw doubts upon the truth of the reported death of Dr. Livingstone . . ." Murchison wrote in mid-March 1867. "I can now scarcely cling to the hope that my dear friend should still be alive."[6]

Murchison produced a letter from E. D. Young, the pilot of the *Pioneer* steamer for two years on the Zambezi expedition. Young knew Livingstone and the Johanna men, and spoke to their character.

> Having had 12 of them in the crew of the Pioneer, and Sir, I can confidently assert that, at all times and under all circumstances, there was the slightest dependence to be placed on them, more especially as far as the truth was concerned, added to which, they were great thieves.
>
> I have, therefore, great reason to hope that their story respecting

the murder of the Doctor will prove a mere fabrication, more especially if they brought nothing belonging to him, for they knew well the
value of books or papers, &c., which the [Mafites] do not.[7]

Other authorities weighed in, and not always with optimism.
Explorer Samuel Baker, a Nile adversary but a man well acquainted with
the African interior, refused to believe any evidence of Livingstone's
safety. The debate raged on.

As the global attention to Livingstone's fate captivated the world,
even the sultan of Zanzibar took personal interest in uncovering the
truth. All the Johanna men and the Indian soldiers who could be gathered were cross-examined and re-examined again by the sultanate.

Under intense scrutiny, Musa's story began unraveling. Now, Musa
claimed not to have witnessed the murder as he once testified but said
he came upon the body shortly after the assault. The Mafites had not
attacked suddenly, but after a quarrel erupted over their demand for cloth.
Finally, his observation of three assailants grew to a war party of two
or three hundred. Inconsistencies multiplied among the explanations
proffered.

With the Johanna story debunked, Livingstone's fate held a rising glimmer of hope. Murchison seized the opportunity, proposing an
RGS-sponsored search party to travel to the interior. The search party
would seek any information on the whereabouts of the explorer and, if
they found him in need, recover him. Murchison appointed E. D. Young
to lead the party. The announcement led to a flood of applicants wishing
to join the endeavor.

"I do not hesitate to say," Murchison wrote, "that this search after
Livingstone would meet with the hearty approval of the country . . . thus
clearing away the painful suspense which hangs over the fate of the illustrious traveller . . ."[8]

———

Livingstone was not dead. He was lost.

After recovering from his collapse, he pushed the expedition forward. But he completely missed Lake Bangweolo. The porter carrying Livingstone's sensitive chronometers slipped on mossy, rock-covered terrain and sent the equipment crashing to the ground. Without working chronometers, Livingstone could no longer access accurate longitudinal readings. He proceeded blindly.

Thus far, the entire journey from the coast had covered thousands of miles and taken much longer than expected—nine months. Livingstone had no interest in following the muddy, treacherous path back to Zanzibar. Attempting the return without medicine and fresh supplies might be more dangerous than proceeding forward. With Lake Bangweolo almost within reach, he preferred to continue his work.

Locating an undocumented lake in remote Africa took fact finding and a fair amount of guesswork. Even if he had had working chronometers, Livingstone did not have any coordinates for the lake. Exploration relied on local knowledge and his own approximations based on elevations and the flow of rivers.

"It is distressingly difficult to elicit accurate information about the Lake and rivers," Livingstone complained, "because the people do not think accurately."[9]

Relying on estimates and local experience, he completely missed Lake Bangweolo. By the time new facts made his error clear, he had already passed one hundred miles northeast of the lake. Instead of backtracking, Livingstone changed course. The expedition continued north to Lake Tanganyika, where Livingstone hoped to find a river flowing in from Lake Bangweolo.

After more than a year of trials, he finally gazed upon waters he suspected might hold a clue to the mysterious source of the Nile. Reaching Lake Tanganyika on April 1, 1867, brought a sigh of relief and a moment to relish.

"I never saw anything so still and peaceful as it lies all the morning,"

Livingstone wrote. "About noon a gentle breeze springs up, and causes the waves to assume a bluish tinge. Several rocky islands rise in the eastern end, which are inhabited by fishermen . . . Its peacefulness is remarkable, though at times it is said to be lashed up by storms."[10]

Despite the achievement, Livingstone could conduct little exploring around Tanganyika due to his health. He used the shores of the lake to recover from the fever precipitating his collapse. For a month he lay bedridden, too weak to write in his journal, much less walk. Chuma and Susi stepped up as Livingstone's personal aids, slowly nursing him back to health.

Livingstone knew nothing of his reported death or of the search party mounting in Britain. As his strength returned, he prepared to march north around Lake Tanganyika to search for the Nile flowing north. Troublesome reports brought new setbacks. Another war—this one between local tribes and Arab traders—raged north along the shores of Lake Tanganyika. Seeking revenge for Arab aggression, the northern tribes indiscriminately murdered every foreigner they encountered. Such reports presented too great a risk, even for Livingstone's characteristic bravery and African diplomacy.

Livingstone's quest for the source of the Nile had delved into obsession. The source consumed his thoughts. Any rumored body of water in the region, even one based on the faintest anecdote, abruptly captured his attention. He wanted to explore every lead.

When reports of a nearby lake surfaced—Lake Moero—he redirected the party. Since the expedition could not safely journey north along Tanganyika to search for an inlet, Moero gave him new hope. While he presumed Lake Bangweolo to be the source, he thought perhaps the westerly Lake Moero was fed from Bangweolo to the south, making Moero a critical body of water. Livingstone knew he would have no firsts at Moero; Portuguese explorers and countless Arabs had visited the lake. But, from Moero, he could trace the river down to Lake Bangweolo.

From Tanganyika, he aimed for a nearby Arab settlement where he might gather information and restock with the aid of the always-well-supplied Arab slave traders. Connecting with the traders also presented the rare opportunity for potential contact with the outside world. With Arab caravans headed toward Zanzibar, he could mail his letters. He wanted to mail a letter to Consul Seward in Zanzibar. He had requested supplies to meet him in Ujiji, on Lake Tanganyika, but given the amount of time his travel consumed, he would need more. While he placed little faith in the traders, he accepted the risk that just one letter might reach Zanzibar intact.

At the Arab settlement, Livingstone struggled to watch as the raiding parties returned from plundering and slaving:

> Slavery is a great evil wherever I have seen it. A poor old woman and child are among the captives, the boy about three years old seems a mother's pet. His feet are sore from walking in the sun. He was offered for two fathoms [four yards of unbleached calico cloth], and his mother for one fathom; he understood it all, and cried bitterly, clinging to his mother. She had, of course, no power to help him.[11]

Slave-raiding parties, led by tribes including the Ajawa, would bring their catch to the settlement to trade. Livingstone noted the ever-decreasing value placed on human life. Due to the desperation of the famine, slave traders purchased boys and girls from raiding parties for mere handfuls of maize.

Remarkably, the slave traders welcomed Livingstone. They sympathetically assisted with mail and basic provisions. As days went on, the slave traders showed him greater kindness—presenting food, beads, cloth, and valuable geographic information. Livingstone slowly started falling in to their company—and the charm of their unexpected kindness. He had nowhere to go. The regional war halted his progress to northern Lake Tanganyika and now Lake Moero as well. Undersupplied and underprotected, Livingstone could only wait at the settlement.

"I trust in Providence a way will be opened," he wrote.[12]

Then came an offer Livingstone could not refuse—an invitation to join a caravan, under the care of the Arab porters and guards, in search of his prized river source.

The caravan prepared to march west past Lake Moero. Short on supplies and medicine, Livingstone could either travel with them or stay and rely on their charity. If he had to rely on their charity either way, at least he could do so continuing his work.

Perhaps Providence had arrived in the unlikely form of an Arab slave trader.

———

Outside Africa, the world had made Livingstone a martyr. His reported death sanctified his image, and the bitter criticism that had overwhelmed the Zambezi expedition vanished. Not only did Livingstone, the man, fascinate the public, but so did the ideals and motivations that drove him to such extreme measures. Among his inspirations, the abolition of the slave trade rose to the fore, and, consequently, Livingstone fervor ushered a revival of African slave trade awareness into the public forum. Activists quickly joined the cause. The Committee of the Church Missionary Society committed to ending the slave trade, enlisting fresh sympathy and arousing public attention.

A campaign to lobby Parliament began, but the British government chose to deal with the fate of Livingstone before addressing his abolition agenda. If not dead, wherever Livingstone was, he faced dire circumstances. With a comrade down in the field—a consul of Her Majesty's crown, no less—Livingstone's safety became an imminent matter of national pride. As such, no one else but Britain's legendary global explorers would be sent to extract this man from deep in the heart of Africa.

Murchison's RGS-bannered search party to determine Livingstone's fate received funding from Foreign Secretary Lord Clarendon. By June

1867, the search party had readied its team and taken possession of a completed steamer. The expedition received state-of-the-art technology. At thirty feet long and weighing more than a ton, the steel-plated boat made a first of its kind for the British navy. As Livingstone had once devised, the boat was designed to be dismantled into sections and carried over land—around the Shiré's Murchison Cataracts.

The search party would sail to the mouth of Zambezi, then make its way toward Nyassa via the Zambezi and Shiré rivers. Carrying the steamer around the rapids, they would sail onto Lake Nyassa and along its shores to confirm Livingstone's status.

Rumors of Livingstone sightings began trickling out of Africa, bolstering the pressure to secure him. Kirk investigated promising leads, including a sighting by one native who, while part of a trading caravan, claimed to have seen a white man deep in the interior: In a village along a major trade route, the white traveller had arrived accompanied by thirteen armed Africans. Dressed in white with cloth wrapped around his head, this peculiar man presented the village chief with a gift but refused to accept any ivory in return. Certainly not a trader, the man gave letters to a caravan headed for Zanzibar and continued his journey north.

The description matched Livingstone.

Attempting to positively identify the explorer, Kirk showed the native photos of Livingstone. The native did not recognize the first portrait. Kirk showed him a second photo.

"That is the man," he replied.[13]

Kirk believed him. By his estimates, this put Livingstone halfway through his expedition and headed for Lake Albert.

"Suspend your opinion for a little," Kirk cautioned in a letter to the *Illustrated London News*.[14] He wanted evidence from the search party or the arrival of Livingstone's letters. He planned to go to the village to inquire.

While they waited, more reports of a white man in Africa's interior continued to arrive. Reports put Livingstone headed toward Lake Tanganyika, then they put him on the west side of Tanganyika. The search party would know more in short order. By October, they were cruising on the waters of the Zambezi River. They would soon be at Nyassa.

———

Tippoo Tib, the great Zanzibari trader, led the Arab caravan, and Livingstone walked by his side. With soft eyes, bulging cheeks, and a broad nose, Tippoo Tib's face had a gentle and welcoming smile, cupped by a short but bushy salt-and-pepper beard. His piteous white Arab garb and white turban stood in sharp contrast to his dark complexion and ruthless ethic.

Known for boasting massive slave caravans, the notorious Tippoo Tib led an aggressive campaign to exploit the vast African interior. His career had only just begun, but he intended to build a trading empire. By the time he met Livingstone, he had made large strides toward such ends.

Despite Tippoo Tib's hand in the slave trade, he showed extreme kindness and generosity to Livingstone. He protected and fed the lost explorer, and more: he befriended him. The men grew to enjoy each other's company.

Tippoo Tib did his best to insulate Livingstone from the worst of his business. Despite overt activities inescapably apparent to Livingstone, the explorer had no options. Helplessness forced Livingstone's reliance on men such as Tippoo Tib, but it also demanded a more nuanced view of slave traders. General traders made use of slaves as they traded ivory. Tippoo Tib might buy slaves to carry his ivory to Zanzibar where they would be sold in the slave market.

Slave traders, on the other hand, raided villages to capture men and women for slavery. Livingstone drew a distinction. He tolerated the general traders, whom he saw as Zanzibari businessmen with relatively mild involvement in slaving. And yet he abhorred the slavers, such as those he found on the Kilwa route massacring the Shiré and Nyassa regions. The distinction had blurred lines, and Livingstone struggled to admit it.

While the general traders did not typically enslave villages, they often contracted with the slavers to do their raiding.

"If one wanted to see the slave trade in its best phases," Livingstone wrote to Murchison, "he would accompany the gentleman subjects of the Sultan of Zanzibar. If he wished to describe its worst form, he would go with the Kilwa traders."[15]

Tippoo Tib's caravan progressed slowly. It stopped frequently to search for ivory. A mere one-hundred-mile journey took a month. By November 8, 1867, the caravan finally reached Lake Moero. Livingstone parted with them to make a short and succinct survey.

By canoe, Livingstone took observations as best he could. What he saw left him convinced a large river flowed northwest out of Lake Moero—the Lualaba River. But flowing into Lake Moero and forming the link to Bangweolo, another river must exist, the Luapula River. This would make Lake Bangweolo the ultimate source of the Lualaba River. If these lakes did connect, it confirmed his suspicion of Lake Bangweolo as the Nile's source. How Bangweolo connected to Lake Tanganyika, if at all, puzzled him.

Livingstone's plan for exploration evolved. He would continue on from Lake Moero to Lake Bangweolo to confirm the source. From there, he would trace the entire water flow north from the Lualaba to the Nile. Short on supplies, Livingstone dared not attempt the journey from Moero to Bangweolo without restocking. In Zanzibar, he had arranged for supplies to meet him in the town of Ujiji, on the shores of Lake Tanganyika; they would have arrived by now. He would rejoin Tippoo Tib's caravan and find a way to Ujiji.

Tippoo Tib promised he would return to Ujiji after briefly visiting one nearby trading center. A captive to his poverty, Livingstone stayed with the caravan under the care of the Arab trader. At the trading center, Tippoo Tib changed course, abandoning his promised return to Ujiji. Livingstone found another Arab caravan heading north, led by a trader named Muhammad bin Salim. Livingstone joined Salim.

Not long after they set out, the winter rains arrived, soaking the region and returning it to a vast swamp. They could proceed no farther and would sit out the rains for several months. Livingstone, who preferred traveling fast, had covered little more than one hundred miles in two months.

Delays finally broke the uncharacteristic patience Livingstone had thus far displayed on the Nile expedition. Old habits resurfaced. He began writing spiteful letters, lashing out at everyone from Murchison and the Royal Geographical Society to the Portuguese.

In his fury, Livingstone struggled with pains of the current expedition and rehashed past failures, including blame for the Zambezi disaster. He blamed the Portuguese for conspiring to destroy the Zambezi expedition. In letters to Britain, he charged Murchison with underfunding his current expedition. He accused the RGS of cheating him by requiring him to make detailed maps that he must simply turn over after the expedition. He threatened to return his salary and keep the maps.

He had heard nothing from his government and, perhaps understandably, felt abandoned. To Livingstone, the world had forgotten him.

"Almighty Father," Livingstone penned in his journal on January 1, 1868, "forgive the sins of the past year for Thy Son's sake. Help me to be more profitable during this year. If I am to die this year prepare me for it."[16]

———

"Livingstone safe."

Headlines in the *Times* shared the news with Britain. "A load is lifted from the national mind," reported the *London Illustrated News*.[17]

"With unspeakable delight," Murchison wrote, "I have just received the following telegram from Mr. Young, 'I have returned from Lake Nyassa. Dr. Livingstone had gone on in safety. The Johanna men deserted him.' There is now, therefore," Murchison continued, "no longer the shadow of a doubt that the white man seen on the west side of Lake Tanganyika was Livingstone."[18]

The search party had proceeded to Lake Nyassa and on to the scene where Livingstone's alleged murder had taken place. The party interviewed villagers and porters in the area. Several villagers produced evidence of a spoon and knife given by Livingstone as gifts. Then, they met villagers who had carried the expedition's baggage for four days after the Johanna men's desertion. The search party felt confident in Livingstone's survival. It appeared the explorer had continued north.

In Zanzibar, Kirk finally received Livingstone's long anticipated letters brought by Arab messenger. The letters fully confirmed his safety. Still, no one knew the unpredictable explorer's next move. Many suspected the next Livingstone news might come from Cairo or Khartoum if he had sailed the Nile north.

———

The world imagined him safe and confidently executing his agenda of discovery. It could not have been further from reality.

Livingstone remained destitute and at the mercy of Salim. But Salim had deceived him. Due to a quarrel with a chief to the north, Salim would not proceed to Ujiji territory and wanted to hold Livingstone back as well.

Livingstone would take no more of Salim's delays. He told his men to prepare to march. Instead of returning to Ujiji for supplies, Livingstone wanted to head south for Lake Bangweolo and only turn for Ujiji once he had confirmed Bangweolo as the Nile's source.

Livingstone's men refused. After several more defections, his party dwindled to just four. Livingstone did not blame the defectors. To many on his team, as well as to Salim, the plan appeared impulsive and suicidal. For the past year, he had not left the Arab caravans and had few supplies to make the journey to Bangweolo. But Livingstone would not change his mind. He began the march south.

Salim made one last attempt to detain Livingstone, sending a messenger after him to persuade him to return and wait out the rains for the Ujiji trip.

"... say to Mohamad [Salim]," Livingstone replied to the messenger, "that I would on no account go to Ujiji, till I had done all in my power to reach the Lake I sought . . ."[19]

Moving toward a significant destination encouraged Livingstone, but the expedition faced miserable conditions. The men found themselves sometimes walking in waist-deep water for as long as four hours at a time. At other times, they had no choice but to slog through fecal, decaying mud.

After a month, Livingstone and his small troop arrived at a trading post along the Bangweolo route. There he met another "gentleman subject of the Sultan," a trader named Bogharib. Bogharib planned to travel to the Bangweolo region in search of ivory and invited Livingstone to join him.

In the company of Bogharib and his slave caravans, Livingstone felt perhaps the most saddened by the suffering of the African people. Livingstone saw six men in chains, singing "as if they did not feel the weight and degradation of the slave-sticks."

"I asked the cause of their mirth," Livingstone wrote, "and was told that they rejoiced at the idea 'of coming back after death and haunting and killing those who had sold them.'"

Livingstone asked how they intended to accomplish this.

"Oh, you sent me off to [the coast]," a slave replied, "but the yoke is off when I die, and back I shall come to haunt and to kill you."

"Then all joined in the chorus," Livingstone noted, "which was the name of each vendor. It told not of fun, but of the bitterness and tears of such as were oppressed, and on the side of the oppressors there was a power: there be higher than they!"[20]

Despite the fact that Bogharib traded slaves, he and Livingstone became friends. Bogharib shared his personal food supplies and cared for Livingstone in sickness. Due to his kindness and generosity, Livingstone spoke admirably about him. Perhaps the contradiction weighed on Livingstone—relying on the generosity of the men he came to stop. His thoughts turned, yet again, to his death.

Happening upon a small, peaceful grave in the forest, Livingstone wrote as if he wished for death: "This is the sort of grave I should prefer:

to be in the still, still forest, and no hand ever disturb my bones. The graves at home always seemed to me to be miserable, especially those in the cold damp clay, and without elbow-room . . ."

He concluded, "I have nothing to do, but wait till He who is over all decides where I have to lay me down and die."[21]

———

"I will announce my discovery to Lord Clarendon," Livingstone wrote as he approached Lake Bangweolo, ". . . but I reserve the parts of the Lualaba and Tanganyika for future confirmation."

Although he had not yet reached the lake, Livingstone felt assured Bangweolo formed the body of water from which the Nile began its journey to Egypt. Despite his confidence, he still needed confirmation that Bangweolo even connected to the Nile.

"I have no doubts on the subject," Livingstone wrote, "for I receive the reports of natives of intelligence at first hand, and they have no motive for deceiving me. The best maps are formed from the same sort of reports at third or fourth hand."[22]

On July 18, 1868, Livingstone walked out into the cool water of Lake Bangweolo. He had finally arrived on the shores of the lake he had thought so much about. He spent the next two weeks making observations, exploring by canoe, and trying to calculate the lake's size.

The size of the lake left Livingstone convinced: he had undoubtedly found the source.

"The discovery of the sources of the Nile is somewhat akin in importance to the discovery of the North-West Passage," Livingstone boasted in his journal:

> . . . the Nile possesses, moreover, an element of interest which the North-West Passage never had. The great men of antiquity have recorded their ardent desires to know the fountains of what Homer called 'Egypt's heaven-descended spring.' . . . Alexander the Great,

157

who founded a celebrated city at this river's-mouth, looked up the stream with the same desire, and so did the Caesars. The great Julius Caesar is made by Lucan to say that he would give up the civil war if he might but see the fountains of this far-famed river.[23]

He journaled extensively about his success and the importance of his observations. Unknown to Livingstone, rainy season flooding had exaggerated his estimates of the size of Lake Bangweolo. His bravado continued.

". . . that which these men failed to find, and that which many great minds in ancient times longed to know, has in this late age been brought to light by the patient toil and laborious perseverance of Englishmen . . . Old Nile played the theorists a pretty prank by having his springs 500 miles south of them all!"[24]

Rejoining Bogharib's caravan on August 1, Livingstone intended to reach Ujiji as soon as possible for his long-requested supplies. Bogharib, however, did not plan on traveling to Ujiji; he would head west to a region known as Manyuema. Although it delayed his restocking, the prospect of Manyuema excited Livingstone. In this region, natives reported, the Lualaba River flowed north. Livingstone suspected the Lualaba might truly be the Nile. If he could prove the Lualaba became the Nile, he would have traced the Nile all the way from its suspected source and made an important, geography-shaping discovery. With the opportunity to visit the Lualaba, Livingstone abandoned his resupply run to Ujiji.

In the Manyuema-bound caravan, Livingstone found himself once again in a slow-moving, slave-binding, miserable procession. Still penniless, he continued to rely on the Arab traders for everything, and as he traveled farther west, the challenges of mailing letters increased dramatically. The world beyond the African interior would know nothing of his whereabouts or safety.

The year closed much as it had opened, with illness and discomfort.

"I have been wet times without number," wrote Livingstone on New Year's Day 1869, "but the wetting of yesterday was once too often."[25]

11 ❖ BROKEN

I never made a sacrifice. Of this we ought not to talk when
we remember the great sacrifice which He made who left
His Father's throne on high to give Himself for us.

—DAVID LIVINGSTONE

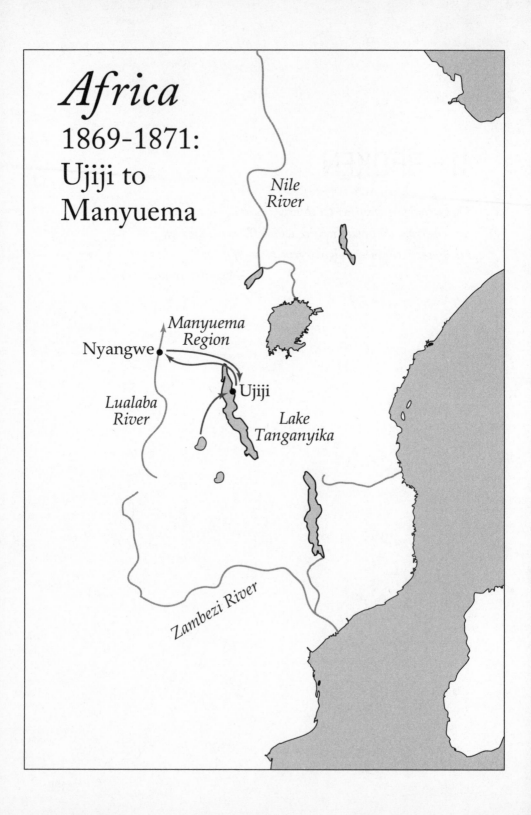

Africa
1869-1871:
Ujiji to
Manyuema

Nile
River

Manyuema
Region

Nyangwe

Ujiji

Lualaba
River

Lake
Tanganyika

Zambezi River

C annot walk," Livingstone wrote. "Pneumonia of right lung, and I cough all day and all night."

Livingstone reached his weakest condition yet in early January 1869. He wondered if he had ever been so sick—even his cognition waivered:

Ideas flow through the mind with great rapidity and vividness, in groups of twos and threes: if I look at any piece of wood, the bark seems covered over with figures and faces of men, and they remain, though I look away and turn to the same spot again. I saw myself lying dead in the way to Ujiji, and all the letters I expected there useless. When I think of my children and friends, the lines ring through my head perpetually:

> *I shall look into your faces,*
> *And listen to what you say,*
> *And be often very near you*
> *When you think I'm far away.*[1]

Family fears added to health concerns. He worried about his children—unable to send or receive letters, he knew nothing of them and they nothing of him.

161

Bogharib's caravan, now with more than one thousand slaves and a massive amount of ivory, decided to travel to Ujiji after all, before continuing on to Manyuema. Livingstone badly needed the Ujiji pit stop. His health had deteriorated rapidly and, adding to pneumonia, other unusual tropical diseases afflicted him:

> I extracted twenty Funyés, an insect like a maggot, whose eggs had been inserted on my having been put into an old house infested by them; as they enlarge they stir about and impart a stinging sensation; if disturbed, the head is drawn in a little. When a poultice is put on they seem obliged to come out possibly from want of air: they can be pressed out, but the large pimple in which they live is painful; they were chiefly in my limbs.[2]

Livingstone held great expectations for the supplies awaiting him at Ujiji, surpassing his want of medicine. In the years since he made the arrangements in Zanzibar, he had sent additional letters to Kirk requesting more supplies and a new team of porters to meet him there. Ujiji would be an oasis. His supplies would be there, letters from the government and news from home would await him, and a new team of porters would not be far behind.

He needed sustenance—both physical nourishment and a lifeline to the outside world. Yet the anticipation of Ujiji did little to heal his weak, failing body. He grew unable to move on his own.

"Mohamad Bogharib offered to carry me," Livingstone admitted, "I am so weak I can scarcely speak. . . . This is the first time in my life I have been carried in illness, but I cannot raise myself to the sitting posture."[3]

Livingstone blistered in the sun as he lay on the shoulders of Bogharib and his porters. A handful of leaves barely provided protection from exposure.

"Mohamad Bogharib is very kind to me in my extreme weakness; but carriage is painful . . . jolted up and down and sideways—changing shoulders involves a toss from one side to the other . . ."[4]

Without Bogharib's attention, Livingstone might not have survived the month.

Arriving at Lake Tanganyika on February 14, the caravan still had some distance left to Ujiji. Livingstone's failing health, however, necessitated more urgent measures—he could wait no longer. The Arab traders sent canoes to paddle him across the lake to the settlement.

"I was here very ill," Livingstone remarked, "and if I did not get to Ujiji to get proper food and medicine I should die."

Livingstone spent more than two weeks in the canoes as they rounded the lake. Each day passed more slowly as he clung to the hopes of what awaited him.

"Patience was never more needed than now: I am near Ujiji, but the slaves who paddle are tired, and no wonder; they keep up a roaring song all through their work, night and day. I expect to get medicine, food, and milk at Ujiji . . . hope to hold out to Ujiji. Cough worse."

Finally he could see the great Arab settlement of Ujiji on the water's horizon. He was still alive.

———

Slavery's perfect storm arrived in 1869. Global demand for ivory soared, and buyers preferred the large, soft tusks of the African elephants. Africa exported 550 tons annually to England alone and killed roughly forty-four thousand elephants. International demand for ivory increased just as Zanzibari traders discovered large untapped sources of ivory in the African interior. A contemporaneous cholera epidemic broke out in East Africa, killing thousands of slaves along the coast and in Zanzibar. The value of a slave skyrocketed—far above the price of the ivory.

Ravenous demand for slaves and a voracious appetite for ivory profited the traders enormously who simultaneously raided for humans and tusks. As the human gold rush struck the African interior, many Zanzibaris gave up on their trade in goods altogether to join in slave raiding. The boom also attracted new slavers from beyond Zanzibar's shores, and they often brought more ruthless tactics.

In Britain, abolitionists carrying Livingstone's torch made headway, encouraging the British government to take small steps toward further restrictions on the East African slave trade. With Sultan Majid's death in Zanzibar in 1870, a transition in leadership made it necessary to approach his successor. Sultan Barghash, the young, open-minded son of Sultan Majid, showed more promise for progress than his father had.

The British government presented a proposal to Sultan Barghash, asking him to affirm all slavery-restricting acts of the last two decades, including agreements allowing British warships to enter Zanzibari waters, to seize dhows, and to stop the transport of slaves during the monsoon season. The proposal still fell short of complete abolition.

Sultan Barghash swiftly rejected the lion's share of the plan. The sultan would not undo one of Zanzibar's greatest sources of profit. He and his subjects believed the slave trade to be a divinely sanctioned institution for the conversion of African heathens.

Despite the rejection, Barghash left the door open for continued dialogue with Kirk about modifying existing treaties. Negotiations started slowly, while the slave trade expanded rapidly.

———

"Plundered."[5] Everything plundered.

The moment Livingstone entered the dirt streets of Ujiji, he learned his supplies had vanished. His stores had indeed arrived months before, but when no one came forth to claim them, the Arab traders presumed the intended recipient had died and that the supplies had been abandoned.

Despite his fury, Livingstone could do nothing but rest in Ujiji. Still, his presence in the booming Arab settlement caused a stir. Livingstone posed a threat. The slavers knew the British had placed increasing pressure on the slave trade by forcing restrictions through the sultan of

Zanzibar. With Livingstone's known government association and his contacts with the sultan, he could not be trusted.

Livingstone walked a fine line with the traders. If he wanted to contact the coast, the traders were his only relay for correspondence. Many traders objected to taking his letters, ostensibly claiming the sultan would order the trader to return to Livingstone with a response. Some outright refused to carry his letters on suspicion Livingstone documented their nefarious activities. Others promised to deliver his letters but destroyed them for the same reason.

"Plunder and murder is Ujijian trading," Livingstone wrote, summarizing the world he saw centered in Ujiji.[6]

"This is a den of the worst kind of slave-traders; those whom I met [to the southwest] were gentlemen slavers: the Ujiji slavers, like the Kilwa and Portuguese, are the vilest of the vile. It is not a trade, but a system of consecutive murders; they go to plunder and kidnap, and every trading trip is nothing but a foray."[7]

Despite the magnitude of the problem, Livingstone remained undeterred:

> The emancipation of our West-Indian slaves was the work of but a small number of the people of England—the philanthropists and all the more advanced thinkers of the age. Numerically they were a very small minority of the population, and powerful only from the superior abilities of the leading men, and from having the right, the true, and just on their side . . .[8]

With no supplies and weakened health, Livingstone debated whether he should return to Zanzibar or go west to explore the Lualaba River in the Manyuema region. Reports from the trail to Zanzibar alleged a tribal war had broken out. A large, well-armed caravan might fight through, but Livingstone and his handful of men had little protection. Given his health, the risks looked too great. And, if he did make it to

Zanzibar, his return would echo the failure of the Zambezi trip. Failure would threaten another recall.

Livingstone chose to push on for Manyuema. He desperately wanted to complete his work, which necessitated a survey of the Lualaba River. But he could not simply measure its depth, he needed to see where the river flowed. In Manyuema, he planned to buy a canoe and trace the river until it clearly became the Nile. Secretly, he feared the Lualaba actually turned into the Congo River and flowed west.

Manyuema had vast, untapped resources of ivory. Arab caravans had only started venturing into the remote eastern region, but traders knew its potential. As the rumor of plentiful ivory began spreading, new caravans of well-armed Ujijian traders flooded the region, eager to hunt.

Livingstone joined one of the Arab caravans headed east to the Manyuema region and its village of Bambarre. He fell in with a ruthless trader named Dugumbe. Dugumbe had amassed large stores of ivory and had men in the region to do his plundering and killing.

As they entered Manyuema country, the landscape changed dramatically from the sparse terrain near Ujiji. Livingstone entered a land previously unexplored. He found it so surpassingly beautiful, he could barely begin to describe the stunning, broad forests between villages and the palm trees crowning the tops of mountains. The caravan walked up and down deep ravines abounding with birds and monkeys. Livingstone found unknown wild fruits and gigantic trees—one twenty feet in circumference.

The people intrigued him as much as the geography. The Manyuema people tattooed their bodies with moons, stars, and crocodiles, and the women wore practically no clothes. Few foreigners had visited Manyuema—and never a white man; Livingstone shocked them. People stared unrelentingly and crowds followed him everywhere.

But despite its beauty, Manyuema exuded a repressing darkness cloaked in fear. At night, Livingstone would hear the voices of people awaking in fright uttering "most unearthly yells."[9]

Terror gripped the members of the trading caravan. The Arab traders refused to leave sight of the camp for fear of being killed by the fiercely protective Manyuema. Notorious for cannibalism, the Manyuema would kill anyone carrying a tusk. And the Manyuema knew how to fight. Every raiding foray would lose at least three or four men, sometimes as many as ten.

The slavers responded by raising the terror to a level of brutality intended to subdue the frightened people. The slave traders bred hatred, cultivating plunder and violence where peace had once prevailed. With no great chief in Manyuema, the traders leveraged disunity. They trained the natives to kill, turning village against village and tribe against tribe in an effort to despoil the land of its ivory. Introducing guns and new fighting methods, they fostered an economy in which the natives did their bidding. Arab traders no longer led the hunt but made it a competition among the tribes. Murder demonstrated the strength of a man, and brother turned on brother. The slavers encouraged competition with deadly consequences; the more people a man could murder, the more likely his life would be of use to the traders.

"Each slave as he rises in his owner's favor," Livingstone explained, "is eager to show himself a mighty man of valor by cold blooded killing."[10]

"You were sent here not to murder but to trade," Livingstone told a slave raider who boasted of taking forty lives during a raid.

"We are sent to murder," the slave raider replied.[11]

Disobedience meant death, or worse—war. A stolen string of beads by a Manyuema man led to nine destroyed villages and one hundred men killed.

Livingstone made vain attempts at civil discussion:

I told some of [the slave traders] who were civil tongued that ivory obtained by bloodshed was unclean evil—"unlucky" as they say: my advice to them was, "Don't shed human blood, my friends; it has guilt not to be wiped off by water." Off they went; and afterwards the bloodthirsty party got only one tusk and a half, while another party, which avoided shooting men, got fifty-four tusks![12]

Uncharacteristically, he longed for home.

"I don't like to leave my work so that another may 'cut me out' and say he has found sources south of mine . . ." Livingstone wrote to a friend, "and while I feel that all my friends will wish me to make a complete work of the exploration I am at times distressed . . . thinking of my family . . . I ought to have been at home . . ."[13]

In Manyuema, Livingstone saw more violence than he had ever seen in Africa, and the increasing violence tied him to the traders. He could not safely travel alone or buy food. His fragile health decreased his options even further. Pneumonia, dysentery, and fever still plagued him, but the constant wet conditions made travel painful. Livingstone developed sores on his feet that would "eat through everything—muscle, tendon, and bone, and often lame permanently if they do not kill."[14] Putting a foot to the ground produced a pain too severe to walk. For three months, he could not move.

The sores plagued the entire caravan.

"The wailing of the slaves tortured with these sores is one of the night sounds of the slave camp," he noted.[15] But Livingstone observed worse pain among the slaves than the sores on their feet:

> The strangest disease I have seen in this country seems really to be broken-heartedness, and it attacks free men who have been captured and made slaves. . . . They ascribed their only pain to the heart, and placed the hand correctly on the spot, though many think that the organ stands high up under the breast bone. Some slavers expressed surprise to me that [their slaves] should die, seeing they had plenty to eat and no work . . . it seems to be really broken-hearts of which they die.[16]

Making his time in Bambarre even more humiliating, Livingstone remained a public spectacle. As the first white person anyone had seen, Livingstone found people regularly trying to catch a glimpse of this strange creature in his hut. To quell curiosity, he began eating in public in a roped-off enclosure. He astounded the crowds by using a knife and fork, writing in his journal, and washing his hair with soap.

The hardships of travel took their toll on his small team of followers as well. By August 1870, his team had shrunk to three. Only Chuma, Susi, and one young porter remained at his side.

In the worst of times, Livingstone held a small scrap of paper to serve as medicine when he had none. "Turn over and see a drop of comfort . . ." Livingstone had scrolled across the front.[17] On the back, he had one of the few encouraging reviews of his book, *A Narrative of an Expedition to the Zambesi and Its Tributaries*, from the *British Quarterly Review*:

> Few achievements in our day have made a greater impression than that of the adventurous missionary who unaided crossed the Continent of Equatorial Africa. His unassuming simplicity, his varied intelligence, his indomitable pluck, his steady religious purpose, form a combination of qualities rarely found in one man. By common consent, Dr. Livingstone has come to be regarded as one of the most remarkable travellers of his own or of any other age.

———

The trip to Bambarre turned into a seven-month stay. Of those months, Livingstone spent eighty-four days sick and unable to move. He read his Bible four times from beginning to end, devoting considerable time to studying the Old Testament and dwelling at length on Exodus. Perhaps he shared a common bond with its themes. The Nile brought life and redemption in Exodus. The Nile, Livingstone believed, would be his redemption as well. Like Moses, Livingstone wanted to rise up against the pharaohs terrorizing Central Africa to let his people go. He felt more African than European now, akin to the slaves near whom he marched—abandoned, unable to move or survive unless at the mercy of a slave trader—reminiscent of his early years of near-slavery in the factories.

His psychological suffering brought on lucid daydreams. He

imagined following the Nile north and discovering the legendary city of Meroe, purportedly founded by Moses in inner Ethiopia.

"I dream of discovering some monumental relics of Meroe," Livingstone confessed, "and if anything confirmatory of sacred history does remain, I pray to be guided thereunto. If the sacred chronology would thereby be confirmed, I would not grudge the toil and hardships, hunger and pain, I have endured—the irritable ulcers would only be discipline."[18]

He now thought much about discovering the Nile and little about ending the slave trade. His own blood loss, coupled with the bloodshed he witnessed daily, distracted him from his purpose. Finding the source of the Nile now consumed him. The quest for glory captivated him. He wrote tirelessly of his search for the river and disapprovingly of Grant and Speke:

> I am a little thankful to old Nile for so hiding his head that all "theo-retical discoverers" are left out in the cold. With all real explorers I have a hearty sympathy, and I have some regret at being obliged, in a manner compelled, to speak somewhat disparagingly of the opinions formed by my predecessors. The work of Speke and Grant is part of the history of this region, and since the discovery of the sources of the Nile was asserted so positively, it seems necessary to explain, not offensively, I hope, wherein their mistake lay, in making a somewhat similar claim. My opinions may yet be shown to be mistaken too, but at present I cannot conceive how.[19]

The legend of the fountains mesmerized him. He began to believe in it and determined no exploration of the Nile could be complete without confirming the fountains' existence.

"I am grievously tired of living here . . . to sit idle or give up before I finish my work are both intolerable; I cannot bear either, yet I am forced to remain by want of people."[20]

Livingstone spent most of his time in Bambarre waiting. He had joined the caravan to explore the area east of Ujiji while new supplies would make their way from the coast. But the caravan became much longer and more violent than he had anticipated. Now, he wanted to return to Ujiji where he expected to receive his second set of supplies, which he had requested from Kirk in 1870, and check for letters from friends and family.

"I am in agony for news from home," Livingstone lamented, "all I feel sure of now is that my friends will all wish me to complete my task. I join in the wish now, as better than doing it in vain afterwards . . . The Lord be my guide and helper. I feel the want of medicine strongly, almost as much as the want of men."[21]

Two weeks later, he wrote: "Mine has been a calm, hopeful endeavour to do the work that has been given me to do, whether I succeed or whether I fail. The prospect of death in pursuing what I knew to be right did not make me veer to one side or the other."[22]

But despite his preoccupation with Nile discoveries, he could not escape the African condition:

The education of the world is a terrible one, and it has come down with relentless rigour on Africa from the most remote times! What the African will become after this awfully hard lesson is learned, is among the future developments of Providence. When He, who is higher than the highest, accomplishes His purposes, this will be a wonderful country . . .[23]

———

Ten porters marched into Bambarre on February 4, 1871. They came from the coast, arranged by a Zanzibari company, but not as part of an Arab caravan or to trade in human life. They came for Livingstone.

The men had arrived in Ujiji as instructed, then were redirected to Bambarre. The British Consulate had hired the caravan in response to Livingstone's request for supplies. Of forty letters entrusted to the traders, only this solitary appeal had made it through. Although considerably less than what he had requested, Livingstone would take any supplies he could get. The men offered a chance to head to the Lualaba River and, more importantly, to escape Bambarre.

He quickly discovered the Zanzibari caravan company hired by the consulate had not sent free men, but slaves. If Livingstone wanted to proceed, he had no option but to take the men, who immediately refused to continue. Desperate, Livingstone threatened the men with force, then offered to pay them twice the monthly salary of a free man in Zanzibar. Reluctantly, they agreed. Livingstone combined the ten new porters with his small team of three aids, and his new party left Bambarre, heading north to the Lualaba River.

Away from the shelter of the traders, he witnessed more desolation and terror in the countryside. Livingstone's team marched through deserted villages. Smoking fires and barricaded doors betrayed the presence of people who fled Livingstone's approach, fearing the small expedition to be a raiding party.

"The prospects of getting slaves overpowers all else, and blood flows in horrid streams. The Lord look on it!" Livingstone lamented. "I am heartsore, and sick of human blood."[24]

"I have no slaves," Livingstone assured himself, refusing to treat his men as slaves—although someone owned them on the coast. Perhaps the close company of slaves under his authority renewed his sense of conviction. He contemplated repaying the traders for all he had received the past several years, so as not to appear complicit.

After a six-week journey, Livingstone arrived at the Lualaba River.

"It is a mighty river truly," he declared.[25]

Livingstone began his usual methodical research, measuring distances, altitudes, depths, and calculating volumes. More than three thousand yards broad with a strong current, the people told him anyone who attempted to ford the river would perish. The Lualaba, he learned, overflowed its banks annually like the Nile, giving Livingstone's theory a boost.

Livingstone wanted to cross by canoe, but no one would take him. If he wanted neither slaves nor ivory, the people inquired, why would any foreigner wish to cross the river? The people could comprehend no other reason than that Livingstone wished to kill or enslave Manyuema people. The Manyuema had good reason to fear his intentions: another foreigner was ravaging them. The region had fallen under the control of Dugumbe.

Livingstone had met Dugumbe in Bambarre, and the men had become friends. When no natives would supply a canoe for Livingstone to cross the two-mile-wide Lualaba, Livingstone approached Dugumbe. He offered him all the money and supplies in his possession in return for passage; Dugumbe took the offer into consideration. Until he could arrange it, Livingstone settled into a grass house in Nyangwe village.

Nested on the Lualaba, the village of Nyangwe existed for trade, boasting a large market. The Zanzibari traders also had a keen interest in securing this village at the center of the slavery and ivory boom. With fierce competition among traders, Dugumbe faced a bitter turf war with a rival in the region. Several villages, including Nyangwe, dealt with both sides, but Dugumbe wanted complete control.

Livingstone often spent his days in Nyangwe's market. The market opened every four days and attracted as many as fifteen hundred people. Livingstone went to the market as often as possible—his pacifying presence would help dispel rumors that he wanted to kill Manyuema people across the river. He also enjoyed watching the market gatherings—counting people walking past his door and marveling at the loads women would carry on their heads. He liked the activity, the bartering, and the business. It seemed a pleasure for the people to haggle, joke, and laugh. A woman would trade dried cassava for salt and pepper; another would barter handmade pottery for fish. This was commerce alive and well in Africa—a microcosm of his dream. On top of that, the market promised a peaceful oasis of respite amid the chaotic violence of the region—market rules prevented anyone from carrying guns.

On one hot and sultry afternoon in mid-July, as Livingstone left the market, he saw three of Dugumbe's armed men enter the market area.

"I was surprised to see these three with their guns, and felt inclined to reprove them, as one of my men did, for bringing weapons into the market, but I attributed it to their ignorance . . ."[26]

No more than thirty yards out of the market, Livingstone heard a spirited argument over a chicken break out behind him. Then two shots rang out in the quiet afternoon. Then another shot, then a wild barrage. Dugumbe's three men had opened fire.

Panic ensued and the crowd began to run, casting away their wares in hurried fright. A throng stampeded toward the creek to reach the cluster of beached canoes.

As the assailants continued their indiscriminate slaughter in the marketplace, an armed party near the creek opened fire on those dashing toward the water. Even as the villagers, mostly unarmed women, attempted to flee across the nearby river, the attackers continued to fire on them. Aiming for their exposed heads, they shot those trying to swim to safety.

"Shot after shot continued to be fired on the helpless and perishing." Livingstone watched in horror as villagers fled into the bloodstained water. "Some of the long line of heads disappeared quietly; whilst other poor creatures threw their arms high, as if appealing to the great Father above, and sank."

Livingstone was filled with rage.

"My first impulse was to pistol the murderers," but before Livingstone could act, he found himself inundated with survivors. At least thirty ran to Livingstone for protection, and Livingstone sent his men out to save others with only the shield of the Union Jack to protect them.[27]

When the chaos in the market finally subsided, the ground was littered with bodies. Dugumbe's men had gunned down four hundred men and women, all unarmed, and even killed two of their own. Then they followed the people back to their homes. The warfare continued. Livingstone counted twelve burning villages.

"As I write I hear the loud wails on the left bank over those who are there slain, ignorant of their many friends now in the depths of Lualaba. Oh, let Thy kingdom come! No one will ever know the exact loss on this bright sultry summer morning, it gave me the impression of being in Hell."[28]

Dugumbe's explanation for the massacre involved a disobedient slave. His men had resolved to punish the slave and make an impression on the town. While Dugumbe had fired no shots himself, Livingstone knew him to be the architect of the massacre. Dugumbe had won—proving he controlled Nyangwe village.

Livingstone confronted him.

"Now for what is all this murder?" Livingstone asked him. Dugumbe blamed the men in the market for acting without orders but advised Livingstone against a blood feud with the vicious slavers.[29] Livingstone did not believe him. He proposed Dugumbe catch the murderers and hang them in the market to demonstrate justice to the region. Dugumbe replied that it was out of his control but promised to send his men over to end the violence in the countryside.

The next day the plunder and arson continued; Livingstone could see smoke pillars rising from seventeen villages. By the time the massacre had run its course, twenty-seven villages were in ashes.

". . . it was terrible that the murdering of so many should be contemplated at all," Livingstone wrote. "It made me sick at heart. Who could accompany the people of Dugumbe . . . and be free from blood-guiltiness?"[30]

Chiefs from the destroyed villages gathered and came to Livingstone. They begged him to come and aid them with rebuilding and resettling in new regions.

"I was so ashamed of the company in which I found myself, that I could scarcely look the [natives] in the face," Livingstone wrote. "I could not remain among bloody companions, and would flee away . . . The open murder perpetrated on hundreds of unsuspecting women fills me with unspeakable horror: I cannot think of going anywhere with [the traders]."[31]

Despite his poor health and shortage of provisions, Livingstone could no longer remain with the trading caravans. He had admired

Dugumbe in some respects and depended on him, but any esteem was now shattered. Livingstone felt ashamed of his friendship and, to a certain extent, complicit for accepting his charity. He could not stand to be near Dugumbe or any of the slave traders, no matter how much he needed their aid. He had to escape.

"'Don't go away,' say the Manyuema chiefs to me; but I cannot stay here in agony."[32]

With only a few men and no supplies, Livingstone saw his only option as returning to Ujiji. He could restock, arrange new porters, then travel on his own free of the porters. The detour back to Ujiji, however, would prevent him from exploring the course of the Lualaba River.

Before Livingstone departed, Dugumbe attempted a peace offering, proposing Livingstone take any supplies he needed. Livingstone wanted nothing from him, only taking a little gunpowder and a goat out of necessity, and accepting beads to carry as currency.

"At last I said that I would start for Ujiji, in three days on foot," Livingstone determined.[33]

With his small band of aids and porters, Livingstone had a long walk in front of him. He expected at least forty-five days—roughly a six-hundred-mile trek with all the twisting and turning for geography.

———

The British public clung to all rumors of Livingstone's possible whereabouts. Updates on the search for the explorer ran in newspapers regularly, and any news of his journey captured attention. New reports surfaced of his death, other reports spoke of Livingstone turning up in South Africa to meet a British ship, and still other tales told of Livingstone marrying an African princess. None were true, but all boosted the Livingstone myth.

Unbeknownst to Livingstone, his abolitionist advocacy from the Zambezi expedition had begun producing results: The Committee of the Church Missionary Society and advocacy groups inspired by Livingstone continued their work and pressure on the government. Queen Victoria, in her biannual address, drew the attention of Parliament to the East African slave trade. Following her speech, a Royal Commission formed a Select Committee of the House of Commons to guide legislative action. Finally, in the House of Commons session of 1871, in collaboration with the Anti-Slavery Society, a motion was made for inquiry into the East African slave trade.

Parliament appointed a committee to investigate the proposition for abolition in East Africa. In July, the committee presented evidence from Livingstone—his 1867 dispatches on the state of the slave trade. Then the committee called and examined fourteen witnesses, from the head of the British Foreign Office's Anti Slavery Department, to past consuls of Zanzibar, to missionaries associated with the Zambezi expedition.

The testimony aimed to prove that past treaties with Zanzibari sultans created "a mere blind"—fictitious action with no effect on the scale of the trade.[34] But testimony quickly grew lively and vivid over the unmitigated loss of human life experienced on the trade routes.

"It is like sending up for a large block of ice to London in the hot weather," Horace Waller, a Universities' Mission member, testified, "you know that a certain amount will melt away before it reaches you in the country as it travels down; but that which remains will be quite sufficient for your needs."[35]

Captain Colomb, commander of a patrol of cruisers in charge of blocking slave dhows, explained how captains of their slave ships about to be captured often threw their slaves into the sea to save its other cargo.

While the witnesses imparted vivid accounts, they offered little encouraging advice for successfully ending the slave trade. All agreed it would be impossible to abolish the trade in Zanzibar. The sultan simply could not do it; the humiliation and economic disaster to come upon him through abolition would invite a coup and assassination.

Then Bartle Frere took the stand, prepared with a different answer. Frere, as a former governor of Bombay, held responsibility for British activities in Zanzibar. Frere spoke clearly, with determination and optimism.

He presented a solution mirroring Livingstone's ideas: technology and commerce.

"You must, to some extent, bring [the sultan] over to your view, that this matter of slave trading is a bad one for him," Frere told the committee. Then, he recommended that a high-ranking negotiator go to Zanzibar "prepared with some authority, and with the dignity of a special envoy to press these points."[36]

Frere had the perfect senior British diplomat in mind: himself.

Frere's recommendations afforded the ammunition the committee needed to press harder for a legislative agenda. The committee boldly produced a report recommending that the British government take measures to secure the entire abolition of the East African slave trade. Although the sultan had already dismissed a much less drastic proposal, in the committee's view, compromise could no longer be entertained.

". . . any attempt to supply slaves for domestic use in Zanzibar will always be a pretext and cloak for a foreign trade," the committee's report concluded.[37]

Despite the committee's proposal, government action ground to a halt. When no news of Livingstone surfaced, the flurry of public interest accompanying his rumored death faded. Frere held public abolition rallies to keep the matter active, but he could not reach a critical mass of national concern. Without overwhelming public support, the government had no reason to go to such great lengths to pressure the sultan.

Then, after the rally for abolition had grown cold, several of Livingstone's letters finally managed to arrive in Zanzibar. Albeit unintentional, Livingstone's years embedded with the slaves in Ujiji and Manyuema had proved strategic. He gained intelligence on the trade, its routes, operations, and weaknesses.

He gave Kirk advice on necessary next steps for fighting the slavers: "The Sultan must get troops who will scour the mainland and catch the bloody thieves inland."[38] Livingstone's vision remained much the same as it had years before on Lake Nyassa: the fight must move from ocean to land.

"The cheering prospect of stopping the East Coast slave trade belongs to you," Livingstone had written to Kirk in one of his itinerant letters, "and therein I do greatly rejoice."[39]

———

Livingstone came upon a downed tree in their Ujiji-bound forest pathway. The rustling of trees to his right heralded the release of a spear—an ambush. The lance nearly grazed his back as Livingstone saw two Manyuema men running off only thirty feet away.

Livingstone's team proceeded ahead, coming upon an area of dense forest where more of the ambushing tribe lay in wait. Another spear flew at Livingstone, missing him by only a foot. A barrage of spears followed, with two lances striking men on Livingstone's team. By the time Livingstone's party could open fire, their aggressors had fled into the forest. Through the thick vegetation, they could hear the Manyuema jeering at them.

"As they are experts with the spear I don't know how it missed," Livingstone remarked, "except that he was too sure of his aim and the good hand of God was upon me."[40]

The fierce Manyuema had mistaken Livingstone for a slave trader. The likeness haunted him and made him a wanted man, the murder of whom would be revenge for the death of thousands of Manyuema.

"From each hole in the tangled mass we looked for a spear," Livingstone wrote, "and each moment expected to hear the rustle which told of deadly weapons hurled at us. I became weary with the constant strain of danger, and—as, I suppose, happens with soldiers on the field of battle—not courageous, but perfectly indifferent whether I were killed or not."[41]

Later the same day, Livingstone looked up at a cracking sound. A giant tree damaged by fire crashed to the earth. He stepped back to watch it fall exactly where he had stood moments before.

Livingstone's scattered attendants yelled as they came running back to find him covered in dust. "You will finish all your work in spite of these people, and in spite of everything."

"Three times in one day was I delivered from impending death," Livingstone reflected. "Like them, I took it as an omen of good success to crown me yet thanks to the 'Almighty Preserver of men.'"[42]

Livingstone spent three punishing months on the trail to Ujiji, passing through a countryside of villages plundered and burned to the ground among a people who wanted him dead. Sleepless nights and the constant fear of attack took their toll. Short on food and absent of medicine, he grew ill again—too weak to write more than a few sentences.

"I felt as if dying on my feet," Livingstone journaled. "Almost every step was in pain, the appetite failed, and a little bit of meat caused violent diarrhea, whilst the mind, sorely depressed, reacted on the body . . . I alone had failed and experienced worry, thwarting, baffling, when almost in sight of the end towards which I strained."[43]

Livingstone survived the next month and, in late October, once again laid weary eyes on Ujiji, urgently in need of the provisions he had requested the previous year from the British consul. Livingstone stumbled into town, suffering much and "reduced to a skeleton."[44] By evening, he learned the tragic news: his provisions had been squandered, again.

His resupply had arrived months earlier in Ujiji, as planned, but the Zanzibari trader in charge of the caravan decided the long overdue recipient must be dead. He appropriated the stores and sold them. Not a single yard of calico out of three thousand yards remained, nor a single string of beads out of three hundred. In the market of Ujiji, Livingstone watched in agony as the trader's slaves carried goods bought with Livingstone's provisions. Twice he had lost his provisions—his hope and lifeline—to Ujiji's anarchy.

"I felt in my destitution as if I were the man who went down from Jerusalem to Jericho, and fell among thieves; but I could not hope for Priest, Levite, or good Samaritan to come by on either side . . ."[45]

Sick, destitute, and exhausted, Livingstone no longer knew where to turn. He hated Ujiji even more than he had before. This time he had no sustenance from powerful traders, nor did he want it. With no supplies nor the health to travel farther, the loss of his provisions reduced him to beggary.

"I am terribly knocked up but this is for your own eye only . . ." Livingstone wrote to a friend. "Doubtful if I live to see you again."[46]

Livingstone had finally reached the end of his journey. Now he awaited death.

12 ❧ HOPE

I think I am in the line of duty . . . I have never
wavered in my conviction that this is the case.

—David Livingstone

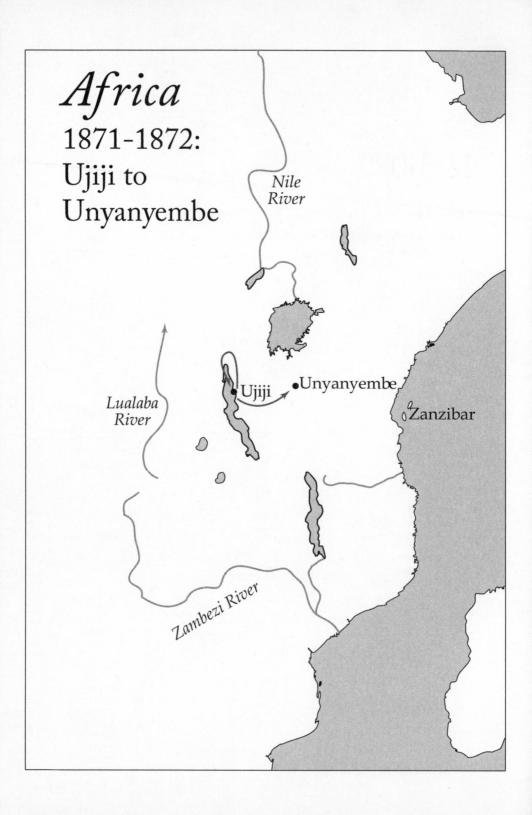

Africa
1871-1872:
Ujiji to
Unyanyembe

Nile
River

Lualaba
River

Ujiji

Unyanyembe

Zanzibar

Zambezi River

Henry Morton Stanley, an accomplished American journalist, had received an important invitation in the fall of 1869. James Gordon Bennett, editor of the *New York Herald*, summoned Stanley to his room at the Grand Hotel in Paris.

Stanley was recognized in publishing circles as a traveling journalist. During the Civil War, he composed notable reports as a ship's writer, then arrived first on the scene to report a successful British rescue operation in Ethiopia. The call from Bennett would mark his most important assignment to date.

"Where do you think Livingstone is?" Bennett asked.

"I really do not know, sir!"

"Do you think he is alive?"

"He may be, and he may not be!" Stanley answered. "What! Do you really think I can find Dr. Livingstone?"[1]

Stanley raised concerns over the cost of the proposed venture—it would be overwhelmingly expensive.

"Draw a thousand pounds now," Bennett replied, "and when you have gone through that, draw another thousand, and when that is spent draw another thousand, and when you have finished that draw another thousand, and so on; but FIND LIVINGSTONE."

Bennett knew a sensational story when he saw one: American journalist finds lost British explorer in vast, uncharted continent for face-to-face interview. Bennett salivated at the thought that an American newspaper could do what self-aggrandizing British derring-do could not. It was almost scandalous. With Livingstone's fate still unconfirmed, it would surely be a dramatic tale. E. D. Young's search party had neither found Livingstone nor certifiably determined his whereabouts; it merely shed skepticism upon his premature obituary.

Although Livingstone's disputed death had revived public interest in Britain's infamous explorer, Livingstone remained a controversial figure. The sour taste of the Zambezi debacle hung in recent memory, and as each day passed with no new news of the man's status, Livingstone sentimentality diminished.

But Bennett thought otherwise. He owned a media empire notorious for sensational stories. He could remake Livingstone—larger than life and bigger than even Murchison could ever dream. If Stanley could find him, Bennett would publish the story along with Stanley's trip reports and letters from Livingstone. Bennett speculated that any Livingstone distaste would immediately vanish, and the explorer would again become a global phenomenon.

Stanley was the perfect choice for the assignment—an adventurer known for concocting wild stunts and reporting from dangerous locations. Orphaned in Wales at an early age, he had joined a merchant ship at age fifteen to cross the Atlantic. In New Orleans, he came to live with a local merchant, adopting the man's last name, then joined the Confederate Army to fight in the Civil War. Stanley had no fear, nothing to hold him back. More important, Stanley desperately wanted to achieve great public notoriety—and an expedition to find Livingstone presented a ticket to fame and fortune. For both Stanley and Bennett, the prospect of finding Livingstone warranted considerable personal gain.

Bennett delayed Stanley's Africa trip one year. Letters from Livingstone arrived in Zanzibar, corroborating his survival and renewing public hope. Then he went silent again. Bennett waited for Livingstone to be fully lost in the public mind before sending Stanley.

When Stanley reached Zanzibar in January 1871, no one had since heard from Livingstone. To the world outside Africa, Livingstone was lost again, or even dead. In the minds of Kirk and the British Consulate, silence meant nothing. Kirk believed Livingstone knew his course and would surface when he pleased. Business as usual in African exploration explained Livingstone's absence. As far as Kirk was concerned, a new letter might arrive tomorrow just as easily as Livingstone might stumble back into town.

In Zanzibar, Stanley kept a low profile about his intentions. He did not want to arouse suspicion over his pursuit of Livingstone, risking an emergency British search party upset, obstruction of his caravan, or public embarrassment if he failed. Stanley fronted a guise: he came to Zanzibar to explore the Rufiji River, an obscure waterway south of Zanzibar on the African mainland.

Kirk presented the largest obstacle to Stanley's plan. Kirk possessed the most information about the explorer's whereabouts, and he pulled the strings at the British Consulate. Stanley left Kirk asking many questions, from his purpose in exploring an insignificant river to his sources of funding. Accordingly, Kirk held his power and knowledge close to his chest. For that, Stanley despised him from the beginning. Kirk was not an ally in the Livingstone search, but an adversary.

Stanley asked if Burton, Grant, or Baker had tried to find the missing explorer, and whether Kirk thought he could be found. Kirk said Livingstone did not want to be found, nor did he want any companionship. If Livingstone heard of any explorer's approach, said Kirk, "[he] would put a hundred miles of swamp in a very short time between himself and them."

Stanley spent nearly a month on Zanzibar building the largest caravan of any exploring party to that time. With no budget cap and no sense for arranging an African expedition, Stanley purchased more of everything than he required and the best of everything he could obtain. He hired approximately two hundred porters and bought boats, a bathtub, and a thoroughbred horse. Setting sail from Zanzibar on February 5, the expedition started for the African interior on March 28.

Stanley's enormous caravan quickly turned into a nightmare. His party passed through the same drought-stricken, disease-infested lands that Livingstone had walked through several years before. Stanley's men trotted through flooded swamps, suffered painful dysentery, and fought off starvation with anything they could find to eat. His thoroughbred horse died within a few days from the bite of a tsetse fly. In the eight months Stanley spent trudging toward Ujiji, two-thirds of his porters deserted or died. Stanley proved as unforgiving as the environment, developing a notorious reputation for beating men who disobeyed him.

Livingstone was Stanley's Nile. With the same unrelenting tenacity of Livingstone's pursuit of the river, Stanley pursued the whereabouts of the explorer.

"I have taken a solemn enduring oath," Stanley wrote en route to Ujiji, "an oath to be kept while the least hope of life remains in me, not to be tempted to break the resolution I have formed, never to give up the search, until I find Livingstone alive, or find his dead body . . . only death can prevent me. But death—not even this; I shall not die, I will not, I cannot die!"[2]

Days after Livingstone's penniless arrival in Ujiji, a salvo of gunfire broke the quiet of the 1871 November afternoon. The near-unison barrage signified not battle, but a caravan's arrival to town.

Susi ran to Livingstone's tent at the top of his speed.

"An Englishman! I see him!" he gasped, and darted off to the road into the town to meet the procession.

The flag at the head of the caravan was not English, but American. Following the flag holders came a giant array of porters outfitted with bales of supplies, huge kettles, tents, tin baths, and a folding boat.

This must be a luxurious traveller, thought Livingstone, *and not one at his wits' end like me.*

Crowds gathered in Ujiji. Stanley, an immaculately dressed stranger, made his way through the mob, by now a long avenue of people. He walked slowly—nervously—unsure how Livingstone, or the crowd, might react. Sporting a spotless safari hat and freshly polished boots, Stanley sensed the entire city yearned to know his purpose. Reaching Livingstone's hut, he parted the sea of people to find Livingstone standing before him. The doctor looked pale and wearied, his beard grey and clothes faded. Yet he proudly wore his blue consular cap and red-sleeved waistcoat.

Stanley removed his hat and walked up to Livingstone.

"Dr. Livingstone, I presume?"

A smile lit up Livingstone's face at Stanley's introduction.

"Yes," the explorer replied, lifting his cap slightly.

"I thank God, Doctor, I have been permitted to see you."

"I feel thankful that I am here to welcome you," Livingstone answered.

———

The accomplishment of finding Livingstone took Stanley awhile to accept. He had devoted years of thought and months of suffering to accomplishing a near-impossible feat. He had risked his own life and sacrificed many other lives along the way. Stanley processed his triumph through little dialogues with himself:

What was I sent for? To find Livingstone. Have you found him? Yes, of course; am I not in his house? Whose compass is that hanging on a peg there? Whose clothes, whose boots, are those? Who reads those newspapers, those "Saturday Reviews" and numbers of "Punch" lying on the floor? Well, what are you going to do now? I shall tell him this morning who sent me, and what brought me here. I will then ask him to write a letter to Mr. Bennett, and to give what news he can spare. I did not come here to rob him of his news. Sufficient for me is it that I have found him. It is a complete success so far. But it will be a greater one if he gives me letters for Mr. Bennett, and an acknowledgment that he has seen me.[3]

As the men sat down for breakfast the next morning, Stanley called for his servants who brought forth bright plates, cups, and saucers, and shining silver spoons, knives, and forks along with a silver teapot. They spread out a rich Persian carpet for the men to sit on. Livingstone had not seen such delicacies in years, nor had he ever traveled in such opulence.

Stanley had much news to share with the lost explorer: global politics, the opening of the Suez Canal, and the Livingstone search parties. The world had changed significantly in recent years. But there was also bad news: the negative press about Livingstone and the disappointment that the bank where Livingstone placed proceeds from the *Lady Nyassa* had failed. Absent a trust he set up for his children, his entire fortune had vanished.

Surprising to Stanley, Livingstone did not want to leave Africa but remained eager to continue his search for the Nile. Stanley not only shared his interest in finding the source, but also offered him means. The men traveled north along Lake Tanganyika at Stanley's expense and with his porters.

Since he began his Nile expedition, Livingstone had felt assured Tanganyika played a critical role in the Nile's watershed. What role, specifically, remained unclear. Livingstone imagined Lake Tanganyika drained north into Lake Albert and from Lake Albert flowed into the Nile.

The journey to Tanganyika gave the men time together. Before Stanley set out, he knew rather little about the man he endeavored to find. What he did know did not sound particularly pleasant. The intervening news and failure of the Zambezi expedition prejudiced Stanley's view of Livingstone. To the American journalist, Livingstone gave Stanley merely an object for pursuit—a story. Who Livingstone was or why he devoted his life to Africa mattered less than being the first to find the lost hero:

> I was led to believe that Livingstone possessed a splenetic, misanthropic temper; some have said that he is garrulous, that he is demented; that he

has utterly changed from the David Livingstone whom people knew as the reverend missionary . . . I respectfully beg to differ with all and each of the above statements. I grant he is not an angel, but he approaches to that being as near as the nature of a living man will allow. I never saw any spleen or misanthropy in him—as for being garrulous, Dr. Livingstone is quite the reverse: he is reserved, if anything; and to the man who says Dr. Livingstone is changed, all I can say is, that he never could have known him . . .[4]

Not a particularly religious man, Stanley was filled with admiration and intrigue by Livingstone's faith:

His religion is not of the theoretical kind, but it is a constant, earnest, sincere practice. It is neither demonstrative nor loud, but manifests itself in a quiet, practical way, and is always at work . . . In him, religion exhibits its loveliest features; it governs his conduct not only towards his servants . . . Religion has tamed him, and made him a Christian gentleman.[5]

From mid-November to mid-January, Stanley joined the survey of Tanganyika. In spite of their best efforts, the men could not find a river exiting from the lake. Livingstone assumed the water traveled underground. Excavations would need to wait until he had proper equipment and had confirmed the existence of the fountains. Despite the new setbacks, Livingstone remained undeterred.

"No one will cut me out after this exploration is accomplished," Livingstone wrote, "and may the good Lord of all help me to show myself one of His stout-hearted servants, an honour to my children, and, perhaps, to my country and race."[6]

With no geographic breakthrough to report at Tanganyika, Stanley grew anxious to share his news with the world. He began preparing to return to the coast. In his weeks spent with Livingstone, Stanley had come to admire him and lamented the departure. During their travels together, Stanley had often fallen ill with fever, and at times had reached a critical condition. Livingstone always kept a watchful eye over him and attended to him, in Stanley's words, "like a father." Perhaps like the father the orphaned boy never had.

"In Livingstone I have seen many amiable traits. His gentleness never forsakes him; his hopefulness never deserts him. No harassing anxieties, distraction of mind, long separation from home and kindred, can make him complain. He thinks 'all will come out right at last;' he has such faith in the goodness of Providence."[7]

Stanley brought out the best in Livingstone, but also the worst. Still upset by Kirk's cold reception in Zanzibar, he wanted to drive a wedge between the men who had previously called each other friend. Stanley convinced the explorer that Kirk had maliciously sent irresponsible porters and inadequate supplies so as to thwart Livingstone's quest. Livingstone believed his explanation and began a barrage of angry letters to friends and colleagues disparaging Kirk.

Stanley ardently tried to persuade Livingstone to return to London with him. His arguments had appeal: Livingstone could regain strength, receive artificial teeth, put together a new expedition, and then come back to finish his search. Livingstone considered the offer.

". . . my judgment said, 'All your friends will wish you to make a complete work of the exploration of the sources of the Nile before you retire,'" wrote Livingstone. "My daughter Agnes says, 'Much as I wish you to come home, I would rather that you finished your work to your own satisfaction than return merely to gratify me.' . . . She is a chip off the old block."[8]

Livingstone refused to leave Africa, but he sent his words with Stanley.

"If indeed my disclosures should lead to the suppression of the East Coast slave-trade," Livingstone penned to friends in Britain, "I would esteem that as a far greater feat than the discovery of all the sources together. It is awful, but I cannot speak of the slaving for fear of appearing guilty of exaggerating. It is not trading; it is murdering for captives to be made into slaves."[9]

As a gesture of thanks to the *Herald*, Livingstone wrote an editorial for Bennett, intended for publication and the leveraging of a new audience.[10] Stanley would reveal the letter when he arrived at the coast, as well as forward Livingstone's letters to friends and family.

On March 14, Livingstone presented Stanley with his letters and sealed journals—positively not to be opened until London and then entrusted strictly to Agnes. With his journals, Livingstone handed over exactly what the world needed to hear: graphic firsthand accounts of a full-blown massacre due to the slave trade and not just a few isolated deaths. The market scene at Nyangwe, in particular, might be indisputable evidence for abolitionists. Beyond firsthand reports and evidence, Livingstone's letters provided encouragement to continue the fight against the slave trade.

Finally, after four months and four days together, Stanley's dreaded departure arrived. The night before parting, Livingstone poured out his gratitude. Stanley wept like a child.

"We had a sad breakfast together," Stanley wrote of the following morning. "I could not eat, my heart was too full; neither did my companion seem to have an appetite."

To savor the last precious moments with Stanley, Livingstone walked with him for the first few miles. As the men walked side by side, they sang together. Stanley took long looks at Livingstone, "to impress his features thoroughly on my memory."

"Now, my dear Doctor," Stanley stopped, "the best friends must part. You have come far enough; let me beg of you to turn back."

"I will say this to you," Livingstone replied, "you have done what few men could do, far better than some great travellers I know. And I am grateful to you for what you have done for me. God guide you safe home, and bless you, my friend."

"And may God bring you safe back to us all, my dear friend. Farewell!"

"Farewell."

"March!" Stanley bellowed at his men, fighting back his emotions. "Why do you stop? Go on! Are you not going home? . . . No more weakness. I will show them such marching as will make them remember me."[11]

Their parting hit Livingstone equally hard. Livingstone's days with Stanley were perhaps some of the happiest of his life. ". . . that good brave fellow has acted as a son to me," Livingstone would tell Agnes in a letter. He so missed the company of Stanley, he sent Susi to catch up with the journalist to bring back any last words.

"My dear Doctor," Stanley wrote in the weeks to come, "very few amongst men have I found I so much got to love as yourself . . ."[12]

The farther Stanley marched, the more he missed Livingstone:

> . . . I wrote the above extracts in my diary on the evening of each day. I look at them now after six months have passed away; yet I am not ashamed of them; my eyes feel somewhat dimmed at the recollection of the parting. I dared not erase nor modify what I had penned while my feelings were strong. God grant that if ever you take to travelling in Africa you will get as noble and true a man for your companion as David Livingstone! For four months and four days I lived with him in the same house, or in the same boat, or in the same tent, and I never found a fault in him. I am a man of a quick temper, and often without sufficient cause, I daresay, have broken the ties of friendship; but with Livingstone I never had cause for resentment, but each day's life with him added to my admiration for him.[13]

The weeks following Stanley's departure, however, brought solemn and reflective moments upon Livingstone. Memories of the Nyangwe massacre rekindled feelings of anger and mourning. They reminded him of his purpose, why he came to Africa in pursuit of the Nile.

"What I have seen of this horrid system," he wrote to a friend, "makes me feel that its suppression would be of infinitely more importance than all the fountains together."[14]

His birthday arrived, signifying another year of his life spent in the wilds of Africa, and another year of unfinished work and failure. He recalled the agonizing walk to Ujiji and shuddered to think how near he came to death's door.

"My Jesus, my king, my life, my all," Livingstone decried in his journal, "I again dedicate my whole self to Thee. Accept me, and grant, Gracious Father, that ere this year is gone I may finish my task. In Jesus' name I ask it. Amen, so let it be."[15]

Eight anxious months passed before Stanley, racing back to Zanzibar, could declare to the world that Livingstone was alive. Stanley would also send Livingstone fresh supplies. From Ujiji to Zanzibar, Stanley's extraordinary dispatch traveled on to Bombay, then to London by telegraph for relay to New York for the *Herald* to break the news.

The world would soon learn of Stanley's remarkable encounter and Livingstone's uncompromising anger.

PART THREE

RESURRECTION

13 ❧ THE LONG WAY HOME

I must finish my work.
> —DAVID LIVINGSTONE

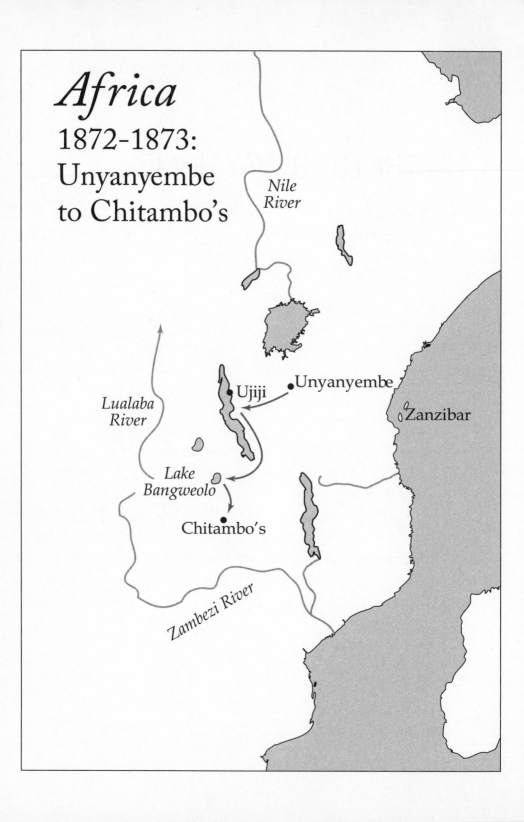

Africa
1872-1873:
Unyanyembe
to Chitambo's

Nile
River

Lualaba
River

Ujiji

Unyanyembe

Zanzibar

Lake
Bangweolo

Chitambo's

Zambezi River

July 2, 1872: The *Herald* publishes Livingstone's letter.
10 months and 4 days until the end of the East African slave trade.

Slaves sold per annum: 20,000
Total victims of the slave trade: 556,000

N ow, that you have done with domestic slavery forever, lend us your powerful aid towards this great object," Livingstone's words resounded in the *New York Herald*. "This fine country is blighted as with a curse in the above, in order that the slavery privileges of the petty Sultan of Zanzibar may not be infringed . . ."[1]

Livingstone's message to his audience across the Atlantic went to press in the *Herald* on July 2, 1872. America: *End the East African slave trade!*

Livingstone's publicity stunt had worked. Although he had not yet found the source, his quest for the Nile had yielded him a voice of authority. Alongside the great sensation of the American journalist's search, Livingstone's letter updated the world on his travels and praised Stanley for coming to his rescue. But its thrust and conclusion elevated the importance of the fight against the East African slave trade above his mission of finding the Nile's source: ". . . if my disclosures regarding the terrible Ujijian slavery should lead to the suppression of the east coast slave trade, I shall regard that as a greater matter by far than the discovery of all the Nile sources together."[2]

Along with letters to the *Herald*, Stanley carried out Livingstone's consular dispatches, including those to the British government describing the slave trade in East Africa. Several letters addressed to the British foreign secretary outlined the problem and proposed a solution:

> Slaves are not bought in the countries to which [slave] agents proceed . . . indeed it is a mistake to call the system of Ujiji slave-"trade" at all; the captives are not traded for, but murdered for, and the gangs that are dragged coastwards to enrich the [slave agents] are usually not slaves, but captive free people. A sultan anxious to do justly rather than pocket head-money would proclaim them all free as soon as they reached his territory.[3]

Livingstone's observations pulled back the veil of the sultan's façade to shed light on what the outside world could not see: the inner workings of the slave trade filled the sultan's coffers. The sultan led the world to believe Zanzibar's variety of slavery was both relatively benign and beyond the scope of his power. Livingstone confirmed that this was not the case.

Corruption challenged any effort to end the slave trade. The traders controlled Zanzibar's customhouse—the door to the exchange in slaves—as well as the island's financial institutions. With such authority, the slavers could conceal everything and support the slave agents in fraudulent activity.

To combat corruption, Livingstone proposed a change in management and strict financial oversight. Turn Zanzibar's income sources over to reputable foreign management, he suggested. Specifically, Livingstone recommended an English or American merchant. Not only would foreign independent oversight guard against the slave trade, it would promote lawful commerce in Zanzibar.

Lawful commerce—the latter effect of Livingstone's oversight proposal—pointed toward his ultimate goal: civility. Livingstone craved a moral force in East Africa—ethical institutions and systems that could battle corruption. In Livingstone's view, this moral force fundamentally included the British system of justice and the Christian church, institutions he believed had contributed beneficially in suppressing the slave trade near English settlements on the west coast of Africa.[4]

Livingstone recommended colonies—not colonization for the sake of building a global empire, but colonies to establish a moral force. He saw few other institutions that could work effectively in the chaotic East African environment. The violent brutality of the Arab traders ruled out the possibility of Arab colonies, which would quickly be commandeered by unscrupulous slavers. The African-born or mixed-ethnic Arab-Africans adopted the violent ethics they witnessed and could not provide a sufficient moral force. Portugal still held interests in slavery. Finally, the Banyans—Indians in Africa—had self-interested financial reasons for continuing the trade, providing credit and outfitting caravans. They had joined in the slaving as well. Besides Britain and America, few nations existed with the power and conscience to truly abolish the trade.

Livingstone returned again to the issue of the sultan's annual subsidy to Muscat. The subsidy Britain imposed on the sultan of Zanzibar in 1861, Livingstone suggested, might hold some culpability in contributing to the sultanate's financial reliance on the slave trade, but could also provide a bargaining chip.

———

"Finished a letter for the *New York Herald*, trying to enlist American zeal to stop the East Coast slave-trade," Livingstone wrote feverishly in his journal from deep in the heart of Africa. "I pray for blessing on it from the All-Gracious."[5]

He grew impatient waiting for fresh supplies and porters to be sent by Stanley. He filled his time writing dispatches and letters to the *Herald*, further expounding on the horrors of slavery in East Africa. With the *Herald* eager to publish all things Livingstone, he now had the ear of

America—a nation gaining power on the world stage and a competitive threat to Britain. Livingstone hoped to leverage this power.

He anticipated opponents who would argue that slavery filled a natural course of human development. Wilberforce had faced similar arguments. Livingstone rehearsed the arguments in his journal:

> When endeavouring to give some account of the slave-trade of East Africa, it was necessary to keep far within the truth, in order not to be thought guilty of exaggeration; but in sober seriousness the subject does not admit of exaggeration. To overdraw its evils is a simple impossibility. The sights I have seen, though common incidents of the traffic, are so nauseous that I always strive to drive them from memory. In the case of most disagreeable recollections I can succeed, in time, in consigning them to oblivion, but the slaving scenes come back unbidden, and make me start up at dead of night horrified by their vividness. To some this may appear weak and unphilosophical, since it is alleged that the whole human race has passed through the process of development. We may compare cannibalism to the stone age, and the times of slavery to the iron and bronze epochs—slavery is as natural a step in human development as from bronze to iron.[6]

He continued, "Some people say, 'If so ancient, why try to stop an old established usage now?' Well, some believe that the affliction that befel the most ancient of all the patriarchs, Job, was small-pox. Why then stop the ravages of this venerable disease in London and New York by vaccination?"[7]

Livingstone placed his letters once again in the hands of Zanzibar traders to deliver them at the coast, then turned his attention back to the geographic problem of the Nile's source. He would not leave Africa until he had answered this question.

But before he could get underway, painful news arrived in a letter from his son, Oswell. Livingstone's unfailing champion and near-surrogate father, Roderick Murchison, had passed away.

"Alas! alas!" Livingstone grieved, "this is the only time in my life I ever felt inclined to use the word, and it bespeaks a sore heart: the best friend I ever had—true, warm, and abiding—he loved me more than I deserved: he looks down on me still. I must feel resigned to the loss by the Divine Will, but still I regret and mourn."[8]

The note from Oswell brought further agony. At only twenty years old, Oswell had joined a search party to reach his father. He intended to convince him to return to England and give up his quest for the Nile. As Oswell's party marched into Africa, they met Stanley on his return from Livingstone. With Stanley's success, Oswell's commanding officer saw the mission fulfilled and disbanded the expedition. Unequipped to continue alone, Oswell had been forced to abandon the search party with them.

On the heels of Stanley's departure, news of Oswell's decision hit Livingstone hard. Stanley, with no family bloodline, had struggled through Africa to reach him not only to bid him return, but to encourage him. Oswell, it appeared to his father, had given up and did not believe in Livingstone's goal.

Of his children, only Agnes cheered him on. And, they were not children anymore. Agnes had turned twenty-five; Thomas, twenty-three; Oswell, twenty; and Anna Mary, thirteen. Only Agnes truly knew her father. With the departure of Stanley, the loss of Murchison, and the withdrawal of Oswell, Livingstone felt more abandoned than ever before. Stanley felt more like family than his own kin.

For the next week, Livingstone wrote almost daily of his weariness. In his weakness, he reflected regularly on faith and matters of the heart:

All the great among men have been remarkable at once for the grasp and minuteness of their knowledge. Great astronomers seem to know every iota of the Knowable. The Great Duke, when at the head of armies, could give all the particulars to be observed in a cavalry charge, and took care to have food ready for all his troops. Men think that greatness consists in lofty indifference to all trivial things. The Grand Llama, sitting in immovable contemplation of nothing, is a good example of what a human mind would regard as majesty; but the Gospels reveal Jesus, the manifestation of the blessed God over all as minute in His care of all. He exercises a vigilance more constant, complete, and comprehensive, every hour and every minute, over each of His people than their utmost selflove could ever attain. His tender love is more exquisite than a mother's heart can feel.[9]

Livingstone expected men from Stanley to arrive within sixty days. By August 9, eighty days had passed. He struggled to focus on anything except their delay.

On August 10, men from the coast began arriving. In all, a troop of fifty-seven porters sent by Stanley came bearing supplies and a new medicine chest to extend Livingstone's expedition and sustain his health. Among the porters came Jacob Wainwright, a young African man who was sold into slavery as a boy, but liberated by British squadron. After liberation, in India Wainwright received an education in English and Christianity. Livingstone now had an aid who could read and write.

With men to help, Livingstone focused his attention back on the Nile.

"In reference to this Nile source I have been kept in perpetual doubt and perplexity. I know too much to be positive. Great Lualaba . . . may turn out to be the Congo and Nile, a shorter river after all—the fountains flowing north and south seem in favour of its being the Nile."

He returned to his grand publicity stunt. He would soon reach the fountains and, with that discovery, return to Britain with the authority to speak for Africa. Livingstone turned his eyes to a southern journey. After two weeks of packing, weighing, and preparing, his expedition team took their first steps toward the fountains.

"No one can estimate the amount of God-pleasing good that will be done, if, by Divine favour, this awful slave-trade, into the midst of which I have come, be abolished," Livingstone wrote to Agnes in the days after the men arrived. "This will be something to have lived for, and the conviction has grown in my mind that it was for this end I have been detained so long."[10]

———

Stanley's valiant arrival in Britain in the late summer of 1872 came with a hero's welcome, securing even greater Livingstone enthusiasm. The Livingstone family thanked him. Queen Victoria praised his success.

Britain's public embarrassment brought out cynics. The Royal Geographical Society stonewalled Stanley, crying forgery over Livingstone's letter and journals. Allegations of a scandal propelled the craving for all things Stanley and Livingstone to an insatiable level. When the RGS accusations proved false, it further bolstered Livingstone fervor and gave Britain another black eye.

Adding to the Livingstone excitement, the *Herald* printed regular reports from Stanley chronicling how he had found the lost explorer, followed by a rapidly published book in 1872. *How I Found Livingstone* proved a smash success, both for Stanley and Livingstone. Stanley painted a picture in the public imagination of a gentle and stately aging man abandoned by the world he dutifully served. The British public loved it. The world devoured it.

Livingstone's second letter to America splashed across the *Herald*:

In now trying to make Eastern African slave trade better known to Americans, I indulge the hope I am aiding on, though in a small degree the good time coming yet when slavery . . . will be chased from the world. If I am permitted in any way to promote [the suppression of the East African slave trade], I shall not grudge the toil and time I have spent. It would be better to lessen this great human woe than to discover the sources of the Nile . . . May Heaven's rich blessing come down on every one, American, English, or Turk, who will help to heal this open sore of the world.[11]

Directing his campaign toward the American public, Livingstone was encouraging America to join the cause, but more importantly, he was attempting to force Britain's hand. On Livingstone's account, Britain had already suffered extreme embarrassment. An American reporter had accomplished what no British explorer could. Now Livingstone challenged Britain's global might. Britain's oversight of Africa, the efficacy of its navy, and, most important, its moral resolve, would be outshined should the United States suppress the trade while Britain ignored it.

With America emerging as a world power, she wanted to shake her own ugly history of slavery. Livingstone's letter gave America ammunition. American publishers relished it, using Livingstone's words to blame Britain for moral indifference in East Africa.

In response to Livingstone's admonition and Stanley's revelation, books and editorials from American commentators flooded stores and newsstands:

It would be unjust to charge the government of Great Britain with intentional criminality in this case [of the East African slave trade through Zanzibar]. But it stands proved, by the failure of English expeditions to find Dr. Livingstone, and by his own positive, earnest testimony, now that an American expedition has succeeded in discovering him, that it is the subjects of the British monarchy who are responsible for the existence of the slave trade of Zanzibar and all the nameless horrors of the interior resulting therefrom. The moral culpability, by reason of neglect not to put the case too strongly of the British government is therefore made manifest; and of this great national turpitude that government must stand convicted before the bar of Christendom.[12]

Livingstone's media gamble worked. England's highest offices took note of the slave trade and responded. Addressing Parliament on August 10, 1872, Queen Victoria acknowledged the East African slave trade and committed the crown to the cause: "My Government has taken steps to prepare the way for dealing more effectually with the slave trade on the East Coast of Africa," she announced.[13]

"Let this awful sacrifice of life be stopped at any cost," declared the *Quarterly Review*, speaking on behalf of the British public in October 1872.[14]

Public uproar compelled the royal crown to move swiftly, attempting to head off its growing image as the slave trade's complacent villain. To broad public support, Britain quickly appointed a special diplomatic mission to negotiate a new treaty in Zanzibar. The government revisited the recommendation of the 1871 Select Committee of the House of Commons.

Frere once again offered to spearhead diplomacy. Parliament appointed him immediately. He possessed the experience, the power, and the prominence. He also had the skill; the problem of Zanzibar slavery would not involve simple negotiations, but nuanced political maneuvering. At the helm of the new diplomatic mission bound for Zanzibar, Frere intended to render the slave trade illegal by sea. Aboard the *Enchantress*, Frere sailed into Zanzibar's harbor in January 1873.

———

"Rain, rain, rain," Livingstone wrote, "as if it never tired on this watershed."[15]

Livingstone's wet march south toward the legendary fountains brought him into a land of broad sponges and plagues of leeches. Everywhere he looked, he saw water. Rivers could only be distinguished from surrounding waters by their deep currents—in these spots the party required canoes.

Even Livingstone had never experienced such extreme weather. His party walked in neck-deep water and plunged deeper when crossing elephant footprints.

Some days the rain prevented any travel at all. Harsh conditions took their toll on the men, and by September, Livingstone's chronic intestinal bleeding had returned. Illness slowed them further.

It was desolate country. The landscape became a grassy sea with tiny islets surrounded by water. The rain wiped out anything edible, and the slave trade had ravaged the population. They saw few people. Small villages had erected fierce stockades to keep out raiders and refused to open their doors for Livingstone's caravan. They could neither find nor buy food.

The depressing human condition returned his mind to the slave trade, as he wrote to his brother John:

> If the good Lord permits me to put a stop to the enormous evils of the inland slave-trade, I shall not grudge my hunger and toils. I shall bless His name with all my heart. The Nile sources are valuable to me only as a means of enabling me to open my mouth with power among men. It is this power I hope to apply to remedy an enormous evil [in the East African slave trade]. Men may think I covet fame, but I make it a rule never to read aught written in my praise.[16]

In spite of desolate country, Livingstone sensed he neared his goal. The wide, seemingly endless swaths of water must have had a birthplace—the fountains.

"The amount of water spread out over the country constantly excites my wonder; it is prodigious."[17]

The water world gave him a glimmer of hope. Writing to James "Paraffin" Young, he anticipated the fulfillment of his duty and relit the rare hope that he might return to Britain:

> I have been led, unwittingly, into the slaving field of the Banians and Arabs in Central Africa. I have seen the woes inflicted, and I must still work and do all I can to expose and mitigate the evils. . . . During

a large part of this journey I had a strong presentiment that I should never live to finish it. It is weakened now, as I seem to see the end towards which I have been striving looming in the distance.[18]

For more than three months, Livingstone's party had crossed wet territory. As the expedition slogged ahead, Livingstone grew increasingly optimistic that he would see the fountains. He needed optimism to keep him going. Through his desperation, he struggled with whether his life amounted to anything more than failure. The horrifying slave trade in East Africa continued—he had not ended it. The source of the Nile remained unsolved—he had not discovered it. The Zambezi expedition ended in a catastrophe—he had caused it. The Livingstone name was tarnished—he had not redeemed it.

"Thanks to the Almighty Preserver of men for sparing me thus far on the journey of life," Livingstone wrote. "Can I hope for ultimate success? So many obstacles have arisen. Let not Satan prevail over me, Oh! my good Lord Jesus. . . . Nothing earthly will make me give up my work in despair."[19]

Eventually illness caught up with him. The intestinal bleeding increased, stealing his energy and sacking his confidence.

"I am pale, bloodless, and weak from bleeding profusely ever since the 31st of March last: an artery gives off a copious stream, and takes away my strength. Oh, how I long to be permitted by the Over Power to finish my work."[20]

Livingstone could no longer stand. He had to lie down. Yet he refused to give up the work. After much urging, his men finally persuaded him to be carried. He proceeded on Susi's shoulders.

Crossing a two-thousand-foot-wide river, the main stream rose to Susi's mouth and soaked Livingstone's legs, who now sat atop Susi's shoulders. When Susi sank into an elephant's footprint, two men pulled them out. Susi carried Livingstone until he ran out of breath, then passed him to another man. Every fifty yards, for the next hour and a half, they passed Livingstone from porter to porter as they slogged through the fast-moving river.

Taking nearly no rest, Livingstone grew weaker in the coming days— unable to move a hundred yards, make geographic observations, or hold a pencil. Eventually he took to riding the donkey—a gift left by Stanley. "It is not at all pleasure this exploration," Livingstone admitted as his health declined.[21]

Days later, he collapsed, falling from the donkey to the ground.

"Chumah," Livingstone muttered, "I have lost so much blood, there is not more strength in my legs: you must carry me."

Chuma and Susi stopped the caravan. They built a platform from two seven-foot branches crossed with smaller timbers and covered with grass. They fashioned a sling to attach the platform to a long pole, carried at either end by two of their strongest men. With their makeshift stretcher, the caravan continued south.

Soon, they neared the village of Chief Chitambo and dry ground. Although finally out of the water and on a plain, Livingstone's strength declined to its lowest point ever. Dehydration grew so severe he could no longer stand and, if lifted, would nearly faint. After weeks of flooded lands, he needed water but none could be found. He became too weak even to speak.

Reaching Chitambo's village on April 29, 1873, his men found a hut for Livingstone. Inside the hut, they fashioned a bed raised from the floor by sticks and grass. A box in the hut became a table for his medicine chest.

Around eleven the next evening, the man assigned the duty of Livingstone's night watch summoned Susi. Loud shouts could be heard in the distance as Susi made his way to Livingstone's hut.

"Are our men making that noise?" Livingstone asked when Susi arrived.

"No," Susi replied. "I can hear from the cries that the people are scaring away a buffalo from their dura fields."

"Is this the Luapula?" Livingstone asked slowly, minutes later.

After Susi explained they had stayed in Chitambo's village, Livingstone went silent again.

"How many days is it to the Luapula?" Livingstone asked in Swahili.

"I think it is three days, master."

An expression of great pain came over Livingstone's face.

"Oh dear, dear!" he exclaimed. Then he fell back to sleep.[22]

———

Public outrage in Britain surged against the slave trade as it waited for word from Frere in Zanzibar. Her Majesty's administration had high hopes for the Frere mission and believed that any day they would learn of his success.

While waiting for news of the sultan's coalescence to the new treaty led by Queen Victoria's biannual address to Parliament in the spring of 1873, Britain strengthened her antislavery tone to show the public she had taken action:

> You were informed, when I last addressed you, that steps had been taken to prepare the way for dealing more effectually with the slave trade on the east coast of Africa. I have now despatched [sic] an envoy to Zanzibar, furnished with such instructions as appear to me best adapted for the attainment of the object in view. He has recently reached the place of his destination, and has entered into communication with the Sultan.[23]

Frere had nondiplomatic tasks in Zanzibar beyond treaty negotiations—specifically, to assist Livingstone. Public concern for Livingstone's safety was coupled with the outcry against the slave trade. Frere could address both. Since Stanley had returned with Livingstone's letters, but not the explorer himself, he gave a boost to concern for Livingstone's livelihood. Britain quickly scrambled together two new relief parties to assist the impoverished explorer in finishing his mission, as well as to show the world that Britain had the capability of reaching him.

The first relief party, arranged by the Royal Geographical Society, launched an expedition from Africa's east coast. Headed for Lake Tanganyika under the command of Lieutenant Cameron, the relief expedition had arrived in Zanzibar on the *Enchantress* in the company of Frere. Frere set them off under his diplomatic instructions.

James "Paraffin" Young, Livingstone's friend and financier of half of the Nile expedition, funded a second relief party. Suspecting Livingstone had continued north, the team started from Africa's west coast, steaming up the Congo River toward Manyuema and Ujiji.

Frere's RGS-sponsored relief party set off into Africa carrying a letter from H. C. Rawlinson, who had succeeded Murchison as the new president of the RGS:

DEAR DR. LIVINGSTONE,

You will no doubt have heard of Sir Bartle Frere's deputation to Zanzibar long before you receive this, and you will have learnt with heartfelt satisfaction that there is now a definite prospect of the infamous East African slave-trade being suppressed. For this great end, if it be achieved, we shall be mainly indebted to your recent letters, which have had a powerful effect on the public mind in England, and have thus stimulated the action of the Government. . . .

I remain, yours very truly, H. C. RAWLINSON.[24]

On Zanzibar, Frere's assignment proved unexpectedly difficult. Sultan Barghash firmly opposed abolition and was not above enlisting the support of other global powers, notably France and the United States, should diplomacy turn into British bullying. In spite of Frere's diplomatic prowess, the sultan emphatically refused a new treaty. Negotiations dragged on for months before finally collapsing.

Three months after the queen had spoken so determinedly about abolition in East Africa, Frere declared his mission to Zanzibar a failure.

He sailed on for Madagascar leaving a political wreck in the hands of John Kirk, now British consul at Zanzibar.

Since the Zambezi expedition, Kirk had remained personally interested in abolishing the East African slave trade. In Livingstone's company, he had witnessed the horrors of the Shiré and Nyassa regions. Livingstone had persistently encouraged him to continue the fight. Before Frere's departure, Kirk had remained a consular subordinate. Now he could take the reins.

Kirk, commanding seven years of firsthand knowledge about Zanzibar's slave trade, understood the sensitivities of Zanzibari politics. He brokered orders from the foreign office, allowing him to give the sultan an ultimatum: consent immediately to the terms of the slave-trade-suppressing treaty, or face a blockade by British naval forces. With its entire economy built on facilitating trade between Africa, Asia, and Arabia, a blockade of Zanzibar would instantly crush the island nation.

Kirk knew the sultan could not abolish slavery unless his council members agreed. The sultan relied on his council to oppose the slave trade so that he could shelter himself under the weight of their decision. If the sultan unilaterally abolished slavery without the consent of the council, the council would condemn him. That could lead to assassination.

Kirk accordingly turned his attention to the council, informing them of the disastrous consequences Zanzibar would face should they reject the treaty. Should they choose the blockade, he promised to make their economically damaging verdict "a matter of public notoriety."[25]

With no practical option but to accept the slavery-suppressing treaty, Zanzibar prepared to relent. For the first time, it appeared Livingstone's dream of abolition might be realized.

———

Susi awoke at four in the morning to the panicked plea of the porter charged with watching over Livingstone.

"I am afraid," the night watchman said. "I don't know if he is alive."

Scrambling out of bed, Susi woke other members of the team on the dark morning of May first. Susi and his five teammates scurried to Livingstone's hut. Their leader, no matter how feeble and exhausted, always recovered, but something in the aid's alarming bid felt different.

Entering the door to Livingstone's hut, they immediately drew back. His bed lay empty. A candle, stuck in its own wax to the top of a box, shed enough light for them to see Livingstone's outline kneeling at the side of his bed. He appeared to be in prayer, as if he had nodded off in conversation with God. His body stretched forward, his head buried in his hands upon the pillow.

"When I lay down he was just as he is now," the aid said, "and it is because I find that he does not move that I fear he is dead."

For a minute, Susi and his companions watched their leader from the doorway. Livingstone did not stir. He showed no signs of breathing. Advancing slowly, one of the men placed a hand upon Livingstone's cheek. His skin felt cold and lifeless. Livingstone was dead.

The men lay his body on the bed and carefully covered him. Gathering the team in the damp night, they had matters of leadership succession to resolve immediately. Livingstone's expedition had reached its deepest point in Africa and its farthest distance from home. Would they return to Zanzibar? What would they do with the body? The sun would rise soon, and a dead body would arouse horrified superstition—belief in the souls seeking vengeance beyond the grave, returning to haunt and destroy.

"What should be done?" Susi and Chuma asked.

"You are old men in travelling and in hardships," responded the porters. "You must act as our chiefs, and we will promise to obey whatever you order us to do."[26]

Under Susi and Chuma's authority, they resolved to return the explorer's body to his homeland. There he could rest with his family, and the British could receive their hero's body. Yet Chuma and Susi knew Livingstone's heart did not belong in England. It belonged in Africa.

They asked Chief Chitambo for permission to build a temporary settlement away from his village, ostensibly to have their own camp. All agreed not to disclose the plan to the chief.

The morning after Livingstone's death, they began clearing ground and building several huts. For preparing the body, they constructed a separate hut. Round and with an open roof, the hut would be tall enough not to see in and strong enough to prevent any beast from breaking through. They set Livingstone's remains inside the new structure. Finally, they erected a stockade around the complex to keep out opportunistic animals.

Sent to the village to buy food, two of Livingstone's men unintentionally divulged the secret death. When Chitambo heard, he set off for the new settlement immediately.

"Why did you not tell me the truth?" Chitambo confronted Chuma. "I know that your master died last night. You were afraid to let me know, but do not fear any longer . . . I know that you have no bad motives in coming to our land, and death often happens to travelers in their journeys."[27]

Chuma told him of the plan to prepare the body and take it to the coast. It would be far better to bury it here, Chitambo replied, for you undertake an impossible task. Chitambo agreed to perform a customary mourning honor for Livingstone.

Leading his people, Chitambo returned to the settlement clad in red cloth. The people carried bows, wailing loudly as they marched. Drummers joined the lamentation while Livingstone's porters fired volley after volley of gunshots into the air.

After the ceremony, Susi and Chuma carefully made an incision into Livingstone's frame of skin and bones. They removed his internal organs and discovered a blood clot in his stomach the size of a fist. To preserve his corpse, they filled his body with salt.

His heart they placed in a tin flour box, which they reverently buried four feet deep beneath a beautiful Mvula tree. Jacob Wainwright read Scripture, then carved Livingstone's name into the tree.

"This is the sort of grave I should prefer: to be in the still, still forest, and no hand ever disturb my bones," Livingstone had written five years before. Echoing his wish, Livingstone's heart came to rest in Africa.

The porters moved his body to the recently erected, open-air structure. For the next two weeks, they repositioned him every day for exposure to the sun. Once dried, they wrapped Livingstone's body in calico cloth and placed it in a cylinder of tree bark. This they placed in a piece of sailcloth, which they sewed shut and lashed to a pole.

In early June, Livingstone's men lifted his bundled body and began the long march toward Zanzibar.

14 ✦ REDEMPTION

I am a missionary, heart and soul. God had an only Son, and He was a missionary and a physician. A poor, poor imitation I am or wish to be. In this service I hope to live, in it I wish to die.

—David Livingstone

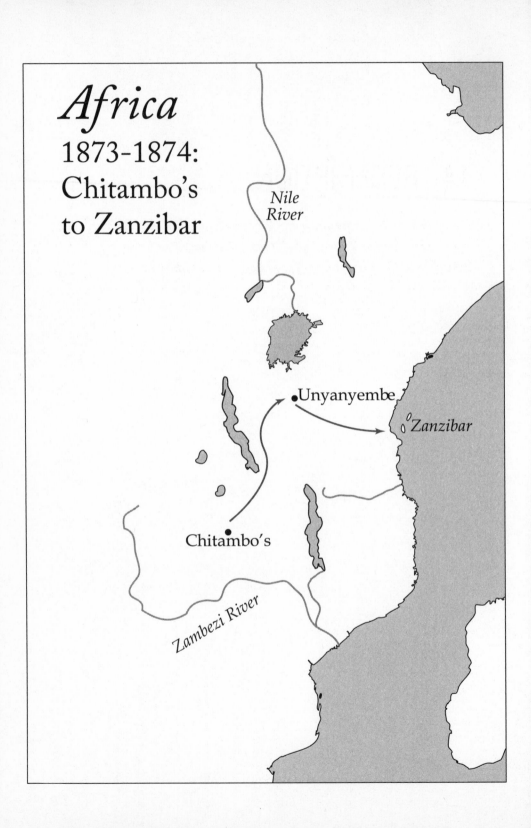

Africa
1873-1874:
Chitambo's
to Zanzibar

*Nile
River*

Unyanyembe

Zanzibar

Chitambo's

Zambezi River

Zanzibar's customhouse posted notice:

To allow our subjects who may see this and also to others, may God
save you, know that we have prohibited the transport of slaves by
sea in all our harbours and have closed the markets which are for sale
of slaves through all our dominions. Whosoever therefore shall ship a
raw slave after this date will render himself liable to punishment and
this he will bring upon himself. Be this known.[1]

Barely one month after Livingstone's death, the great Zanzibar slave
market closed forever. The notice of June 5, 1873, shut down more than
a market, it formally and legally ended the slave trade. The sultan's council had assented to Kirk and, protecting their power, chose to end the
slave trade rather than face the British naval blockade. The sultan signed
Britain's treaty.

Queen Victoria announced the success to Parliament: "Treaties have
been concluded with the Sultan of Zanzibar . . . which provide means
for the more effectual repression of the slave trade on the east coast of
Africa."[2]

———

Livingstone's body traveled from Chitambo's village toward the coast through a land now legally free of slavery. With the treaty so recently passed, neither the men nor the region's slavers were yet aware of it.

For five months, Livingstone's weary aids pushed north through the treacherous wasteland. The procession secretly concealed the contents of their slung cloth as they passed the many villages. They survived an attack by a lion, which took the life of the donkey that carried Livingstone in his last miles. They defused a hunting accident where a misfire injured a young villager. They had done the impossible.

As they closed in on Unyanyembe, the porters heard news of a relief party led by two Englishmen. Chuma ran ahead to meet them. On October 20, he found Lieutenant Cameron in Unyanyembe. Cameron's relief expedition had run very short on supplies, but Cameron remained willing to relieve Chuma and Susi's efforts.

When the procession reached Unyanyembe, Cameron voiced his concerns about carrying the corpse. They debated whether Livingstone should be buried with his wife along the Zambezi or returned to Britain. He had come so far, all felt it worth the risk of continuing.

Four months later, the procession reached the Indian Ocean. From there a British cruiser would take Livingstone's body to Zanzibar. The long, arduous nine-month journey had reached its end.

———

To investigate the remaining vestiges of the slave trade on the mainland, Kirk sent his deputy to gather a firsthand account and establish a network of secret agents. Conditions had grown worse than he expected.

"'[P]laces of skulls' mark the various roads upon which the traffic continues to flourish," Kirk's deputy reported from mainland Africa, "and skeletons lie thick scattered on the beach . . ."[3]

One gang of lads and women, chained together with iron neck-rings, was in a horrible state, their lower extremities coated with dry mud and their own excrement and torn with thorns, their bodies were mere frameworks, and their skeleton limbs slightly stretched over with wrinkled parchment like skin. One wretched women had been flung against a tree for slipping her rope, and came screaming up to us for protection, with one eye half out and the side of her face and bosom streaming with blood.[4]

An old man living along the slave trade route, and well acquainted with its history, recounted how "he had never seen anything so shameful, it was only killing men not trading."[5]

Clearly, the fight for the end of the slave trade had not truly ended. While Kirk's treaty significantly thwarted the East African slave trade by prohibiting the shipment of slaves over a seaboard of nearly a thousand miles, it only prohibited it by sea. The pact left an ambiguity: a potential overland route through the sultan's territories along the East African seaboard. Slave traders had never attempted the treacherous overland route. Shipping slaves by sea from the closest coast to Zanzibar offered both convenience and economy. The overland route had always been considered far too dangerous.

But desperate to resume their trade, the slavers conspired to circumvent the treaty by smuggling humans overland. Their coastal march became the notorious Kisiju Road. Winding from Kilwa north to Lamu, the Kisiju Road ended at a checkpoint beyond the sultan's territory.[6] From there, dhows would ship slaves by sea to the Arabian Peninsula.

The arduous journey and significantly longer route hindered less determined slave traders. Still, reports estimated that the slave trade forced ten thousand to twelve thousand victims along the route annually, with numbers steadily rising as the route became more established. For the slave traders who endured the Kisiju Road, the horrific overland conditions worsened their brutality on an already appalling passage. Unimaginably, the horrors of the East African slave trade intensified.

The Kisiju Road deliberately avoided large towns and the watchful eyes of the sultan's forts. It followed back-road trails, crossing remote creeks and diverting its course through mangroves—anything to evade view. The slave traders carefully prepared the route, establishing regular watering holes equipped with cooking trenches and stocking depots with spare gang irons. In the villages they passed through, they constructed slave stockades, and at river crossings they built ferries to shuttle their haul.

Determined to end the slave trade over land as well, Kirk marshaled the British government. As he wrote the Foreign Office on March 9, 1877:

> It must be borne in mind that we are engaged in a campaign with an enemy who has little to lose and everything to gain in his contest with us; who is therefore ever on alert to take advantage of our mistake; whose information is far superior to our own; and who by the very necessities of the case, must exercise ceaseless craft, vigilance, and activity.[7]

Kirk's resolve met with little reciprocity in London. He found waning government support in the wake of its successful treaty. Britain had satisfied the public outcry for action against the slave trade, and its champions had moved on to other matters. The new foreign secretary, Lord Derby, "didn't care 'a farthing about the suppression of the slave trade from conviction.' "[8] He would only attend to it if the public insisted on carrying it out.

In the eyes of the British public, far removed from the Kisiju Road, the fight against the slave trade had been won. They had achieved victory for Livingstone. They imagined him alive in the remote jungle, soon to return home to celebrate his well-earned victory. Kirk and the abolitionists hoped that his return would reignite public sentiment to quash the remaining remnants of the slave trade.

———

"Death of Dr. Livingstone."

These four bold words stole the lead headline of the *Times* on January 27, 1874. This time, it was true.

England received news from Zanzibar that her beloved Livingstone was confirmed dead; his corpse had irrefutably arrived on the African coast. His death resulted in "an almost unprecedented outpouring of national mourning."

"The nation's most saintly hero had returned after his weary pilgrimage, and the cause for which he had given his life, the fight against slavery, had been sanctified by his death."[9]

Cold and damp, April 15 befit a day of national mourning in London. The casket had arrived by boat from Africa only two days earlier, for immediate delivery to Britain's Royal Geographical Society. Jacob Wainwright had accompanied the casket from Africa. Crowds gathered at the docks to meet the steamer while a band played Handel's "Dead March" from *Saul*. A special train brought the casket to London for delivery to the headquarters of the Royal Geographical Society. It waited at the society's headquarters for official identification.

Colleagues arrived for the somber but necessary task. The body, barely recognizable from its tree-sap embalmment, had traveled nine long months under the blazing equatorial sun from Central Africa to the coast. The shriveled, sunbaked corpse demanded attention to detail. Friends and doctors examined him. Only those who knew him well could make out his features—but not easily. His left arm, shattered many years ago in the powerful jaws of a lion, confirmed his identity: it was indeed the body of David Livingstone.

Three days later, the funeral procession assembled outside the Royal Geographical Society. A chaotic mass of carriages swelled, accompanied by horse artillery and a military band. Leading the march, empty carriages sent by both Queen Victoria and the Prince of Wales commanded the long convoy.

Rain and cold posed no barrier to his devotees. The April 18 funeral, paid for by the British government, drew massive crowds. Shoulder to shoulder, throngs of admirers poured into the streets on a gloomy London day to bid farewell to the explorer and catch a glimpse of their hero's casket.

As the Queen's carriage advanced to begin the formal procession to Westminster Abbey, it was clear this would be no ordinary funeral. All of England seemed to mourn him.

Missionaries passionately claimed him. But was he a missionary? Despite unapologetically resigning his celebrated missionary post, Livingstone was imagined by the world as proselytizing Africans by the thousands. Yet, his converts to Christianity numbered only one—and even this singular believer had relapsed into animism. No missionary had ever received such a funeral.

Science unequivocally claimed him. But was he a scientist? The world watched him chase the source of the Nile with relentless obsession; a discovery that would have made him the greatest explorer of his time. He never found it. No unsuccessful explorer had ever received such honors.

At Westminster Abbey, Henry Morton Stanley, E. D. Young, John Kirk, and Jacob Wainwright met the procession. The men, honored as Livingstone's pallbearers, carried his coffin from carriage to cathedral. In the crowded abbey, they laid Livingstone to rest in a special place in the nave.

With standing room only, crowds crammed into the halls of Westminster Abbey. The Queen sent a wreath; high society turned out in droves. A dry eye could not be found. When the ceremony began, Livingstone's friends had to physically restrain Jacob Wainwright from throwing himself into the grave.

In the abbey, the inscription on his stone would read:

BROUGHT BY FAITHFUL HANDS OVER LAND AND SEA HERE REST
DAVID LIVINGSTONE, MISSIONARY, TRAVELLER, PHILANTHROPIST,
BORN MARCH 19. 1813, AT BLANTYRE, LANKARKSHIRÉ.
DIED MAY 1. 1873, AT CHITAMBO'S VILLAGE, ULALA.

FOR 30 YEARS HIS LIFE WAS SPENT IN AN UNWEARIED EFFORT TO EVANGELIZE THE NATIVE RACES, TO EXPLORE THE UNDISCOVERED SECRETS, TO ABOLISH THE DESOLATING SLAVE TRADE, OF CENTRAL AFRICA, WHERE WITH HIS LAST WORDS, HE WROTE, "ALL I CAN ADD IN MY SOLITUDE, IS, MAY HEAVEN'S RICH BLESSINGS COME DOWN ON EVERY ONE, AMERICAN, ENGLISH, OR TURK, WHO WILL HELP TO HEAL THIS OPEN SORE OF THE WORLD."

On its side, etched in Latin, the gravestone offered a quote from the Roman poet, Lucan: "So great is my love of truth that there is nothing I would rather know than the sources of the river which lay hid for so many centuries."

Punch, one of London's typical humorist magazines, published a sober, but fitting, tribute to Britain's hero. (Please see following page.)

Droop half mast colors bow bareheaded crowds
As this plain coffin o er the side is slung
To pass by woods of masts and ratlined shrouds
As erst by Afric's trunks liana hung

Tis the last mile of many thousands trod
With failing strength but never failing will
By the worn frame now at its rest with God
That never rested from its fight with ill

Or if the ache of travel and of toil
Would sometimes wring a short sharp cry of pain
From agony of fever blain and boil
Twas but to crush it down and on again

He knew not that the trumpet he had blown
Out of the darkness of that dismal land
Had reached and roused an army of its own
To strike the chains from the slave's fettered hand

Now we believe he knows sees all is well
How God had stayed his will and shaped his way
To bring the light to those that darkling dwell
With gains that life's devotion well repay

Open the abbey doors and let him in
To sleep with king and statesman chief and sage
The missionary come of weaver kin
But great by work that brooks no lower wage

He needs no epitaph to guard a name
Which men shall prize while worthy work is known
He lived and died for good be that his fame
Let marble crumble this is Living stone[10]

15 ❧ TRIUMPH

All will come right at last.
                    —DAVID LIVINGSTONE

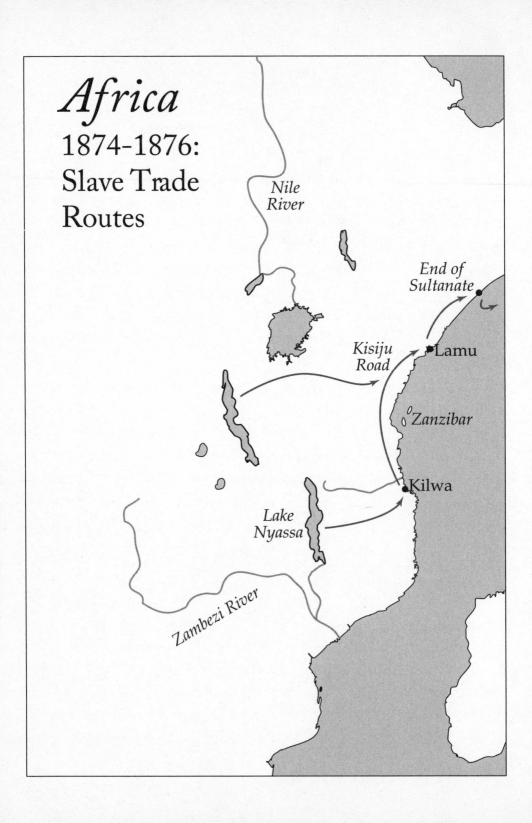

Africa
1874–1876:
Slave Trade
Routes

Nile
River

End of
Sultanate

Kisiju
Road

Lamu

Zanzibar

Kilwa

Lake
Nyassa

Zambezi River

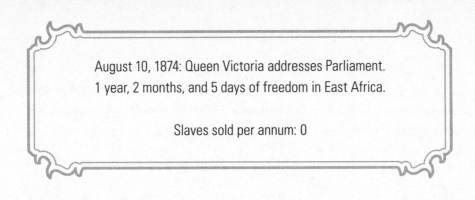

The treaty signed by the sultan of Zanzibar, Queen Victoria told Parliament in August 1874, "having for its object the suppression of the East African slave trade, has been faithfully observed, and has already done much to put an end to that traffic as carried on by sea. [Our efforts] will not be relaxed until complete success has been obtained."[1]

Although Sultan Barghash had avoided near-certain death by deflecting blame upon his council, the Zanzibari slavers knew British pressure held ultimate responsibility for the economic loss to the island. Championing the treaty, Kirk stood square in their crosshairs. Sultan Barghash laughed at Kirk and told him: "If anyone is to be killed you are the one!"[2]

Despite the risks, and resistance from the Foreign Office, Kirk continued his fight. Between the successful negotiation of the over-sea treaty and the arrival of Livingstone's body in London, Kirk had been hard at work. He visited slave trade sites along the Indian Ocean as far north as the Somali coast and made a trip to England—his first leave from Zanzibar in seven years.

Although Lord Derby had remained ambivalent toward the slave trade without public pressure, the broad sentiment surrounding Livingstone's death now captured him. Britain now wanted the slave trade to end. Antislavery organizations rallied, Jacob Wainwright toured the country telling of Livingstone and the slave trade, and the public took a keen interest in Africa. All this came in the name of Livingstone. Derby could benefit politically from association with Livingstone's cause. He conceded, authorizing Kirk to pursue the slave trade over land as he deemed fit.

With permission granted and a blank slate, Kirk started with diplomacy. He had twin goals: curry the sultan's favor and build Zanzibar's dependence on Britain. With Kirk's prompting, the Foreign Office invited Barghash on a state visit to England, where they would flatter and honor him on the world stage as a virtuous opponent of the slave trade. Barghash had an unquenchable thirst for power; the visit and attention were meant to inspire him to bend toward justice if it increased his international respect.

Britain welcomed the sultan with open arms. Politicians entertained him. Clergy greeted him. Crowds followed him, and the *Times* covered his trip on a near-daily basis. Organizations showered him with honors and ovations. The Anti-Slavery Society even expressed their gratitude to him for supporting the treaty. The sultan responded as though he saw not only the advantage, but also the merit in pursuing justice. Sultan Barghesh appeared to be a new champion for abolition:

> To the members of the British and Foreign Anti-Slavery Society . . . we shall always endeavor, God willing, to fulfill our treaty arrangements with Great Britain. Nevertheless, as you must be aware, a traffic of very long standing, having ramifications through a vast extent of country, cannot be eradicated at once. . . . Still we are doing our best, and we are intent on causing our people to carry out our views . . .[3]

When the sultan finally departed London, he left with the reputation of a reformer—a partner with Britain for the full suppression of the slave trade. He now publicly agreed to work toward such ends. The thrill of contemporary London convinced him of the necessity of abolition to promote modern industry and global influence in his territory; the honors tempted him with the prospect of leaving his mark in history as a great eradicator of slavery.

For Kirk, the sultan's visit was a triumph. He accompanied the sultan everywhere, and the stay ended successfully. But though the sultan spoke well of his intentions in public, Kirk knew he might act differently in private, especially back in the climate of Zanzibar. While he had the sultan's goodwill, Kirk still needed a bargaining chip. An opportunity quickly presented itself.

Soon after the sultan departed England, Egyptian forces invaded his northern territories along the Somali coast. Egypt was no mere nuisance, but a serious threat. She had ambitions to gain territory and power in the Arab world. The east coast of Africa, even Zanzibar itself, made an attractive acquisition.

Kirk jumped aboard a British cruiser and sailed north to Egyptian-occupied territory. As Kirk anchored, Egyptian forces lined the beach. He set ashore, and the Egyptian troops stopped him at gunpoint. Not to be defied, Kirk threatened to begin bombarding the occupied town at two o'clock in the afternoon. At half past one, the Egyptian forces yielded.

In town, Kirk gathered information from his informants on Egypt's interests. Egypt encouraged the slave trade. The land along Africa's east coast strategically aided Egypt's slaving opportunities. With this land, Egypt could continue drawing on the supply of slaves from Africa's interior.

Kirk now had leverage with the sultan. The Egyptian incursion prevented the sultan's public commitment to ending the slave trade overland in his territories, but if the sultan's promises to end slavery held true, then British diplomacy could flex its muscles in his support. If not, then Britain could withdraw its protection and the sultan's meager forces would face an Egyptian onslaught.

Britain put on a show of force for the sultan, pressuring for the withdrawal of Egyptian troops. The sultan peacefully regained his territory. He could not defend his sultanate without British protection, but protection would come at a price.

Sultan Barghash issued a proclamation in the summer of 1876 out-lawing the traffic of slaves by land and giving Kirk the authority to pursue offending caravans. Ennobled with this new power, Kirk began an unforgiving siege on the slave trade. He sent fleets of ships out to capture more dhows and took troops to the mainland to patrol the Kisiju Road.

Kirk's method played to a weakness of the slave traders: shame. With an Arab-influenced culture founded upon honor, he turned the trade into a venture too risky for respectable citizens. Kirk's efforts began influencing the culture to view slave trading as a route to dishonor.

Kirk would jail any slave trader, no matter his social status. Once capturing six slave owners and a dhow captain, Kirk had them all flogged in public before the sultan's palace. He would put anyone, even the most influential citizens of Zanzibar, in irons and imprison them.

On mainland Africa, Kirk's troops captured a coffle of slaves and their owners. After interrogation, the slave owners named their superior: Saeed Bin Abdulla. Abdulla held powerful rank in Zanzibari society. As a relative of the sultan, a member of his council, and a former governor of Kilwa, Abdulla believed himself to be above the law. He controlled a key region of the sultan's territories, land strategic to routes north for the slave trade.

Abdulla directly supported the purchase of slaves from Lake Nyassa, and that discovery gave Kirk momentum. Determined to hold the most high profile Zanzibar families accountable to the treaty, Kirk now had the most prominent Zanzibari aristocrat in his grasp. Armed with this intelligence, Kirk planned to take extraordinary measures to make an example of Abdulla. The sultan's public durbara, a formal council meeting, took place in mid-February. Abdulla would be there, seated next to the sultan.

On the day of the public durbara, Kirk entered the palace forum without warning. Behind Kirk followed the men captured on the mainland—Abdulla's slave agents and slaves.

In open court, in front of the sultan, the council, and the public,

Kirk called a witness: an old slave taken from Abdulla's chain gang. Kirk demanded this man be allowed to speak. The man shared his story of Abdulla's inhumanity. After the testimony, Kirk confronted Abdulla about his involvements in the slave trade. Abdulla could give no answer.

Kirk had Abdulla arrested immediately, placing him in the same slave irons Abdulla used on his captives. Then Kirk moved Abdulla to the common prison where he shared company with the slave agents who had driven his captives up Kisiju Road—slave agents who were once Abdulla's slaves themselves.

Although Abdulla's agents drove the slave gangs, they only followed commands at the threat of flogging or death for disobedience. To humiliate Abdulla further, Kirk asked the sultan to release Abdulla's slaves. The sultan obliged. All Zanzibar, and the slave trade, took notice.

Abdulla's demise was the deathblow to the East African slave trade. The Kisiju Road, which took thousands of lives a year, dwindled to a close. Kirk and his men could now deal with the trade in small, localized areas.

By August 1877, Kirk readied a declaration he had wanted to write for more than a decade, a declaration Livingstone would have been proud to hear: ". . . the foreign slave trade from Zanzibar territory has been for practical purposes totally abolished."[4]

EPILOGUE

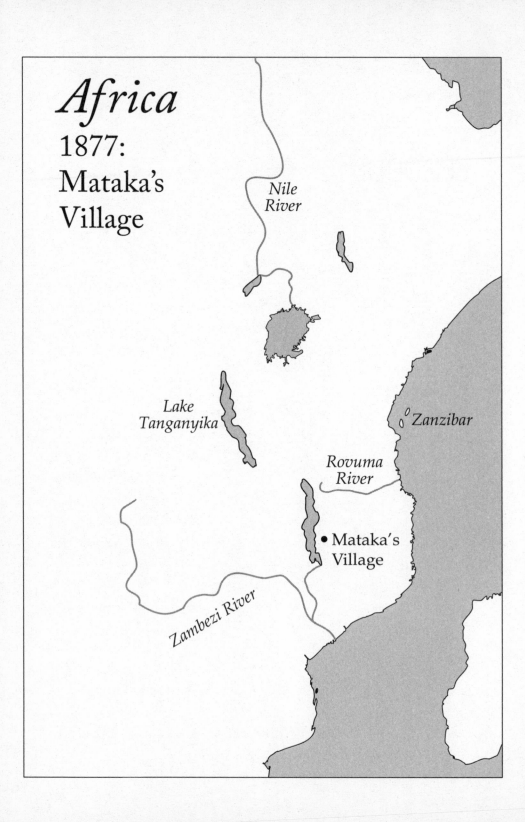

Africa
1877:
Mataka's
Village

Nile
River

Lake
Tanganyika

Zanzibar

Rovuma
River

• Mataka's
Village

Zambezi River

n August of Kirk's 1877 declaration, an African messenger arrived at the door of the small, square house where Chauncy Maples stayed.

Twenty-five-year-old Chauncy Maples had traveled to the African interior from Britain as a new representative of the Universities' Mission to Central Africa. He came to establish villages, clinics, and schools for freed slaves—in a land now free of slavery. Maples had only arrived on the mainland via Zanzibar within the past year. He had traced the Rovuma River to the UMCA's recently reestablished post near Lake Nyassa, where he found himself in a town known as Mataka's Village.

The messenger told Maples of a village elder who insisted on seeing him. The elder had met a white man in "old days"—an Englishman—and, if at all alike, wanted to make Maples's acquaintance.

Maples stepped out of the small house and onto the sunbaked, reddish clay streets. He made his way to the house of the old man, passing through the town's sprawling gardens and beds of English peas.

Here, in Mataka's Village in 1866, Livingstone had spent a fortnight on his last journey. Livingstone died perhaps believing he had failed in every aspect. Yet, in the few short years after his death, everything Livingstone had worked for had come to fruition. Maples, a young English missionary building a colony in Central Africa to support freed slaves, embodied all Livingstone's dreams.

At the door to the house, the old man called Maples inside and stepped forward to welcome him. In dignified speech, he told of the white man who had visited Mataka's Village ten years before:

> A white man who treated black men as his brothers, and whose memory would be cherished all along the Rovuma Valley after we were all dead and gone. A short man with a bushy moustache, and a keen piercing eye, whose words were always gentle, and whose manners were always kind, whom as a leader it was a privilege to follow, and who knew the way to the hearts of all men.

Then the old man pointed to a coat hanging behind him. Ragged and deteriorating, the trappings of English tailoring were recognizable to Maples.

The man treasured the coat, having kept it for the past decade in memory of the giver. He had parted with it for no one, for no offer.

The old man removed the coat from the wall and carefully cradled it.

Extending his arms, he presented Livingstone's coat to Maples. "As one of Livingstone's brothers," he said.[1]

AFTERWORD

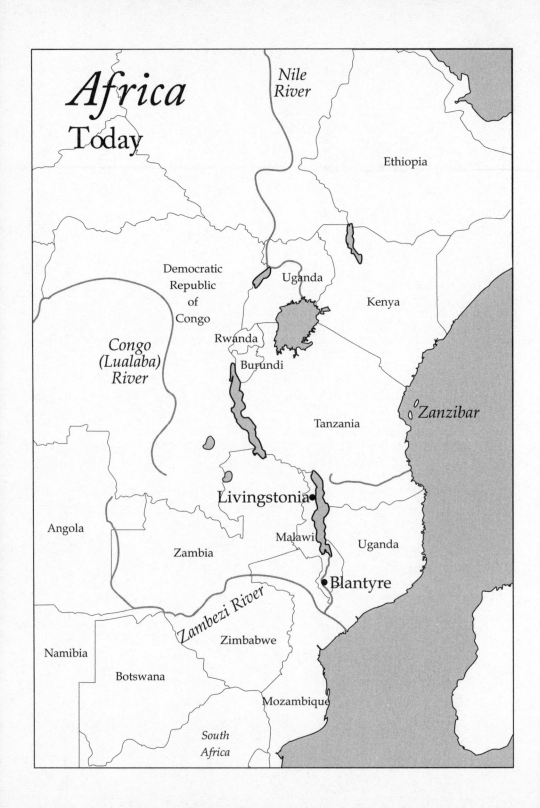

Africa
Today

Nile
River

Ethiopia

Democratic
Republic
of
Congo

Uganda

Kenya

Congo
(Lualaba)
River

Rwanda

Burundi

Tanzania

Zanzibar

Livingstonia

Angola

Malawi

Uganda

Zambia

Namibia

Zambezi River

Zimbabwe

Botswana

Blantyre

Mozambique

South
Africa

T he future will justify my words and hopes," Livingstone remarked in 1864, after the failed Zambezi expedition.[1] While likely more of a vindictive pronouncement than a well-reasoned prophecy, the future would, indeed, support many of Livingstone's dreams and visions:

HENRY MORTON STANLEY

Stanley returned to Africa in 1874 to finish Livingstone's work by tracing the Lualaba north. He proved that the Lualaba eventually became the Congo River, thus confirming Livingstone's fear.

After exploring the Congo region, Stanley tried to find a nation willing to colonize the Congo. He found a willing taker in King Leopold II of Belgium, who wanted to expand his empire. The result eventually became the Belgian Congo.

On the same expedition, Stanley circumnavigated Lake Victoria and came into agreement with Speke that the Nile began there. On the northern side of Lake Victoria, the King of Buganda asked Stanley to send missionaries to help stave off Egyptian expansion into the kingdom. Stanley made a public appeal in 1875 on the king's behalf. Anglican and Catholic missionary orders responded. The "Scramble for

Africa" had also begun and, with rival European nations vying for territory, competition for Uganda grew fierce. Britain annexed Uganda in 1894 to safeguard its claim.

Death and destruction marked Stanley's expeditions, particularly his forays into the Congo and the relief team organized to rescue Emin Pasha, governor of Equitoria in southern Sudan. His expeditions sustained significant loss of life—and many allegations point to Stanley's direct involvement in the violence. Nonetheless, he is credited with several discoveries, including the Rwenzori Mountains (Ptolemy's "Mountains of the Moon") and Lake Edward.

Stanley settled in Britain, married, and was elected to the House of Commons in 1895. He was knighted in 1899 and passed away in 1904 at age sixty-three. He expected to be buried at Westminster Abbey next to Livingstone, but the dean of the church denied his body, ostensibly for violence committed on his expeditions.

LIVINGSTONE'S COMPANIONS

CHUMA traveled to Britain after Livingstone's funeral, then returned to Africa to work for the Universities' Mission to Central Africa. He was baptized in Livingstone's presence in 1865 and, by the time he died in 1882, had spent half his life on expeditions.

SUSI also traveled to Britain after Livingstone's funeral, then returned to Africa to work for the Universities' Mission to Central Africa as a caravan leader. He joined Stanley on expeditions to the Congo, helping cofound a station that would become Kinshasa. Born a Muslim, Susi converted to Christianity in 1886. He died in 1891.

JACOB WAINWRIGHT's command of the English language opened doors for him to work as the official scribe for the court of Kabaka Mutesa, the king of Uganda. He later dedicated his life to spreading Christianity in Uganda, working for the Church Missionary Society of Uganda until his death in 1892.

THE SOURCE OF THE NILE

The hotly debated geographic question remains, ultimately, unanswered to this day. Modern expeditions continue to search and extend the length of the Nile. To a certain degree, everyone in the debate answered the question correctly. In 1858, Speke claimed Lake Victoria in modern-day Uganda as the source of the Nile. Indeed, Lake Victoria is conventionally considered the point at which the Nile becomes a definable river. Explorers, however, look beyond Lake Victoria to the Nile's true headwaters. Geographers have located springs in the mountains of Burundi, between lakes Tanganyika and Victoria. Livingstone was perhaps correct in his search for the "fountains," but he explored too far south.

AFRICAN RIVERS

Livingstone imagined rivers as God's highway for Christianity. The Shiré proved navigable with a boat disassembled and carried as Livingstone had envisioned. E. D. Young did just that on his Livingstone Search and Relief Expedition. To this day, the Zambezi River remains unnavigable beyond the Kebrabasa Rapids. Navigation up to Victoria Falls remains a dream, with active proposals to construct a channel around the rapids.

THE UNIVERSITIES' MISSION TO CENTRAL AFRICA

After Bishop Mackenzie's death, his successor, Bishop Tozer, retracted the Shiré highlands mission and relocated the project to Zanzibar. The Universities' Mission had significant success there. A mere six months after closing the great Zanzibar slave market, it was razed and, on Christmas Day 1873, the foundation stone for Christ Church was laid on its former grounds. The cross in the church is made from the Mvula tree under which Livingstone's heart was buried.

In 1874, after Livingstone's death, the next bishop directed the Universities' Mission to reestablish a presence at Lake Nyassa. Chauncy Maples eventually became the Bishop of Nyassa. Maples tragically drowned in a storm on Lake Nyassa while performing his duties. In his honor, the MV *Chauncy Maples* was launched on Lake Nyassa in 1901, the first steamship on the lake. The ship served as a hospital and missionary school, as well as an emergency refuge from the slave trade. The MV *Chauncy Maples* was sailed up the Zambezi to the Shiré, then disassembled and carried overland. It accomplished what Livingstone dreamed for the *Lady Nyassa*.

The ship remains on Lake Malawi (Nyassa) today, the oldest ship afloat in Africa.

COLONIZATION OF AFRICA

Livingstone long envisioned a British colony in the African interior, particularly near Lake Nyassa. Despite the British government's insistence that it would not happen, his dream came true in the decade following his death.

Established in 1877, the Livingstonia Central Africa Company, eventually renamed the African Lakes Company, set up trading outposts on the shores of Nyassa and in the Shiré Valley. Blantyre, the chief town of Nyasaland, earned its name from Livingstone's hometown, Blantyre, Scotland, and on the west shore of Lake Nyassa, Livingstonia was named in his honor. Nyasaland was declared a British protectorate in 1891.

A CHRISTIAN CONTINENT

Livingstone envisioned a Christian Africa and intended to spread the gospel through the continent with his work. Ultimately this vision also succeeded. As of 2012, a Pew Foundation study reported 63 percent of Sub-Saharan Africa as identifiably Christian, with the highest population percentages in Congo, Uganda, Malawi, Tanzania, and Kenya—all territories indirectly influenced by Livingstone or in which he traveled.

THE SLAVE TRADE

Kirk effectively quashed the East African slave trade through successive restrictions, but all-out abolition was not yet the law of Zanzibar in 1877. Although the trade ceased, Zanzibar's citizens could still own slaves. But Britain would finish the task. In 1897, Zanzibar became a British protectorate, and the institution of slavery itself was finally, and legally, abolished.

ACKNOWLEDGMENTS

I am deeply thankful for the team at Thomas Nelson. I am indebted to Joel Miller who caught the vision for this project. I am grateful for my editor, Janene MacIvor, who carefully stewarded this manuscript toward excellence. I am thankful for the work of our copy editor, Zachary Gresham, who gave the manuscript meticulous attention to detail. I appreciate the expertise of Belinda Bass, art director for the cover, and of James Phinney, interior page designer.

I remain indebted to Sealy Yates and the team at Yates & Yates whose friendship and guidance continue to bear fruit.

I am thankful for many friends at Pepperdine University. Bob Cochran provided immense encouragement and scholarly guidance. Darryl Tippens was one of the first to lend an ear to this story and challenged me to pursue it. And my accomplices in global justice: Jim Gash and Dana Hinojosa.

I am thankful for the support of Bethel University and my department.

I am grateful for the friendship of Tim Jones, my sounding board for more lunchtime Livingstone discussions than could be counted.

I delight in bringing students into these projects, and I appreciate the important research assistance that they lend. A special thanks goes to Mark Reinhardt, who dove deep into the Livingstone adventure with

ACKNOWLEDGMENTS

me. At Bethel: Stephanie Johnson. At Pepperdine: Emily Chu, Bethany Bennick, and Eric Cox.

I am thankful for my family who encourages my writing projects: my grandparents, Bob and Pat Ludlow; my parents, Kim and Sarah Milbrandt; and my sister and her husband, Eliza and Eric Raum.

Finally, I am grateful to my wife, Lisa, who, for the last several years, has patiently listened to my continuous musings on all things Livingstone.

STUDY QUESTIONS

PART ONE: RISE

CHAPTER 1: HERO

1. Livingstone arrived in Africa with an idealistic vision for how he would change Africa. Is this a common mistake today?
2. If so, why don't we learn from it? Or is it a necessary part of the learning process?
3. Clearly Livingstone did not begin his first trip to South Africa with fame in mind—it came from organizations that recognized him. How should one handle fame if received without request? Should one turn away from fame?
4. Can fame be used for good? What about for the good of an organization, such as a spokesperson?
5. What if fame is exaggerated? Do we have a duty to mitigate our fame if it exceeds reality? What, if anything, should Livingstone have done differently?

CHAPTER 2: THE COST OF FAME

1. Was the London Missionary Society wrong to ask Livingstone to work at its base and not in the field among unreached peoples?

2. Did Livingstone have a duty to continue working with the London Missionary Society even when they changed his mission?

3. Should Livingstone have resigned from the London Missionary Society or handled it another way?

4. Do you agree with Livingstone that his work with the government was accomplishing both mission and scientific purposes?

CHAPTER 3: GREAT EXPECTATIONS

1. Was Livingstone's vision for European colonies in Central Africa a plan that would help or do more harm than good?

2. Based on what Livingstone promised, should the government have funded the expedition?

PART TWO: FALL

CHAPTER 4: TURBULENCE

1. One definition of leadership is "leading people into places they can't see or don't want to go." Was Livingstone a bad leader, or a good leader with bad people skills?

2. How should Livingstone have handled his first realization that the Zambezi expedition was a loss?

3. Could public relations have been salvaged by returning from the Zambezi sooner?

4. Should Livingstone have left Mary and Oswell in South Africa? Jesus asks us to be willing to follow Him even if it means leaving our families. He did so, but at the expense of his wife and children.

CHAPTER 5: SATAN'S SEAT

1. The Transatlantic Slave Trade is well-known due to the involvement of the United States and Europe. Were you familiar with

the East African slave trade prior to this book? What did you know about it?

2. What responsibility does the world have? Britain and the United States had no direct role in the East African slave trade. Should they have gotten involved?

3. Was the British government wrong to refuse to take serious action to halt the slave trade?

4. Should Portugal have taken responsibility for the slave trade in its territories? What could it have done?

CHAPTER 6: INTERFERENCE

1. Should Livingstone have taken aggressive actions against the slave raiders?

2. Was he wrong to burn their villages?

3. Livingstone wrestled with whether to liberate people who would be quickly enslaved again. The re-enslavement, he reasoned, might take a great toll on them. Are there times when we should not set captives free?

4. Livingstone also struggled with liberation because he had no aftercare resources. What is our duty to liberate when we can't help any further?

5. Livingstone believed that missionaries could carry guns and defend themselves with force. Do you agree?

CHAPTER 7: RETURNING TO RAGS

1. Did Livingstone make the right decision to try other rivers when the Zambezi failed?

2. Do you see the Zambezi expedition as a total loss? Do you see any redeeming or scientific gains?

3. Would the public perception of the Zambezi expedition have been different had Livingstone recalled it earlier?

STUDY QUESTIONS

CHAPTER 8: THE SOURCE

1. When Livingstone claimed he was pursuing the Nile for the purpose of bringing recognition to the slave trade, did you believe him? Or did you believe he was pursuing fame?
2. Livingstone believed he had a God-given duty to return to Africa. Should he have left his family in pursuit of this? What would you do if God called you to something similar?
3. Do you agree that Livingstone was the right man to solve the Nile riddle?

CHAPTER 9: DESPERATION

1. Livingstone had left his family before on the Zambezi expedition. For the Nile journey, he now left his children without their mother. Should Livingstone have left his family in Britain to make this trip?
2. Did Livingstone make the right decision not to take European men?
3. How would you compare and contrast his Zambezi and Nile expedition teams?
4. How would you characterize the sultan's position on slavery and his offer to help Livingstone?

CHAPTER 10: LOST

1. Should Britain have mounted a search party sooner, or at all?
2. What do you think led to Livingstone's popularity?
3. Should Livingstone have joined Tippoo Tib and the traders? Do you think he had a choice, given his circumstances? Would you have made the same choice?
4. Was Livingstone's friendship with Tippoo Tib and the traders a moral oversight, purposeful ignorance, or did he really see the good in them?
5. Did Livingstone's proximity to the slave trade implicate him?

CHAPTER 11: BROKEN

1. How did Livingstone continue to justify his reliance on the slave traders?
2. How should Livingstone have handled the massacre?
3. Does Livingstone's departure from the slave traders relieve any of his culpability?
4. Was Livingstone wrong to employ the slaves sent to him?

CHAPTER 12: HOPE

1. How has the role of the media changed since the days of Stanley?
2. What role should the media play in global crises today?
3. Should Livingstone have left with Stanley to return to Britain?
4. Do you agree that Livingstone was still focusing his attention on the slave trade at the time, or was he too captivated by the Nile?
5. Why do you think Livingstone felt he had to finish his work?

PART THREE: RESURRECTION

CHAPTER 13: THE LONG WAY HOME

1. Should the United States have gotten involved in the slave trade, as Livingstone was requesting? Does the United States have a responsibility? Does it have a duty?
2. Do you agree with the argument that a period of slavery is part of the course of human development?
3. How would you have handled Zanzibari diplomacy if you were Kirk or Frere?
4. How would you have responded to pressure from Britain if you were the sultan?

CHAPTER 14: REDEMPTION

1. Should Livingstone's body have been returned to Britain or buried in Africa? What do you think Livingstone would have wanted?
2. The ban on maritime slave shipping arguably made the slave trade more dangerous and violent along the Kisiju Road. Should another approach have been taken to end the trade?
3. Did Livingstone deserve his heroic welcome and public mourning? Does later information about his relationship with the slave traders diminish him?

CHAPTER 15: TRIUMPH

1. What is the relationship between commerce and law? Could commerce, on its own, have supplanted slavery, as Livingstone originally intended? Or is the rule of law a necessary first step?
2. What is the place of advocacy in responding to injustice? Can you name other examples in which advocacy has made a considerable change?
3. Kirk forced the sultanate legally to end slavery, rather than win it over to a just worldview. How should we measure his success? Is a legal restriction sufficient? Or should Kirk have worked to convince the council it was the right thing to do?
4. Do you see Livingstone as a continuation of William Wilberforce and the abolitionist movement?

NOTES

CHAPTER 1: HERO

Epigraph: George Seaver, *Livingstone's Life and Letters*, 632–33. This source applies to all chapter epigraphs unless otherwise indicated.

1. Edward A. Alpers, *Ivory & Slaves in East Central Africa: Changing Pattern of International Trade in East Central Africa to the Later Nineteenth Century* (Berkley: University of California Press, 1975); William Gervase Clarence-Smith, *The Economics of the Indian Ocean Slave Trade* (London: Frank Cass and Company, 1989), 23–31; Christopher Lloyd, *Navy and the Slave Trade* (London: Frank Cass and Company, 1949), 278. Note: There are no exact accounts of the number of individuals taken captive for the East African slave trade. Scholars disagree, and the best estimates are deduced from import and export documents in Zanzibar and other ports. This book is utilizing estimates from several sources in an effort to represent the size and scope of the slave trade. This note applies for slave statistics at the beginning of all chapters.
2. Timothy Jeal, *Livingstone* (New Haven: Yale Nota Bene, 2001), 158.
3. David Livingstone, *Dr. Livingstone's Cambridge Lectures: Together with a Prefatory Letter by the Rev. Professor Sedgwick* (London: Deighton, Bell, 1858), 85.
4. Ibid., 2.

CHAPTER 2: THE COST OF FAME

1. Jeal, *Livingstone*, 158; quoting the *Times*, August 8, 1854.
2. Ibid., 156.
3. William Garden Blaikie, *The Personal Life of David Livingstone: Chiefly from His Unpublished Journals and Correspondence in the Possession of His Family* (London: John Murray, 1880), 28.
4. Ibid.
5. Ibid., 185.
6. David Livingstone and Charles Livingstone, *Narrative of an Expedition to the Zambesi and Its Tributaries* (New York: Harper and Brothers Publishers, 1866), 625.

NOTES

7. David Livingstone, *The Last Journals of David Livingstone, in Central Africa, from 1865 to His Death, Vol. 1, 1866–1868*, Horace Waller, ed. (London: John Murray, 1874).
8. Blaikie, *The Personal Life of David Livingstone*, 182.
9. Ibid., 195.
10. Livingstone to Clarendon, in Andrew C. Ross, *David Livingstone: Mission and Empire* (New York: Continuum, 2006), 119.
11. Blaikie, *The Personal Life of David Livingstone*, 47.
12. David Livingstone, *Missionary Travels and Researches in South Africa* (London: John Murray, 1857), 21.
13. Ibid., 12.
14. Ibid.

CHAPTER 3: GREAT EXPECTATIONS

1. Blaikie, *The Personal Life of David Livingstone*, 229.
2. Ibid., 182.
3. Ibid., 216.
4. Livingstone to Kirk, March 18, 1858, in *The Zambesi Doctors: David Livingstone's Correspondence with John Kirk, 1858–1872*, R. Foskett, ed. (Edinburgh: Edinburgh University Press, 1964), 40–41.
5. "Farewell Banquet to Dr. Livingstone," *Times*, Feb. 15, 1858. The remaining quotes in chapter 3 are from this article.

CHAPTER 4: TURBULENCE

Epigraph: David Livingstone, *Missionary Correspondence, 1841–56*, Isaac Schapera, ed. (London: Chatto and Windus, 1961), 48.

1. Blaikie, *The Personal Life of David Livingstone*, 202.
2. Ibid., 204.
3. Jeal, *Livingstone*, 75.
4. Seaver, *Livingstone's Life*, 129.
5. Jeal, *Livingstone*, 96.
6. Ibid., 97.
7. Ibid., 197.
8. Livingstone, *Narrative*, 14.
9. Ibid., 27.
10. David Livingstone, *A Popular Account of Dr. Livingstone's Expedition to the Zambesi and Its Tributaries And of the Discovery of the Lakes Shirwa and Nyassa (1858–1864)*, (London: John Murrary, 1894).
11. Jeal, *Livingstone*, 206.
12. Livingstone, *Narrative*, 60.
13. Letter to John Washington, Dec. 18, 1858. Livingstone Online: http://www .livingstoneonline.ucl.ac.uk.

14. George Seaver, *David Livingstone: His Life and Letters* (New York: Harper and Brothers Publishers, 1864), 25, 333.
15. Ibid.
16. Seaver, *Livingstone's Life*, 330.
17. Livingstone, *Narrative*, 88.
18. Jeal, *Livingstone*, 212.
19. Blaikie, *The Personal Life of David Livingstone*, 214.
20. Ibid., March 3, 1859.

CHAPTER 5: SATAN'S SEAT

1. Livingstone, *Narrative*, 122.
2. Blaikie, *The Personal Life of David Livingstone*, 216.
3. Livingstone, *Narrative*, 137.
4. Ibid., 141.
5. Ibid., 392.
6. Lake Nyassa is now known as Lake Malawi.
7. Livingstone, *Narrative*, 372.
8. Ibid., 413.
9. Ibid.
10. Livingstone, *A Popular Account*, 474.
11. Livingstone, *Narrative*, 413.
12. Jeal, *Livingstone*, 219.
13. G. W. Clendennen, ed., *David Livingstone's Shiré Journal 1861–1864* (Aberdeen: Scottish Cultural Press, 1992), 4.
14. Seaver, *David Livingstone*, 330.
15. Jeal, *Livingstone*, 226.
16. Foskett, *The Zambesi Doctors* (Edinburgh: Edinburgh Univ. Press, 1964), 156.
17. J. P. R. Wallis, ed., *The Zambezi Expedition of David Livingstone, Vol. 1, 1858–1863* (London: Chatto & Windus, 1956), 83.
18. Seaver, *David Livingstone*, 345.
19. Jeal, *Livingstone*, 229.
20. Ibid., 232.

CHAPTER 6: INTERFERENCE

1. Jeal, *Livingstone*, 222.
2. Ibid.
3. George Shepperson, *David Livingstone and Rovuma* (Edinburgh: Edinburgh University Press, 1965), 22.
4. Livingstone, *Narrative*, 351.
5. Harvey Goodwin, *Memoir of Bishop Mackenzie* (London: Bell and Daldy, 1865), 285–86.
6. Livingstone, *Narrative*, 357.
7. Ibid., 378.

8. Ibid., 331.

9. Ibid., 378.

10. Ibid.

11. Ibid., 360.

12. The word used was *Chibisa*, which Livingstone translated to "great conqueror or general," and which I am rendering as *savior*.

13. I made this a quote out of what Livingstone said his men said.

14. Livingstone, *Narrative*, 361.

15. Ibid., 382.

16. Ibid., 383.

17. Ibid.

18. Goodwin, *Memoir of Bishop Mackenzie*, 286.

19. Clendennen, *David Livingstone's Shiré Journal*, 5.

20. *Times*, Nov. 26, 1862.

21. Clendennen, *David Livingstone's Shiré Journal*, 5.

CHAPTER 7: RETURNING TO RAGS

1. Clendennen, *David Livingstone's Shiré Journal*, 25.

2. Blaikie, *The Personal Life of David Livingstone*, 248.

3. Jeal, *Livingstone*, 258.

4. Clendennen, *David Livingstone's Shiré Journal*, 22–23.

5. Jeal, *Livingstone*, 259.

6. Clendennen, *David Livingstone's Shiré Journal*, 22–23.

7. James Stewart, *The Zambesi Journal of James Stewart, 1862–1863* (London: Chatto and Windus, 1952), 62.

8. Blaikie, *The Personal Life of David Livingstone*, 253.

9. Shepperson, *David Livingstone and Rovuma*, 65.

10. J. P. R. Wallis, ed., *Zambezi Expedition of David Livingstone, Vol. 2, 1858–1863* (London: Chatto and Windus, 1956), 376.

11. Stewart, *Zambesi Journal*, 59.

12. Jeal, *Livingstone*, 261.

13. Kirk's Zambezi Journal, September 16 & 18, 1862, in Shepperson, *David Livingstone and Rovuma*.

14. R. J. Campbell, *Livingstone* (New York: Dodd, Mead, 1930), 267.

15. Stewart, *Zambesi Journal*, 220.

16. Jeal, *Livingstone*, 264.

17. Stewart, *Zambesi Journal*, 228.

18. Ibid.

19. David Livingstone, unpublished private journal, National Library of Scotland, in Jeal, *Livingstone*, 265.

20. Livingstone, *Narrative*, 475.

21. Ibid.

22. Editorial, *Times*, Jan. 20, 1863.

23. *Times*, Wednesday, Oct. 14, 1863.

24. *Times*, Friday, Apr. 1, 1864.
25. *Times*, Friday, Apr. 8, 1864.
26. Livingstone, *Narrative*, 584.
27. Jeal, *Livingstone*, 272.
28. Blaikie, *The Personal Life of David Livingstone*, 264.
29. Editorial, *Times*, Jan. 20, 1863.
30. Editorial, *Times*, July 23, 1864.
31. Jeal, *Livingstone*, 271.

CHAPTER 8: THE SOURCE

1. Blaikie, *The Personal Life of David Livingstone*, 296–297.
2. Livingstone, *A Popular Account*, Preface.
3. Livingstone, *Narrative*, Postscript to Preface.
4. Ibid.
5. Ibid.
6. Jeal, *Livingstone*, 294.
7. *British and Foreign State Papers, Vol. 65, 1873–1874* (London: William Ridgeway, 1874), 1086.
8. Blaikie, *The Personal Life of David Livingstone*, 349.
9. Ibid., 349–350.
10. David Livingstone to Agnes Livingstone, July 1, 1872. Unpublished. Available in the British Museum Additional Manuscripts.
11. David Livingstone to James Young, November 30, 1864, in Timothy Holmes, *David Livingstone: Letters & Documents, 1841–1872* (Suffolk: James Currey, 1990).
12. Blaikie, *The Personal Life of David Livingstone*, 351.
13. Foskett, *The Zambesi Doctors*, 109.
14. Livingstone to James Young, Jan. 7, 1865.
15. Foskett, *The Zambesi Doctors*, 109.
16. Letter from David Livingstone to John Kirk, January 1, 1866 *Livingstone Online*, http://www.livingstoneonline.ucl.ac.uk.
17. Ibid.
18. Blaikie, *The Personal Life of David Livingstone*, 353.
19. Letter to James Atlay, December 6, 1864, http://www.livingstoneonline.ucl.ac.uk/view/transcript.php?id=LP52.
20. Letter to Charles Alington, February 3, 1865, http://www.livingstoneonline.ucl.ac.uk/view/transcript.php?id=LETT1719.
21. Livingstone, *Last Journals of David Livingstone, Vol. 1*, 13.

CHAPTER 9: DESPERATION

1. Blaikie, *The Personal Life of David Livingstone*, 368.
2. Livingstone to Agnes, February 8, 1966 *Livingstone Online*, http://www.livingstoneonline.ucl.ac.uk/view/transcript.php?id=LP117.

3. Livingstone, *Last Journals*, Vol. 1, 7.

4. Ibid.

5. Livingstone to Agnes, February 8, 1966, *Livingstone Online*, http://www
.livingstoneonline.ucl.ac.uk/view/transcript.php?id=LP117.

6. Livingstone to Frere, March 7, 1866, in Holmes, *Letters & Documents*, 155.

7. Livingstone, *Last Journals*, Vol. 1, 59.

8. Ibid., 63.

9. Ibid., 72.

10. Ibid., 74.

11. Ibid.

12. Livingstone, *Last Journals*, Vol. 1, Sept. 26, 1866; Sir Reginald Coupland,
Livingstone's Last Journey (London: Collins, 1945), 50.

13. Livingstone, *Last Journals*, Vol. 1, 142.

14. Ibid., 201.

15. Ibid., 149.

16. Livingstone to Consul Seward, January 2, 1867.

CHAPTER 10: LOST

1. *New York Times*, March 22, 1867, http://www.rarenewspapers.com/view/563124
?list_url=/list/inventions?page=3.

2. "Reported Murder of Dr. Livingstone," *Illustrated London News*, March 9, 1867.

3. "Death of Dr. Livingstone," *Otago Daily Times*, September 10, 1867.

4. "Reported Murder of Dr. Livingstone," *Queanbeyan Age and General Advertiser*,
April 26, 1967. Available at http://trove.nla.gov.au/ndp/del/article/31681971.

5. Ibid.

6. "The Fate of Dr. Livingstone," *Times*, April 24, 1867.

7. Ibid.

8. Ibid.

9. Livingstone, *Last Journals*, Vol. 1, 207.

10. Ibid., 204.

11. Ibid., 222.

12. Ibid., 210.

13. "The Fate of Dr. Livingstone," *Illustrated London News*, November 30, 1867.

14. Ibid.

15. Livingstone to Murchison, December 18, 1867.

16. *Last Journal of David Livingstone, Vol. 1*, 268.

17. *London Illustrated News*, January 25, 1868.

18. *Times*, January 20, 1868.

19. Livingstone, *Last Journals*, Vol. 1, 287.

20. Ibid., 307.

21. Ibid.

22. Ibid., 309.

23. Ibid., 338.

24. Ibid.
25. David Livingstone, *The Last Journals of David Livingstone, in Central Africa, from 1865 to His Death, Vol. 2, 1869–1873*, Horace Waller, ed. (London: John Murray, 1875), 285.

CHAPTER 11: BROKEN

1. Livingstone, *Last Journals*, Vol. 2, 285.
2. Ibid., 287.
3. Ibid.
4. Ibid., 288.
5. Blaikie, *The Personal Life of David Livingstone*, 328.
6. Livingstone, *Last Journals*, Vol. 2, 333.
7. Ibid., 292.
8. Ibid., 291.
9. Ibid., 299.
10. Ibid., 342.
11. Ibid., 318.
12. Ibid., 319.
13. Holmes, *Letters & Documents*, 168.
14. Livingstone, *Last Journals*, Vol. 2, 320.
15. Ibid.
16. Ibid., 353.
17. Ibid., 330.
18. Ibid., 329.
19. Ibid., 322.
20. Ibid., 343.
21. Ibid., 334.
22. Ibid., 337.
23. Ibid., 344.
24. Ibid., 363–364.
25. Ibid., 113.
26. Ibid., 133.
27. This incident at Nyangwe has attracted recent controversy, as a letter Livingstone wrote about the events has recently been analyzed through spectral imaging technology. Livingstone had run out of supplies, including paper and ink, and was forced to write over other documents with ink made from berries. Due to age, environmental conditions, and the nature of the ink, the letters were previously indecipherable. According to the team involved in imaging the pages, there is evidence that members of Livingstone's party may have been involved in the massacre. Livingstone's extreme remorse may have been due to his party being involved and his failure to intervene. This may also indicate why Livingstone chose to break off and travel alone after the incident. The research team further suggests that Livingstone removed such "problematic" passages,

including an attitude of disgust toward liberated slaves in his party, when he transferred these writings to his 1871 journal. Media has used these early reports of the letter's contents to vilify Livingstone. In my view, these matters do not show a dark side, but further indicate the complexities he faced. For more on this, see "Experts shed light on David Livingstone massacre diary," *BBC News*, Nov. 1, 2011. Available at http://www.bbc.co.uk/news/uk-scotland-edinburgh-east-fife-15536564.

28. Livingstone, *Last Journals*, Vol. 2, 135.
29. Ibid., 384.
30. Ibid., 135.
31. Ibid., 386.
32. Ibid., 139.
33. Ibid.
34. Alastair Hazell, *The Last Slave Market: Dr. Kirk and the Struggle to End the African Slave Trade* (London: Constable, 2011), 219.
35. Ibid., 217.
36. Ibid., 223.
37. Ibid., 155.
38. Ibid.
39. Livingstone to Kirk, March 25, 1871, in Foskett, *The Zambesi Doctors*, supra note __, 145, 148.
40. Livingstone, *Last Journals*, Vol. 2, 393.
41. Ibid.
42. Ibid.
43. Ibid., 398.
44. Ibid., 399.
45. Ibid., 400.
46. "David Livingstone's 'Lost Letter' Deciphered," *BBC News*, July 1, 2010. Available at http://www.bbc.co.uk/news/10459263.

CHAPTER 12: HOPE

1. Henry Morton Stanley, *How I Found Livingstone* (London: Sampson Low, Marston, Low, and Searle, 1872), xvii, xviii, 15, 411.
2. Livingstone, *Last Journals*, Vol. 2, 400.
3. Stanley, *How I Found Livingstone*, 421.
4. Ibid., 430.
5. Ibid., 434.
6. Livingstone, *Last Journals*, *Vol. 2*, 411.
7. Stanley, *How I Found Livingstone*, 560, 432.
8. Livingstone, *Last Journals*, Vol. 2, 169.
9. Livingstone to Sir Thomas Maclear and Mr. Mann, Nov. 18, 1871, in Blaikie, *The Personal Life of David Livingstone*, 426.

10. Martin Dugard, *Into Africa: The Epic Adventures of Stanley and Livingstone* (New York: Doubleday, 2003), 274n35.
11. Henry Morton Stanley, *The Autobiography of Henry Morton Stanley*, Dorothy Stanley, ed. (Boston: Houghton Mifflin, 1909), 279.
12. Jeal, *Livingstone*, 358.
13. Stanley, *How I Found Livingstone*, 627.
14. Livingstone to Wilson, Jan. 24, 1872, in Jeal, *Livingstone*, 355.
15. Livingstone, *Last Journals*, 414.

CHAPTER 13: THE LONG WAY HOME

1. Livingstone to James Gordon Bennett, Esq., Jr., November 1871, in L. D. Ingersoll, ed., *Explorations in Africa* (Chicago: Union, 1872), 324, 328–29.
2. Ibid.
3. Livingstone to Earl Granville, Feb. 20, 1872, in David Livingstone, *Livingstone's Africa: Perilous Adventures and Extensive Discoveries in the Interior of Africa* (Philadelphia: Hubbard Brothers, 1872), 574, 575.
4. Ibid.
5. David Livingstone, *Livingstone's Africa: Perilous Adventures and Extensive Discoveries in the Interior of Africa* (Philadelphia: Hubbard Brothers, 1872), 582.
6. Livingstone, *Last Journals*, Vol. 2, 419.
7. Ibid., 473.
8. Ibid., 437.
9. Livingstone *Last Journals*, Vol. 2, 31.
10. David Livingstone to Agnes Livingstone, August 15, 1872, in Ross, *Mission and Empire*, 232.
11. Livingstone to James Gordon Bennett, Jr., Esq., telegraphed from London on July 26, 1872, in Livingstone, *Livingstone's Africa*, 515, 516–17.
12. Ingersoll, *Explorations*, 324, 328–29.
13. F. Sidney Ensor, ed., *The Queen's Speeches in Parliament* (London: W. H. Allen & Co., 1882), 268.
14. *Quarterly Review*, October 1872, in Edward Moss Hutchinson, *The Slave Trade of East Africa* (London: Sampson Low, Marston, Low, and Searle, 1874), 45.
15. Livingstone, *Last Journals*, Vol. 2, 483.
16. David Livingstone to John Livingstone, December 1872, in Blaikie, *The Personal Life of David Livingstone*, 444.
17. Livingstone, *Last Journals*, Vol. 2, 292.
18. Blaikie, *The Personal Life of David Livingstone*, 443.
19. Livingstone, *Last Journals*, Vol. 2, 497.
20. Ibid., 503.
21. Ibid., 505.
22. Ibid., 511–512.
23. Ensor, *The Queen's Speeches*, 271–72.

24. Rawlinson to Livingstone, November 20, 1872, in Blaikie, *The Personal Life of David Livingstone*, 450.
25. Ibid.
26. Livingstone, *Last Journals*, Vol. 2, 516.
27. Ibid., 517.

CHAPTER 14: REDEMPTION

1. Hazell, *The Last Slave Market*, 271. The notice originally read "raw" slaves, meaning humans brought from Africa, thereby creating a loophole for the resale of humans already in slavery. The word *raw* was immediately removed.
2. Ensor, *The Queen's Speeches*, 275–76.
3. Prideaux to British Foreign Office, February 17, 1874, in Hazell, *The Last Slave Market*, 275.
4. James Frederic Elton, *Travels and Researches Among the Lakes and Mountains of Eastern & Central Africa*, Henry Bernard Cotterill, ed. (London: John Murray, 1879), 82–83.
5. Prideaux to British Foreign Office, February 17, 1874, in Hazell, *The Last Slave Market*, 275.
6. Kilwa is in present-day Tanzania. Lamu is in present-day Kenya.
7. Kirk to British Foreign Office, March 9, 1877, in Hazell, *The Last Slave Market*, 272.
8. W. H. Wylde to Kirk, February 11, 1876, in Hazell, *The Last Slave Market*, 277.
9. Ibid., 277–278.
10. In Louise Seymour Houghton, *David Livingstone: The Story of One Who Followed Christ* (Philadelphia: Presbyterian Board of Publication, 1882), 331.

CHAPTER 15: TRIUMPH

1. Ensor, *The Queen's Speeches*, 283.
2. Kirk to W. H. Wylde, July 3, 1873.
3. *Week's News*, June 26, 1875, Vol. 5, 234, at page 819.
4. Kirk to Lord Derby, August 24, 1877, in Hazell, *The Last Slave Market*, 292.

EPILOGUE

1. Ellen Maples, *Chauncy Maples, D.D., F.R.G.S.* (London: Longmans, Green, & Co., 1897), 17.

AFTERWORD

1. Jeal, *Livingstone*, 271.

SELECTED BIBLIOGRAPHY

Admiralty Letter Book: East African Anti Slave Trade Campaign 1868-1871: http://www
.jjhc.info/HeathLeopold1907admiraltyletterbook1868.htm.
BBC News. "David Livingstone's 'lost letter' deciphered." July 1, 2010: http://www.bbc
.co.uk/news/10459263.
———. "Experts shed light on David Livingstone massacre diary." November 1, 2011:
http://www.bbc.co.uk/news/uk-scotland-edinburgh-east-fife-15536564.
Blaikie, William Garden. *The Personal Life of David Livingstone: Chiefly from His
Unpublished Journals and Correspondence in the Possession of His Family.* London: John
Murray, 1880.
British Museum. Additional Manuscripts.
Chadwick, Owen. *Mackenzie's Grave.* London: Wipf and Stock, 2009.
David Livingstone Museum. "Lady Nyassa": http://atschool.eduweb.co.uk/blantyre
/living/lady.html.
Dugard, Martin. *Into Africa: The Epic Adventures of Stanley and Livingstone.* New York:
Doubleday, 2003.
Elton, James Frederic. *Travels and Researches Among the Lakes and Mountains of Eastern &
Central Africa.* Edited by Henry Bernard Cotterill. London: John Murray, 1879.
Ensor, F. Sidney, ed. *The Queen's Speeches in Parliament.* London: W.H. Allen & Co., 1882.
Fay, Robert. "Nile River." In *Encyclopedia of Africa.* Edited by Anthony Appiah & Henry
Louis Gates. Oxford: Oxford University Press, 2010.
Ferguson, Niall. *Empire: The Rise and Demise of the British World Order and the Lessons for
Global Power.* London: Allen Lane, 2002.
Foskett, R., ed. *The Zambesi Doctors: David Livingstone's Correspondence with John Kirk,
1858–1872.* Edinburgh: Edinburgh University Press, 1964.
Hazell, Alastair. *The Last Slave Market: Dr. Kirk and the Struggle to End the African Slave
Trade.* London: Constable, 2011.
Howard, Michael C. *Transnationalism and Society: An Introduction.* Jefferson, NC:
McFarland, 2011.
Hutchinson, Edward Moss. *The Slave Trade of East Africa.* London: Sampson Low,
Marston, Low, and Searle, 1874.
Ingersoll, L. D., ed. *Explorations in Africa.* Chicago: Union, 1872.
Jeal, Timothy. *Livingstone.* New Haven: Yale Nota Bene, 2001.
Klein, Herbert S. *The Atlantic Slave Trade.* New York: Cambridge University Press, 2010.

SELECTED BIBLIOGRAPHY

Kliot, Nurit. *Water Resources and Conflict in the Middle East.* London: Routledge, 2013.

Livingstone, David. *A Popular Account of Dr. Livingstone's Expedition to the Zambesi and Its Tributaries And of the Discovery of the Lakes Shirwa and Nyassa (1858–1864).* London: John Murray, 1894.

———. *Dr. Livingstone's Cambridge Lectures: Together with a Prefatory Letter by the Rev. Professor Sedgwick.* London: Deighton, Bell, 1858.

———. *Livingstone's Africa: Perilous Adventures and Extensive Discoveries.* Philadelphia: Hubbard Brothers, 1872.

———. *Livingstone's Missionary Correspondence 1841–1856.* Edited by Isaac Schapera. London: Chatto and Windus, 1961.

———. *Missionary Travels and Researches in South Africa.* London: John Murray, 1857.

———. *The Last Journals of David Livingstone, in Central Africa, from 1865 to His Death.* 2 vols. Edited by Horace Waller. London: John Murray, 1874.

Livingstone, David, and Charles Livingstone. *Narrative of an Expedition to the Zambesi and Its Tributaries.* New York: Harper and Brothers Publishers, 1866.

Livingstone Online: http://www.livingstoneonline.ucl.ac.uk/.

Maples, Ellen. *Chauncy Maples, D.D., F.R.G.S.* London: Longmans, Green, & Co., 1897.

Mønsted, Mette, and Parveen Walji. *A Demographic Analysis of East Africa: A Sociological Interpretation.* Nordic Africa Institute, 1978.

Mwachiro, Kevin. "Remembering the East African slave raids." *BBC News.* March 30, 2007: http://news.bbc.co.uk/2/hi/africa/6510675.stm.

New York Times. "Death of Dr. Livingstone." March 22, 1867: http://www.rarenewspapers .com/view/563124?list_url=/list/inventions?page=3.

Nwulia, Moses D. E. *Britain and Slavery in East Africa.* Washington, DC: Three Continents Press, 1975.

Page, Melvin E. "David Livingstone, the Arabs, and the Slave Trade." In *Livingstone: Man of Africa.* Edited by B. Pachai. London: Longman, 1973.

Ross, Andrew. "David Livingstone." *Études écossaises*: http://etudesecossaises.revues.org /index151.html.

———. *David Livingstone: Mission and Empire.* New York: Continuum, 2006.

Royal Archives. *Queen Victoria's Journals*: http://www.queenvictoriasjournals.org/home.do.

Seaver, George. *David Livingstone: His Life and Letters.* New York: Harper & Brothers Publishers, 1957.

Simmons, Jack. *Livingstone and Africa.* New York: Collier, 1955.

Stanley, Henry Morton. *How I Found Livingstone.* London: Sampson Low, Marston, Low, and Searle, 1872.

Stevenson, James. *The Water Highways of the Interior of Africa, with Notes on Slave Hunting and the Means of Its Suppression.* Glasgow: James Maclehose & Sons, 1883.

Treaty between Her Majesty and the Sultan of Zanzibar for the Suppression of the Slave Trade: http://www.pdavis.nl/FrereTreaty.htm.

Waller, Horace, Verner Lovett Cameron, Joseph Cooper, and Colonel C. Chaille Long. "Slavery in Africa." In *Westminster Review.* Vol. 51. London: Trübner & Co., 1877.

Zeleza, Tiyambe. *A Modern Economic History of Africa. Vol. 1, The Nineteenth Century.* Kampala: East African Publishers, 1997.

INDEX

ABOUT THE AUTHOR

Jay Milbrandt is a professor at Bethel University in St. Paul, Minnesota. He is a Senior Fellow in Global Justice with the Nootbaar Institute at Pepperdine University School of Law where he formerly directed the Global Justice Program. He travels throughout the world as a human rights lawyer, manages global initiatives in Africa and Southeast Asia, and consults with organizations engaged in human rights and legal development efforts. Jay produces documentaries and photography exhibits and blogs about justice, service, adventure, and travel.

JAYMILBRANDT.COM